Introduction to configural frequency analysis

Introduction to configural frequency analysis

The search for types and antitypes in cross-classifications

ALEXANDER VON EYE

Department of Human Development and Family Studies
College of Health and Human Development
The Pennsylvania State University

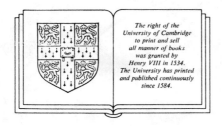

The right of the
University of Cambridge
to print and sell
all manner of books
was granted by
Henry VIII in 1534.
The University has printed
and published continuously
since 1584.

CAMBRIDGE UNIVERSITY PRESS

Cambridge

New York   Port Chester   Melbourne   Sydney

Published by the Press Syndicate of the University of Cambridge
The Pitt Building, Trumpington Street, Cambridge CB2 1RP
40 West 20th Street, New York, NY 10011, USA
10 Stamford Road, Oakleigh, Melbourne 3166, Australia

First published 1990

Printed in Canada

British Library Cataloguing in Publication Data
Von Eye, Alexander
  Introduction to configural frequency analysis.
  1. Contingency tables. Statistical analysis.
  Applications of loglinear models
  I. Title
  519.5'3

  ISBN 0-521-38090-1 hard covers

TO G. A. LIENERT
WHOSE ENTHUSIASM IS CATCHING

Contents

Preface   *page*   xiii

Part I: Concepts of configural frequency analysis   1

1 The analysis of contingency tables   3

  1.1 Basic forms of CFA   6

2 Testing for types and antitypes   16

  2.1 The binomial test and its approximations   17

    2.1.1 Approximation of the binomial test using Stirling's formula   20

    2.1.2 Approximation of the binomial test using the DeMoivre-Laplace limit theorem   22

    2.1.3 Standard normal approximation of the binomial test   23

    2.1.4 Chi-square approximation of the z-test statistic   23

    2.1.5 Heilmann and Schütt's F-approximation of the binomial test   26

  2.2 Asymptotic CFA tests based on distributional assumptions   28

    2.2.1 Lehmacher's asymptotic hypergeometrical test   29

    2.2.2 Küchenhoff's continuity correction of Lehmacher's asymptotic test   30

2.3 Comparison of CFA tests using empirical
    data   31
2.4 The problem of simultaneous testing in
    CFA: procedures for alpha adjustment   35
    2.4.1 Alpha adjustment using Bonferroni's
          inequality   37
    2.4.2 Holm's method for alpha
          adjustment   38
    2.4.3 Hommel, Lehmacher, and Perli's
          modifications of Holm's method   39
2.5 Application and comparison of procedures
    for alpha adjustment in CFA testing   41
3 Models of CFA: concepts and assumptions   46
3.1 The hierarchy of global CFA models   48
    3.1.1 Zero order CFA   48
    3.1.2 First order CFA   49
    3.1.3 Second order CFA   50
3.2 Regional CFA models   51
    3.2.1 Interaction structure analysis   52
    3.2.2 Variations of ISA   53
    3.2.3 CFA of directed relations   54
    3.2.4 Comparison of DCFA, ISA, and
          PCFA   56

Part II: Applications and strategies of CFA   59
4 Global models of CFA: applications and
  examples   63
4.1 Zero order CFA   63
4.2 First order CFA   68
4.3 Second and higher order CFA   74
5 Regional models of CFA: applications and
  examples   82
5.1 Interaction structure analysis   82
    5.1.1 Estimation of expected frequencies   84

5.1.2 Goals of ISA 86

5.1.3 Models of ISA and data examples 86

5.2 ISA strategies 92

5.3 Special ISA application: independence of factorially defined test scales 97

5.4 Prediction CFA 99

5.5 Applications of PCFA: special issues 104

    5.5.1 Conditional prediction CFA: stratifying on a variable 104

    5.5.2 Biprediction CFA 108

    5.5.3 Prediction coefficients 112

5.6 Comparison of k samples 116

    5.6.1 Two-sample CFA 116

    5.6.2 k-sample CFA 124

    5.6.3 Combination of ISA and k-sample CFA 128

5.7 CFA of directed relationships 136

5.8 Aggregation of types and antitypes 140

Part III: Methods of longitudinal CFA 143

6 CFA of change over time 145

6.1 CFA of differences 146

6.2 CFA of shifts in location 153

6.3 CFA of first, second, and higher differences 159

    6.3.1 CFA of first differences between t observation points 159

    6.3.2 CFA of second and higher differences between t observation points 164

6.4 Considering both level and trend information 168

    6.4.1 CFA of categories of trend and location 168

6.4.2 CFA of orthogonal polynomial
coefficients for equidistant time
points   173
6.4.3 CFA of orthogonal polynomial
coefficients for nonequidistant time
points   182
6.5 CFA of time series of different length   186
6.6 CFA in the analysis of treatment effects   189
6.7 CFA of treatment effects in control group
designs   195
6.8 CFA of patterns of correlation or distance
sequences   197

**Part IV: Strategies of CFA and computational
issues**   205
7 Exploratory and confirmatory search for types
and antitypes   207
7.1 Exploratory and hybrid CFA   207
7.2 Confirmatory CFA   213
8 CFA and log-linear models   216
9 Computational issues   222
9.1 Programs for pocket calculators   222
9.2 Programs for microcomputers   223
9.3 Programs for main frame computers   227
Appendix A: Computational issues. The
estimation of tail probabilities for the
standard normal and the F distributions   239
Appendix B: Estimation of expected
frequencies in $2 \times 2 \times 2$ tables under the
assumption that main effects and first order
interactions exist   242

Appendix C: Critical alpha levels under Holm
    adjustment for up to 330 cells and a priori
    alphas 0.05 and 0.01   245
References   249
Subject index   265
Author index   268

Preface

Log-linear modeling focuses on the variables that make up a contingency table. Results typically are expressed in terms of associations among variables. This book deals with methods that focus on groups of subjects in contingency tables. Results are expressed in terms of the characteristics of the subjects in particular cells, and in terms of the number of these subjects, relative to some expectancy. The methods for the analysis of single cells are labeled configural frequency analysis (CFA).

In a 1973 monograph, Krauth and Lienert first summarized CFA developments since the initial presentation of the method by Lienert in 1969. Since 1969, CFA has developed from an eye-balling technique to a many-faceted statistical method. This book gives an overview of CFA including the developments up to 1988.

CFA is of interest chiefly in differential psychology. However, as the examples in this book and the literature show, there are many applications in psychiatry, medicine, sociology, education or history. In general, CFA is useful whenever categorial variables are analyzed.

This book is aimed at readers with a minimal background in statistics. Advanced undergraduate or graduate students with one course in statistics will be able to follow the text without major problems. There are only a few passages that are more technical and require more knowledge in algebra or statistics. The begin and end of these passages are marked by a ▼ and a ▲, respectively. During the first reading, the reader may skip these passages without losing track.

Part I outlines the general problem and defines concepts of CFA. It presents statistical tests and gives an overview of CFA models. Part II introduces the reader to models and applications of CFA, describing the models in more detail. Each model has at least one data example. Part III is concerned with the analysis of longitudinal data. It offers solutions to problems with dependent data and the exponential increase in the number of cells of contingency tables when repeated observations are crossed. In addition, it shows how to decompose time series and to analyze treatment effects. The final part discusses CFA as a complement to log-linear modeling, and appropriate computer programs are presented.

My thanks are due to all those who supported my writing of this text. There is first Gustav A. Lienert who convinced me of the usefulness of CFA and who read and commented on the entire manuscript. Phil Wood and Connie Jones also read the entire manuscript and gave insightful comments. Richard Lerner and Mike Rovine provided encouragement and useful discussions of parts of the manuscript. An anonymous reviewer hired by the publishers read the manuscript very carefully and gave helpful comments and suggestions. Susan Milmoe and Laura Dobbins of Cambridge University Press were encouraging and supportive during all phases of the production of this book. Most of all, I am indebted to Donata, Maxi, Lise, and Juli for all their love.

Any errors in the book reflect my lack of insight. Please do not hesitate to bring these errors to my attention.

Part I:
Concepts of configural frequency analysis

1

The analysis of contingency tables

In empirical sciences, many data are categorical, that is nominal or ordinal in nature. Examples of nominal variables, which are essentially qualitative, include membership in political parties, religion, sex, and presence or absence of illness. Examples of ordinal variables, which rank observational units according to the relative degree to which they possess a particular attribute, include grades in school, severity of illness, and psychometric scores as measures of cognitive complexity or creativity.

The states of categorical variables are mutually exclusive. Therefore, every individual can be assigned to only one state per variable at a time. When two or more categorical variables are measured they can be cross-classified so that every variable may be observed under every state of every other variable. When d variables are cross-classified, a d-dimensional contingency table results (with $d \geqslant 2$).

Consider, for instance, the three variables extraversion (E), criminal behavior (C), and intelligence (I), with categories as follows: $E1 = $ extravert, $E2 = $ introvert, $C1 = $ presence of criminal record, $C2 = $ absence of criminal record, $I1 = $ high intelligence, and $I2 = $ low intelligence. These three variables can be crossed to form a three-dimensional contingency table that has $2 \times 2 \times 2 = 8$ cells. Table 1.1 presents the eight elementary cells of the present example in tabular form, along with labels specifying the states of each variable.

As can be seen from Table 1.1, every cell contains a group of individuals who are alike with respect to the variables considered, and who differ from the individuals in the other

3

Table 1.1. *Cross-classification of the variables extraversion (E), criminal record (C), and intelligence (I).*

Configuration	Specification
E1 C1 I1	Highly intelligent extraverted criminals
E1 C1 I2	Less intelligent extraverted criminals
E1 C2 I1	Highly intelligent extraverted noncriminals
E1 C2 I2	Less intelligent extraverted noncriminals
E2 C1 I1	Highly intelligent introverted criminals
E2 C1 I2	Less intelligent introverted criminals
E2 C2 I1	Highly intelligent introverted noncriminals
E2 C2 I2	Less intelligent introverted noncriminals

groups in at least one characteristic. For example, the individuals in the first group in Table 1.1 differ from the ones in the second group in their intelligence. However, they differ from the individuals in the eighth group in all respects. In the present context, combinations of states of variables will be called *configurations*.

There are two main approaches to the analysis of tables such as the one given in the first example. These approaches are not necessarily exclusive.

Relationships among variables. The first approach focuses on the structure of relationships between and among the variables that constitute a table. Measures of relationships in contingency tables include coefficients of association that can be interpreted in a manner analogous to correlations, or interactions that indicate that associations differ across states of variables (cf. von Eye 1985). Methods for the analysis of relations among variables in contingency tables include log-linear modeling (Bishop, Fienberg, and Holland 1975), information theory (Kullback 1959; Krippendorff 1986), and chi-square decomposition techniques (Lancaster 1969; Lienert 1978).

Results generated from these methods typically describe relations that include every category of every variable. For the example in Table 1.1, consider the correlation between intelligence and criminal record. Using the methods listed above, the correlation would be assumed to hold for all levels of intelligence and for all levels of criminal record. In sum, this first approach yields results that target variables and their interrelationships as the units of analysis.

Patterns of characteristics. The second approach focuses on groups of subjects. These groups contain subjects who differ from all other subjects in that they display a unique pattern of characteristics or configuration. Examples of methods that allow one to identify such groups include cluster analysis (Hartigan 1975), prediction analysis of cross-classifications (Hildebrand, Laing, and Rosenthal 1977), and *configural frequency analysis* (CFA) (Lienert 1969; Lienert and Krauth 1975; Krauth 1985a; Krauth and Lienert 1973a, 1982b; cf. Haberman's (1973) residual analysis). This second approach, in particular CFA, is the topic of this book.

The following paragraphs give a description of criteria used to describe groups. These criteria are applied to CFA. Comparisons are made to other methods of classification, in particular cluster analysis (Krauth 1981b, 1982).

Criteria for the description of groups. Subjects can be grouped such that the groups are either *disjunctive* or *overlapping*. In disjunctive classifications subjects belong to only one group; in overlapping classification subjects may belong to two or more groups. Because CFA operates with contingency tables consisting of categorical variables, CFA groups, by definition, are disjunctive. Every subject can belong to only one cell of a contingency table. If, as is the case in repeated measurement designs, a subject could be assigned to several cells, suitable techniques must be applied to transform data such that multiple assignment is avoided.

Groups of subjects can be analyzed with respect to either *similarity* or *spatial distance* among group members. In the former case, one uses coefficients of similarity to determine the similarity between subjects. In the latter case, one uses distance measures. In contingency table analysis, cells of a contingency table can be regarded as sectors of the data space. Accordingly, cells differing in one parameter represent adjacent sectors. Cells differing in more than one parameter may lie at opposite borders of the data space. CFA targets single cells. Therefore, CFA analyzes groups of subjects who lie spatially close to each other. The data space in which the subjects lie may be based on either similarity or distance measures.

A third characteristic of groupings is that the classification may be either *exhaustive* or *nonexhaustive*. In exhaustive classifications every subject belongs to at least one group. In nonexhaustive classifications, a certain number of subjects remain unassigned to any group. When applying CFA, the researcher starts the analysis with an exhaustive, disjunctive classification. Every individual belongs to a configuration of characteristics. However, the results of CFA typically include only a subset of subjects. Therefore, the results of CFA are often nonexhaustive.

1.1 Basic forms of configural frequency analysis

There are both *hierarchical* and *nonhierarchical* versions of CFA. Hierarchical CFA systematically excludes variables from the analysis that contribute little or nothing to the constitution of types and antitypes. Nonhierarchical CFA uses all variables simultaneously. In contrast to strategies of forming clusters, these methods do not refer to the process of defining groupings. Rather, they refer to the process of including or excluding variables.

Again in contrast to methods of cluster analysis such as Ward's (1963) hierarchical method, CFA does not lead to solely descriptive statements. Results of CFA are both *descriptive* and *inferential*. They are descriptive in that they result in labels for a configuration (see Table 1.1). They are inferential in that they assign a probability to the frequency of a given configuration relative to some expected frequency.

The strategy for the analysis of contingency tables may be either *confirmatory* or *exploratory*. Confirmatory approaches answer precise substantive questions by applying significance tests to statistics describing samples drawn from well-defined populations. Such tests include attempts to reject null hypotheses. Exploratory approaches do not determine a priori what questions are to be answered. Rather, they utilize characteristics of given data sets to generate hints and hypotheses that help to structure subsequent investigations. CFA can be used to pursue both confirmatory and exploratory goals. Exploratory CFA typically tests simultaneously all possible local null hypotheses under some general null hypothesis (see Chapter 2). More specifically, exploratory CFA tests whether in each cell the observed frequency differs significantly from the expected frequency that is estimated to meet with assumptions on the relations among the variables under study. Confirmatory CFA restricts testing to an a priori specified number of configurations (see Section 7.2). The next section presents the general approach and basic concepts of CFA.

To summarize, CFA is a multivariate statistical method that

- identifies groups of individuals that are, statistically, special
- analyzes groups of individuals who lie spatially close to each other
- typically leads to nonexhaustive results
- includes variables either simultaneously or hierarchically
- may be applied in either a confirmatory or exploratory fashion.

The concepts of types and antitypes. Configural frequency analysis compares the observed to expected frequencies in a cross-tabulation. The goal of this comparison is to determine whether the difference between the observed and the expected frequency for a given configuration is larger than some critical value and is statistically significant. Significant differences suggest the existence of groups that contain either more or fewer individuals than expected under some model. CFA is a method to identify such groups. This book introduces CFA and explains how to interpret these groups.

Let o denote the observed frequency of a given cell, and e the respective expected frequency. (Explanations detailing how to estimate expected frequencies are presented in Sections 4 and 5). The configuration of variable states defining this cell is called a *type* if, statistically,

$$o > e, \tag{1.1}$$

and it is called an *antitype* if, statistically,

$$o < e. \tag{1.2}$$

To interpret types and antitypes the researcher must consider the set of assumptions under which expected cell frequencies were estimated. "Classical" CFA (Lienert 1969, 1971a; cf. Krauth and Lienert 1973a, 1975, 1982b; Hommers 1987) estimates expected frequencies under the assumption of total independence of all variables under study. As in traditional chi-square testing, the variables are allowed to have only main effects. In other words, the categories of each single variable are not required to display the same frequencies. Expected frequencies are estimated so that they fulfill the assumption of total independence. Therefore, any significant difference between o and e indicates that in this particular sector of the data space the variables under study are (locally) associated with each other.

The following two kinds of local associations are to be considered: *Types* indicate that the states that define the cell under study "go together well" such that more subjects display this pattern of states than expected under the assumption of total independence. Examples of types include patients who are both inhibited and depressed. In a sample of patients this pattern of characteristics will occur more often than expected under the assumption of independence between inhibition and depression. *Antitypes* indicate a conceptual misfit between the independence assumption that underlies the estimation of expected frequencies and the data. This results in fewer subjects than expected displaying the particular pattern of states. An example of antitypes would include extrovert schizophrenics. Extraversion and schizophrenia practically never co-occur.

The following extreme example illustrates the concepts of types and antitypes, and the difference between CFA and methods that focus on relationships between variables (cf. Meehl 1950; Krauth and Lienert 1973a; Lienert 1971a; Jannarone and Roberts 1984). Consider two items that can be either true (T) or false (F) and a sample of schizophrenics (S) and normals (N). Item 1, Item 2, and diagnosis are crossed to form a $2 \times 2 \times 2$ cross-tabulation. Table 1.2 gives this cross-tabulation.

The upper panel of Table 1.2 gives a layout containing the cross-tabulation of diagnostic status with Item 2 for each category of Item 1. This layout is convenient for two or three variables. Later, however, CFA will be applied to more than three variables (see, e.g., Table 5.12). For designs this complex, the tabular format is more convenient.

From a CFA perspective, a second advantage of the tabular format is that it allows the researcher to place the observed frequencies, expected frequencies, test statistics, and tail probabilities next to each other. In this way, the tabular format is easier to read. The lower panel of Table 1.2 contains the same data as the upper panel, but in tabular format.

With a few exceptions, the tabular format of Table 1.2 is used throughout this book. The column on the left-hand side gives the configurations. The next columns contain the observed frequencies (o) and the expected frequencies (e) for each configuration. (The expected frequencies were estimated under the assumption of total independence among the items and group membership. Later, equations will be given to calculate es under this and other assumptions. In subsequent chapters, tables will contain additional columns that display the results of significance tests.) The last column in Table 1.2 gives the differences between o and e.

The structure represented in Table 1.2 is an example of what is known as *Meehl's paradox*. Note that this structure can equivalently be expressed by a contingency cube whose edges

Table 1.2. *Meehl's paradox from the perspective of CFA in cross-tabulation* (*upper panel*) *and tabular format* (*lower panel*) (N = 200).

Cross-tabulation format

Item	Item 2	S	N
	T	50	0
T	F	0	50
	T	0	50
F	F	50	0

Tabular format

Configurations[a] 12P	Frequencies		Differences
	o	e	o − e
TTS	50	25	25
TTN	0	25	−25
TFS	0	25	−25
TFN	50	25	25
FTS	0	25	−25
FTN	50	25	25
FFS	50	25	25
FFN	0	25	−25

Marginal sums

$T.. = 100, \quad F.. = 100$
$.T. = 100, \quad .F. = 100$
$..S = 100, \quad ..N = 100$

[a]Column 1, Item 1: T denotes true, F false. Column 2, Item 2: T denotes true, F false. Column 3, Diagnosis: S = schizophrenic, N = normal.

represent the cells in Table 1.2. Figure 1.1 gives such a cube. The paradoxical aspect of this structure is that usual statistical tests of association used to correlate single items with the criterion and with each other, for example, phi coefficient, tetrachoric correlation, difference of proportions, lead to the conclusion that neither item is useful in distinguishing between the two diagnostic groups. Both the correlation of Item 1 with the criterion (see upper panel of Table 1.3) and the correlation of Item 2 with the criterion (middle panel of Table 1.3) are zero. In addition, the correlation between the two items is zero (lower panel in Table 1.3). Nevertheless, it is apparent there is a clear structure in these data.

With respect to Figure 1.1, the upper panel of Table 1.3 corresponds to the surface that results from adding the back to the front side of the cube. This surface conserves Item 1 and Item 2 as variables, and eliminates subject status. The middle panel of the table corresponds to the surface that results from adding the right-hand side to the left-hand side of the cube. This surface conserves Item 1 and subject status as variables,

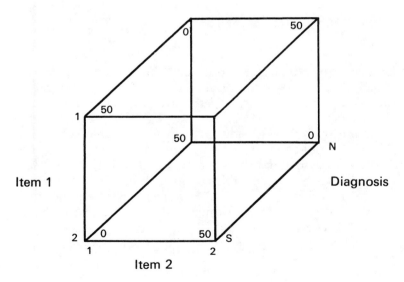

Figure 1.1

Table 1.3. *Subtables from Meehl's paradox.*

Configurations	Frequencies	
	o	*e*
Item 1–Item 2		
TT	25	25
TF	25	25
FT	25	25
FF	25	25
Item 1–subject status		
TS	25	25
TN	25	25
FS	25	25
FN	25	25
Item 2–subject status		
TS	25	25
TN	25	25
FS	25	25
FN	25	25

an eliminates Item 2. Accordingly, the lower panel corresponds to the surface that results from "stepping on the cube," thus conserving Item 2 and subject status as variables, and eliminating Item 1.

To illustrate the association structure in Table 1.2 we use Pearson's phi-coefficient. This coefficient measures the strength of association between two binary variables. When crossed, two binary variables form a 2×2 table with cells $11 = a$, $12 = b$, $21 = c$, and $22 = d$. Table 1.3 gives the three 2×2 tables that can be formed with the three variables in Table 1.2. The phi-coefficient is

$$\Phi = (ad - bc)/((a + b)(c + d)(a + c)(b + d)^{1/2}. \qquad (1.3)$$

For each of the three pairwise combinations of variables

possible in Table 1.3 one obtains

$$\Phi = (25 \cdot 25 - 25 \cdot 25)/((25 + 25)(25 + 25)(25 + 25)(25 + 25))^{1/2}$$
$$= 0/2500 = 0.0.$$

From Φ, we conclude that there is a complete lack of interaction between these three variables. However, this conclusion is based on a coefficient that measures only pairwise relationships. By considering the interaction among all three variables, the frequency distribution can be fully explained. This result can be obtained with log-linear models or information theory.

Despite these results, from the perspective of CFA, there is an obvious structure in this data set. It is clear from Table 1.2 that subjects who display either true scores in both items or false scores in both items belong to the sample of schizophrenics. Subjects who display true for Item 1 and false for Item 2, or false for Item 1 and true for Item 2, in other words, different scores in the two items, belong to the sample of normals.

Configural frequency analysis uses the differences between e and o calculated in the fourth column of Table 1.2 (significance tests will be discussed in Chapter 2) to show that for particular configurations the assumption of total independence between Items 1 and 2 and subject status does not hold true. Rather, each configuration indicates a local association. For example, configuration $11S$ contains 50 subjects. However, under the independence assumption only 25 were expected. Using significance tests (see Chapter 2) one can show that configuration TTS constitutes a type of schizophrenics who score true for both items. Accordingly, configuration TTN constitutes an antitype. No normal subject is observed to display true scores for both items; however, 25 were expected.

To conclude, the pattern of types and antitypes supports the assumption that there is a clear structure in the data set presented here. CFA shows local associations between the two items and group membership. As a result, group membership can be determined based on response to the two items. The pattern of associations is reflected by the presence of statistically significant types and antitypes. Each of these represents a unique configuration of states of the three variables.

In the present example and in the first version of CFA (Lienert 1969; Krauth and Lienert 1973a) only main effects of variables, assuming total independence among all variables, were considered for the estimation of expected frequencies. Chapter 3 gives a classification of models of CFA based on different assumptions that can underlie the estimation of expected frequencies.

A first practical application of CFA. The first real data example given here involves a sample of 362 psychiatric patients (Krauth and Lienert 1973a). The patients were observed for symptoms of depression (D) and hysteria (H), and were or were not treated with sedatives (S). All three variables have categories 1 = present and 2 = absent. Table 1.4 gives the joint frequency distribution of D, H, and S, along with the expected frequencies estimated under the assumption of total independence. (Equations for the estimation of expected frequencies are given in Chapter 4.) The fourth column of Table 1.4 contains standardized residuals, z (see Haberman 1973; Chapter 2), which can be calculated by

$$z = (o - e)/e^{1/2}. \tag{1.4}$$

Each z-value is approximately standard normally distributed. The fifth column in Table 1.4 contains the two-sided tail probabilities of z. The last column of Table 1.4 labels significant z values as either types (T) or antitypes (A).

Table 1.4 shows that three observed cell frequencies differ significantly from their expectancies. Read from the top to the bottom of the table, the first of these is the frequency of configuration 112. It indicates that depression and hysteria are observed together far more often than expected under the assumption of total independence. This applies in particular to the group of patients who do not take sedatives. Configuration 112 may be called a type or a syndrome of untreated agitated depressed patients. In the group of patients who do take

Table 1.4. *Configural frequency analysis of psychiatric patients* ($n = 362$).

Configuration DHS	Frequencies		Significance Tests		Type/ antitype
	o	e	z	$p(z)$	
111	38	37.70	0.049	0.9609	
112	52	33.01	3.304	0.0010	T
121	23	48.14	3.623	0.0003	A
122	48	42.15	0.901	0.3676	
211	39	47.07	1.176	0.2396	
212	30	41.22	1.747	0.0806	
221	93	60.09	4.245	0.00002	T
222	39	52.62	1.878	0.0604	

Marginal sums

$1.. = 161,\quad 2.. = 201$
$.1. = 159,\quad .2. = 203$
$..1 = 193,\quad ..2 = 169$

sedatives the observed frequency of depression and no hysteria was lower than expected (configuration 121).

Configuration 121 is an antitype of nonagitated depression which occurs under the influence of sedatives. The third type, configuration 221, indicates that far more often than expected sedated patients show neither depression nor hysteria. Thus, the data support the notion that sedatives suppress both hysterical and depressive phenomena.

The following chapters give detailed information on significance testing and estimation of expected frequencies. Beginning with Section 4.2, detailed examples of strategies and applications of CFA are given.

2

Testing for types and antitypes

This chapter discusses tests that allow the researcher to decide whether the deviation of an observed from an expected frequency is large enough to suggest the presence of types and antitypes. Let o denote the observed and e the expected frequency of a given configuration. Then, for all tests the null hypothesis is

$$H_0 : o = e. \tag{2.1}$$

In *exploratory CFA* the alternative hypothesis is

$$H_1 : o \neq e. \tag{2.2}$$

Exploratory CFA applies the null hypothesis to every cell in a contingency table.

Confirmatory CFA applies significance tests to an a priori determined subset of cells. In many instances, one knows before data analysis that the difference between o and e should be positive. In this case, one tests for types. If types are expected, the alternative hypothesis is one-sided, and one tests

$$H_1 : o > e. \tag{2.3}$$

If antitypes are expected, one tests

$$H_1 : o < e. \tag{2.4}$$

Two groups of hypothesis tests have been developed in CFA. Section 2.1 discusses the first group, including binomial tests and approximations through z-tests, chi-square tests, the F-distribution, and numerical methods (Krauth and Lienert 1973b; Heilmann and Schütt 1985; Bergman and von Eye

16

1987; von Eye and Bergman 1987). Section 2.2 discusses the second group including tests that require stronger assumptions (Lehmacher 1981; Lehmacher and Lienert 1982). After a comparison of significance tests, the last section of Chapter 2 considers the problem of applying several tests to the same sample.

2.1 The binomial test and its approximations

When testing the null hypothesis (2.1), one assumes the probability of a given configuration is $p = e/n$ with n the sample size. This probability is estimated under assumptions that concern the relations among the variables making up the cross-tabulation under study (see Chapter 3). An exact test for the comparison of the observed frequency with p is the binomial test. Krauth and Lienert (1973b) (cf. Haberman 1973) introduced the binomial test as a method for the identification of types and antitypes in CFA. The random model used in the application of the binomial test, assumes under the null hypothesis that each observation of a configuration constitutes an independent trial of a Bernoulli experiment that is an independent realization of a configuration. Under this assumption, a sample of n observations can be viewed as n independent trials, each of which can result in either of two outcomes. The first outcome is that a particular configuration is observed. The other outcome is that another configuration is observed.

Using the binomial test the point probability of o under expectancy e is given by

$$B'(o) = \binom{n}{o} p^o q^{(n-o)}, \tag{2.5}$$

where p is the probability that the configuration under study occurs, that is, $p = e/n$ and $q = 1 - p$. To check the null hypothesis, the joint probability of o and of all more extreme observed frequencies are compared with alpha, the significance level. A frequency o' is more extreme than o if

$$o' > o \quad \text{for } o > e, \tag{2.6}$$

or

$$o' < o \quad \text{for } o < e. \tag{2.7}$$

Using (2.6) and (2.7) the one-sided tail probability of o with respect to e is

$$B_1(o) = \sum_{i=a}^{l} \binom{n}{i} p^i q^{(n-i)}, \tag{2.8}$$

where $a = o$ and $l = n$ if (2.6) applies, and $a = 0$ and $l = o$ if (2.7) applies. The one-sided test given in (2.8) is applied when the alternative hypothesis is either (2.3) or (2.4). If the alternative hypothesis is (2.2),

$$B_2(o) = 2 \sum_{i=a}^{l} \binom{n}{i} p^i q^{(n-i)}. \tag{2.9}$$

To illustrate the use of the binomial test, Table 2.1 portrays a data set with the same structure as the one in Table 1.2. The only difference between these two frequency distributions is the sample size. To ease computations, n was set to 80 in Table 2.1.

Table 2.1 shows that for all cells there is a large difference between o and e. (The expected frequencies e were estimated, as in Table 1.1, under the assumption of total independence of the variables under study.) In addition, for each cell the two-sided tail probability is smaller than the usual $\alpha = 0.05$. (Section 2.3 will show that these tail probabilities are smaller than α even if adjusted for multiple testing.) The results in Table 2.1 demonstrate that the heuristic interpretation given for the results in Table 1.2 can be justified inferentially. Every cell constitutes either a type or an antitype. Therefore, there is a perfect discrimination between normals and schizophrenics.

The binomial test is an exact test, relatively easy to compute when the sample size is small, and can be reasonably applied even for small sample sizes and small cell frequencies. Despite these advantages, there are two reasons why this test is replaced in most instances by approximations. First, the number of computational steps is large when – as in most

Table 2.1. *CFA binomial tests in a data set that displays Meehl's paradox* ($N = 80$).

Configurations 12P	Frequencies		$B_2(o)$
	o	*e*	
TTS	20	10	0.00005
TTN	0	10	0.00005
TFS	0	10	0.00005
TFN	20	10	0.00005
FTS	0	10	0.00005
FTN	20	10	0.00005
FFS	20	10	0.00005
FFN	0	10	0.00005

$T.. = 40, \quad F.. = 40$
$.T. = 40, \quad .F. = 40$
$..N = 40, \quad ..S = 40$

applications of CFA – samples are large. Second, and more importantly, integer multiplications in the term $\binom{n}{i}$ quickly lead to numbers that are so large that they cause arithmetic overflow, for example, if the program is written in BASIC for a 16 (or fewer) bit processor (see Equation (2.10), below). Because programs written, for instance, in compiled BASIC or in interpreted GW BASIC give an overflow message on the screen only and continue executing the program with inexact values, it is recommended that the researcher use either approximations of the binomial test, approximations through other tests, recurrence formulas (see Abramowitz and Stegun 1970), or other tests when the sample is large. Other alternatives are programs written using more powerful compilers (e.g., FORTRAN77), or programs in which the components of the $n!$ terms in the numerator are divided by the respective components in the denominator before arithmetic overflow leads to mis-estimations.

Thus, the following section presents a numerical approximation of the binomial test. This approximation uses Stirling's

formula which provides a very close representation of the
binomial distribution, especially in the extreme tails of the
distribution. Later, other approximations are presented that
take advantage of the fact that the binomial distribution is
similar to both the standard normal and the chi-square
distribution.

▼

2.1.1 Approximation of the binomial test using Stirling's formula (see Feller 1957; Weber 1967; von Eye and Bergman, 1987)

The repeated calculation of the term $\binom{n}{o}$ requires the largest
number of steps in the application of the binomial test. This
term may be rewritten as

$$\binom{n}{o} = \frac{n!}{(n-o)!\, o!},$$
(2.10)

where $n! = n \times (n-1) \times (n-2) \times \cdots \times (n-(n-2))$.   The
factors for $o!$ are developed accordingly. By summing over the
logarithms of these factors, a very good approximation to this
term can be obtained. This approximation, however, is time
consuming (even with an arithmetic coprocessor). Therefore,
the approximation provided by Stirling's formula might be
considered (cf. Hu 1988). Stirling's formula states that

$$\lim_{n \to \infty} \frac{n!}{n^n e_u^{-n}(2\pi n)^{1/2}} = 1$$
(2.11)

where $e_u = 2.71828\ldots$ is Euler's constant, and $\pi = 3.14159\ldots$.
Using (2.11) we obtain

$$n! \approx n^n e_u^{-n}(2\pi n)^{1/2}.$$
(2.12)

Developing the products in $\binom{n}{o}$ using (2.12) and inserting into
(2.5) yields

$$\hat{B}'(o) = \left(\frac{n}{2\pi o(n-o)}\right)^{1/2} \left(\frac{np}{o}\right)^o \left(\frac{nq}{n-o}\right)^{n-o}.$$
(2.13)

This expression does not contain terms that require calculations as tedious as for $n!$.

For instance, suppose $n = 80$, $o = 41$, $p = 0.4$, and $q = 0.6$. Inserting these values into (2.5) yields

$$B'(o) = \frac{80!}{41!\,(80-41)!}\,(0.4)^{41}(0.6)^{80-41}.$$

Using this expression, the exact value of the point probability is $B'(o) = 0.011330$. Inserting these values into (2.13) yields

$$\hat{B}'(o) = \left(\frac{80}{2\pi 41(80-41)}\right)^{1/2}\left(\frac{80\times 0.4}{41}\right)^{41}\left(\frac{80\times 0.6}{39}\right)^{39},$$

and as an approximation of the point probability $\hat{B}'(o) = 0.011335$. The approximation differs from the exact value only in the sixth decimal place. It is less powerful than the exact test in that the estimated probability is greater than the exact one. In a series of simulations, von Eye and Bergman (1987) showed that numerical approximation using Stirling's formula

(1) generally provides a test slightly less powerful than the exact test,
(2) is weakest when the differences between o and e are small, and
(3) is best when p is small, as is the case in most CFA applications, and when the difference between o and e is large.

For instance, if $p = 0.04$, $n = 50$, and $o = 49$, the results obtained with (2.5) and (2.13) differ in only the 67th decimal place.

The conditions described in (3) are the typical conditions under which CFA is applied. Therefore, the approximation presented in (2.13) is virtually equivalent to the binomial test in CFA and is more parsimonious to calculate.

2.1.2 Approximation of the binomial test using the DeMoivre-Laplace limit theorem (see Feller 1957; Bergman and von Eye 1987)

Using the strong version of the DeMoivre-Laplace limit theorem a good approximation of the binomial test can also be obtained through

$$\hat{B}_1(o) = \Phi(z_{l+0.5}) - \Phi(z_{a-0.5}), \qquad (2.14)$$

where Φ denotes the area of the standard normal distribution that lies beyond a, and a and l are defined as in (2.8). To estimate the z-values, one must estimate the standard deviation of the normal distribution. Here

$$s = (npq)^{1/2}.$$

This expression is known as the standard deviation of the binomial distribution. In large samples, the first term on the right-hand side of (2.14) is approximately $\Phi(z_{l+0.5}) = 1$. Therefore, in large samples, a reasonably good approximation of the binomial test is

$$\hat{B}_1(o) = 1 - \Phi(z_{a-0.5}). \qquad (2.15)$$

Consider the same example as above. We then obtain

$$z_{l-0.5} = (80.5 - (80 \times 0.4))/(80 \times 0.4 \times 0.6)^{1/2}$$
$$= 11.06856$$

and

$$z_{a-0.5} = (40.5 - (80 \times 0.4))/(80 \times 0.4 \times 0.6)^{1/2}$$
$$= 1.939851.$$

The one-sided tail probability of the difference between the expected and the observed frequency is, according to (2.14), $\hat{B}_1(o) = 1 - 0.973197$. The point probability is $B'(o) = 0.06077$. The corresponding one-sided tail probability is 0.026190. In the present example, (2.14) is less powerful than the approximation with Stirling's formula. However, at the extreme ends of the distribution, and when p assumes smaller values, the approximation given in (2.14) can be more powerful (see Bergman and von Eye 1987; von Eye and Bergman, 1987).

▲

2.1.3 Standard normal approximation of the binomial test

It is well known that the binomial distribution can be sufficiently approximated using the standard normal distribution if n is large and p is not too small. The rule of thumb is that the z-test statistic

$$z = (o - np)/(npq)^{1/2} \qquad (2.16)$$

can be applied instead of the binomial test if $np \geqslant 10$. Osterkorn (1975) gives more detailed information on the approximation of the binomial test by z. The goodness of fit of this approximation for a given n depends mainly on the value of p. Equation (2.16) is a more powerful version of (2.14). A continuity correction, recommended if

$$5 \leqslant np \leqslant 10,$$

(Krauth and Lienert 1973a) gives

$$z = (o - np - 0.5)/(npq)^{1/2}. \qquad (2.17)$$

This approximation of the z-test can be more powerful than the one given in (2.14). (Nelder (1974) and Perli, Hommel, and Lehmacher (1987) give additional normally distributed test statistics useful for CFA.) Application of (2.16) to the example in which $n = 80$, $p = 0.4$, and $o = 41$ yields $z = 2.05396$ and $B'(o) = 0.04897$. Application of (2.17) yields $z = 1.939851$ and $B'(o) = 0.06077$. This last value is identical to the one obtained from (2.15) because we had set $\Phi(z_{80+0.5}) := 1$.

2.1.4 Chi-square approximation of the z-test statistic

The last paragraph showed that the binomial test can be approximated sufficiently exactly by the z-test. If one uses standard scores, that is, $x = 0$ and $s = 1$, the ordinate at point x is given by the standard normal

$$\Phi(x) = (2\pi)^{-1/2} e_u^{-x^2/2}. \qquad (2.18)$$

The sum of the squared observations, Σx^2, is called chi-square and is given by

$$\chi^2 = \sum_{i=1}^{t} x_i^2, \tag{2.19}$$

where t is the number of values under study. The distribution of is given by

$$\Phi(\chi) = C\, e_u^{-\chi^2/2} \chi^{t-1}, \tag{2.20}$$

where

$$C = \left(\frac{1}{((t-2)/2)!\,2}\right)^{1/2(t-2)}.$$

In CFA we have $t = 1$ because only one cell is evaluated at a time. Hence we obtain

$$\Phi(\chi) = C\, e_u^{-\chi^2/2}. \tag{2.21}$$

Equation (2.21) describes the positive values of a standard normally distributed variable. The χ^2 curve has only positive values because it consists of squared components. Therefore, (2.21) describes only one half of a normal distribution.

Thus, the following relation can be used for testing in CFA

$$z^2(\alpha/2) = \chi^2(\alpha). \tag{2.22}$$

It follows from this relation that the square of the test statistic given in (2.16),

$$z^2 = (o - np)^2/(npq) \tag{2.23}$$

is distributed as chi-square with one degree of freedom. (For fourfold tables this relation is described by Fienberg (1980, pp. 8–10).)

Notice that the z^2 statistic given in (2.23) is not equivalent to the well-known Pearson X^2 statistic used to approximate χ^2 (see Krauth and Lienert 1973a; von Eye and Bergman 1987; von Eye, Rovine, and Wood 1990; the decomposability of Pearson's X^2 was shown, for instance, by Gilula and Krieger 1983). X^2 is defined as

$$X^2 = (o - e)^2/e = (o - np)^2/(np). \tag{2.24}$$

This expression, however, is equivalent to (2.23) only in the numerator. The multiplication with q is omitted in the denominator of (2.24). Since the X^2 approximation of the binomial test is the easiest to perform, it is important to understand the differences between (2.23) and (2.24). A numerical example depicting these differences appears in Figure 2.1.

Figure 2.1 was generated by defining a series of corresponding expected and observed frequencies. The expected frequencies e varied from 20 to 1 in steps of 1. The observed frequencies o varied from 1 to 20 in steps of 1. The abscissa represents the observed frequencies. The expected frequency for each observed frequency was determined by the formula $21 - o = e$.

Figure 2.1 shows that as long as $np = e$ is less than o, the X^2 values estimated using (2.23) and (2.24) are roughly equivalent. Figure 2.1 depicts examples of the relation $e < o$ on its right-hand side. The estimator (2.24) yields consistently smaller values than (2.23). However, this difference is frequently too small to affect the results of significant tests. On the left-hand side of Figure 2.1, the values for e are greater than the values for o. The examples of this relation show that (2.24) generates

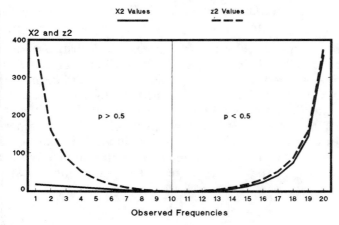

Figure 2.1. Please supply caption.

results increasingly discrepant from those of (2.23). Therefore, we may expect (2.24) to yield evaluations of possible types and antitypes in CFA in an increasingly conservative manner as e increases relative to o.

To illustrate the use of (2.24) consider the same example as in previous sections with $n = 80$, $o = 41$, $p = 0.4$, and $q = 0.6$. Inserting these values into (2.24) yields $X^2 = (41 - (80 \times 0.4))^2 / (80 \times 0.4) = 2.5313$, or, equivalently, $z = 1.59099$. This value is smaller than the z-value obtained with the standard normal approximation and is, therefore, more conservative. The point probability associated with $z = 1.59099$ is $p = 0.11270$. The corresponding one-sided tail probability is $p = 0.055917$. This value gives the most conservative estimation of all tests discussed thus far.

Usually, application of the X^2-test is recommended in CFA if $e > 5$. However, Wise (1963) considers the test still valid if $e \geqslant 2$, provided all e are about equal. Everitt (1977) cites references that allow $e = 1$. Larntz (1978) (cf. Koehler and Larntz 1980) showed that Pearson's X^2 performs better than other approximations even if the sample size is as small as $n = 8$ and expected frequencies are as small as $e = 0.5$.

2.1.5 Heilmann and Schütt's F-approximation of the binomial test

There is a functional relation between the F-distribution and the binomial distribution (Hald 1965). Heilmann and Schütt (1985) suggested using the resulting F-approximation mainly for two reasons. First, the F-approximation is far easier to compute than the binomial test. (Although later, it will be shown that computing the tail probabilities of extreme F-values is tedious.) Second, the approximation is valid even if the sample size is small. It may be applied under the same conditions as the binomial test. The value for F can be determined by

$$F = \frac{o(n - e)}{e(n - o + 1)} \tag{2.25}$$

with $df1 = 2(n - o + 1)$ and $df2 = 2o$. If o is close to n, it is recommended that numerator and denominator and $df1$ and $df2$ be interchanged as well. Since for $o = 0$ the binomial probability is readily computed by

$$B_1(o) = (1 - p)^n$$

(cf. (2.8)), there is no need to replace the binomial test in this particular case.

▼

The relation between the F and the binomial distribution is given by

$$B_2(o) \leqslant \alpha$$

as long as

$$F \geqslant F_{1-\alpha}(2(n - o + 1), 2o),$$

for $i = a, \ldots, e$ (see (2.8)), and, accordingly,

$$B_2(o) \leqslant \alpha$$

as long as

$$\frac{n - o}{o + 1} \frac{p}{1 - p} \geqslant F_{1-\alpha}(2(o + 1), 2(n - o))$$

for $i = 0, \ldots, o$ (see (2.8); Heilmann and Schütt 1985).
The density function for $F > 0$ is

$$p(F) = \frac{(\frac{1}{2}(df1 + df2 - 2))! F^{\frac{1}{2}(df1 - 2)} df1^{\frac{1}{2}df1} df2^{\frac{1}{2}df2} dF}{(\frac{1}{2}(df1 - 2))! (\frac{1}{2}(df2 - 2))! (df2 + df1 F)^{\frac{1}{2}(df1 + df2)}} \qquad (2.26)$$

(cf. Weber 1967).

For the conventional levels of alpha (0.05 and 0.01) and $df1$ and $df2$ ranging from 1 to 500, the critical values of F are tabulated in most introductory statistical textbooks (e.g., Hays 1981) or in textbooks for analysis of variance (e.g., Kirk 1982). However, since in CFA, alpha typically is adjusted to the number of configurations tested (see Section 2.4), either tables for more extreme alpha levels such as those published by

Heilmann and Schütt (1985) must be used, or the tail probability for each F must be calculated. (Appendix A gives a
computationally simpler formula for the calculation of $p(F)$.)

▲

For a numerical example, again suppose $n = 80$, $o = 41$,
$p = 0.4$, and $q = 0.6$. Inserting these values into 2.25 yields
$F = 41(80 - 32)/32(80 - 41 + 1) = 1.5375$. For $df1 = 2(80 -
41 + 1) = 80$ and $df2 = 82$ the corresponding tail probability
is approximately $p = 0.0271$. This result indicates that the F
approximation can lead to more conservative estimations of
tail probabilities than the binomial test. Notice, however, that
numerical differences between the binomial test and the F-test
are solely due to differences in the accuracy of the computational algorithms. Because of the functional relation
between the two tests they should, in principle, yield the same
results.

The F-test may be applied under the same conditions as the
binomial test, that is, even if $e \leqslant 5$. However, even though the
F-distribution can describe both tails of the binomial distribution, the F-test was introduced only for type testing, that is,
for testing $o > e$ (see Heilmann and Schütt 1985). Therefore, F
may best be used in confirmatory CFA when the researcher
determines a priori the configurations to be tested.

2.2 Asymptotic CFA tests based on distributional assumptions

This section discusses CFA tests based on distributional
assumptions. In particular, tests based on the fixed margins
model are presented here. This model was introduced into
CFA by Lehmacher (1981). It assumes the margins are
determined before data collection. If the null hypothesis holds
true, all cell frequencies are randomly assigned under the
constraint of fixed margins. The probability of a given cell
frequency can then be estimated using a generalized hypergeometric distribution.

Two versions of a hypergeometric test for CFA testing are
introduced. Both of these tests are asymptotic in nature; they

approximate the values of the underlying distributions rather than exactly calculate these values. Lehmacher (1981) and Lindner (1984) introduced exact tests for CFA. However, since Lehmacher's exact hypergeometrical test is tedious to compute, and Lindner's test was described only for dichotomous variables, the following sections emphasize the more general and convenient asymptotic tests.

2.2.1 Lehmacher's asymptotic hypergeometrical test

Lehmacher (1981) and Lehmacher and Lienert (1982) introduced an asymptotic test based on the hypergeometrical distribution. The derivation of this test starts from the well-known relation

$$X := (o - e)/(e)^{1/2} \approx N(o, \sigma^2) \quad \text{with } \sigma^2 < 1, \qquad (2.27)$$

which holds true under the null hypothesis, that is, if the null hypothesis cannot be rejected (cf. Haberman 1973). This relation indicates that X is approximately normally distributed with $\sigma^2 < 1$. To avoid unnecessarily conservative decisions in the search for types and antitypes, Lehmacher (1981) deduces the exact variance under the assumption that the marginals are fixed. This variance replaces the estimator e in the denominator in (2.27). The exact variance is

$$\sigma^2 = np(1 - p - (n - 1)(p - \tilde{p})). \qquad (2.28)$$

p is estimated from the marginals under the assumption of complete independence of all variables by

$$p = n_{i...} \times n_{.j..} \times \cdots \times n_{...k}/n^d. \qquad (2.29)$$

For the sake of simplicity of notation, (2.29) expresses p for $d = 4$ variables. Using the same principle, one can estimate p for any number of variables $d > 1$. The probability $\tilde{p}$ in (2.28) is estimated by

$$\tilde{p} = (n_{i...} - 1)(n_{.j..} - 1)\ldots(n_{...k} - 1)/(n - 1)^d. \qquad (2.30)$$

Equation (2.30) uses also, as an example, four variables. Inserting (2.28)–(2.30) into (2.27), the asymptotically normally distributed test statistic z becomes

$$z_L = (o - e)/\sigma. \tag{2.31}$$

Because $(p - \tilde{p}) > 0$, the relationship between the test statistics z (see (2.23)), X (see (2.24)), and z_L is as follows:

$$|X| < |z| < |z_L|. \tag{2.32}$$

Therefore, Lehmacher's asymptotic test always yields the greatest numerical values for the estimation of the standard normal z. The test (2.31) is best applied if sample sizes are very large.

2.2.2 Küchenhoff's continuity correction of Lehmacher's asymptotic test

Küchenhoff (1986; cf. Perli et al. 1987) performed calculations to determine the smallest difference $o - e$ that leads to the detection of a type. For samples varying from $n = 10$ to $n = 100$, results show that the asymptotic test statistic given in (2.31) is often too liberal. Differences between o and e are labelled as significant when they are not significant using the exact hypergeometric test. Simulations by Lindner (1984, p. 401) show that tail probabilities estimated using (2.31) are in some instances by a factor of $1 : 730,000$ smaller than tail probabilities computed under the binomial test. Both results indicate the nonconservative characteristics of Lehmacher's test in its original form. Lindner (1984) showed also that nonconservative results with Lehmacher's asymptotic test occur more often when sample sizes are small.

To avoid nonconservative decisions, Küchenhoff (1986) suggests using Yates' (1934) continuity correction (cf. Lautsch, Lienert, and vcn Eye, in press). Using this correction,

$$o' = \begin{cases} o - 0.5 & \text{if } o > e, \\ o + 0.5 & \text{if } o \leqslant e. \end{cases} \tag{2.33}$$

Küchenhoff's (1986) numerical examples show that the continuity corrected test provides very good approximations of the exact generalized hypergeometrical distribution. Thus, the number of nonconservative decisions is much smaller than without the correction.

2.3 Comparison of CFA tests using empirical data

This section will perform an example configural frequency analysis to compare significance tests. The example data set was used before by Krauth and Lienert (1973a), Lehmacher (1981), Lindner (1984), Heilmann and Schütt (1985), and Ludwig, Gottlieb, and Lienert (1986). The data describe $n = 65$ students who were treated with LSD 50. The students were observed for $C =$ narrowed consciousness, $T =$ thought disturbance, and $A =$ affective disturbance. Each of the symptoms had the categories present $(+)$ or absent $(-)$. Table 2.2 gives the resulting cross-tabulation. The observed frequencies are analyzed using all significance tests discussed in the previous sections. The table contains the one-sided tail probabilities rather than the test statistics themselves. The expected frequencies for this data set were estimated under the assumption of total independence of all symptoms.

Table 2.2 illustrates the characteristics of the significance tests discussed in the present chapter. These characteristics are:

(1) *Binomial test.* The binomial test is an exact nonparametric test. It makes no assumptions concerning underlying distributional parameters. This test can be considered conservative. It is tedious to compute for large samples.

(2) *Approximative binomial test using Stirling's formula.* This test provides a very good approximation of the binomial test, even in small sample sizes. It is only marginally more conservative, and is computationally easier to perform than the binomial test, especially when sample sizes increase.

(3) *z approximation of the binomial test.* This test results from approximating the binomial with the standard normal distribution. It is more powerful than the binomial test. It provides good approximations only if expected frequencies in

Table 2.2. *Comparison of eight different CFA tests using a data set from experimental psychosis research* ($n = 65$).

Symptom CTA	Frequencies		Probabilities of			Significance tests (one-tail)			
	o	e	B_2	B'_2	z	X^2	F	z_L	z'_L
+ + +	20	12.51	0.0177	0.0177	0.0092	0.0170	0.0177	0.0003	0.0007
+ + −	1	6.85	0.0062	0.0067	0.0091	0.0127		0.0011	0.0026
+ − +	4	11.40	0.0069	0.0070	0.0079	0.0142		0.0003	0.0007
+ − −	12	6.24	0.0199	0.0201	0.0077	0.0106	0.0200	0.0010	0.0024
− + +	3	9.46	0.0104	0.0108	0.0115	0.0178		0.0009	0.0020
− + −	10	5.18	0.0325	0.0328	0.0137	0.0172	0.0324	0.0032	0.0073
− − +	15	8.63	0.0214	0.0215	0.0099	0.0150	0.0215	0.0008	0.0019
− − −	0	4.73	0.0074	0.0074	0.0120	0.0149		0.0030	0.0070

+ . . = 37, − . . = 28
. + . = 34, . − . = 31
. . + = 42, . . − = 23

each cell are greater than five (Krauth and Lienert 1973a). It is computationally simple, and tail probabilities can be determined sufficiently exact.

(4) X^2 *approximation of the binomial test.* This test is based on the fact that $z^2(\alpha/2) = \chi^2(\alpha)$ if $df = 1$. It is computationally as simple as the z-test. However, it can lead to distortions, especially in the search for antitypes. It requires a minimal expected frequency of only $e = 0.5$ for each cell (Larntz 1978). The test can be conservative. Tail probabilities can be determined as for z-test statistic.

(5) *F approximation of binomial test.* This test is functionally equivalent to the binomial test. The F-test statistic is easy to compute. However, the tail probability is tedious to determine if tables for extreme alpha levels are not available. Even though the F-distribution describes both sides of the binomial distribution, the F-test statistic was described only for $o > e$ (Heilmann and Schütt 1985).

(6) *Lehmacher's asymptotic hypergeometrical test.* This test is extremely powerful. However, it tends to suggest nonconservative decisions concerning the null hypothesis, in particular when sample sizes are not very large. The test is computationally simple. Tail probabilities are determined as for z-test. The test requires that the expected frequencies be estimated under the total independence model (see Chapter 3).

(7) *Lehmacher's test with Küchenhoff's continuity correction.* This version of Lehmacher's test is still very powerful but the number of nonconservative decisions is much smaller. The test is computationally simple. Tail probabilities are determined as for z-test. This test requires the expected frequencies to be estimated under the assumption of total independence of variables.

Substantively, Table 2.2 shows that the tail probability for each of the configurations is smaller than $\alpha = 0.05$. The highest frequency was observed for configuration $+ + +$. This configuration characterizes those subjects who showed narrowed consciousness, thought and effective disturbances after intake of LSD 50. Both the high absolute frequency of this

syndrome and the overrepresentation of this configuration –
relative to the assumption of total independence of the three
symptoms – support the notion of *Leuner's syndrome* (Leuner
1962; Krauth and Lienert 1973a). According to Leuner, LSD
most often leads to the basic response pattern + + +.

In addition to Leuner's trisymptomatic type, three mono-
symptomatic types were observed. These types are characterized by the presence of only one of the three measured
symptoms. The first of these types includes subjects who
reported only narrowed consciousness. The subjects in the
second of these types showed only thought disturbances, e.g.,
black-outs. The third type contains subjects who showed only
affective disturbances. All monosymptomatic patterns occurred more often than expected under the independence
assumption.

Table 2.2 shows also that all patterns characterizing subjects showing either two symptoms or none are less likely to
occur than expected under the independence assumption.
Therefore, these patterns constitute antitypes. If the independence assumption holds true it is very unlikely that a
subject is not affected in any way by LSD. One may assume
there are relations among the three symptoms such that an
occurrence of the pattern – – – is relatively unlikely. Accordingly, one may expect only a small number of subjects to show
a combination of only two symptoms.

The substantive interpretation of the experimental psychosis data in Table 2.2 is based on the tail probabilities of the
significance tests discussed in this chapter. It should be
emphasized that this interpretation is heuristic for two reasons. First, overfrequentations of certain patterns imply that
other patterns are necessarily underrepresented. Therefore, the
simultaneous tests in Table 2.2 may be dependent upon each
other. Second, as is well known from analysis of variance
testing, multiple testing increases the risk of "capitalizing on
chance." Section 2.4 presents methods to solve both of these
problems (cf. Krauth and Lienert 1973a; Lienert 1978).

2.4 The problem of simultaneous testing in CFA: procedures for alpha adjustment

Usually, the alpha level is determined *before* conducting a statistical data analysis. It is generally not acceptable to assign alpha levels after looking at the data. Krauth and Lienert (1973a) call the usual procedure of assigning one asterisk when $P < 0.05$, two asterisks when $P < 0.01$, or three asterisks when $P < 0.001$ to test statistics, descriptive rather than inferential.

In applications of CFA, because several statistical tests are performed using the same data set, two major problems arise. The first problem can be characterized as the *mutual dependence of multiple tests*. When one applies just one test to a data set, the a priori specified alpha level indicates that area of the underlying distribution that represents the tolerable risk or error. The probability that the test statistic under study falls in this area, is alpha. When more than one test is performed upon the same sample, it cannot be excluded that these tests are dependent upon each other. Steiger, Shapiro, and Browne (1985) showed that chi-square tests, for example, sequentially applied to the same data, have an asymptotic intercorrelation which often is quite high. This dependency can lead to a heavy underestimation of the actual alpha level, and, therefore, to faulty rejections of true null hypotheses.

For instance, suppose data are analyzed twice with an a priori nominal alpha $= 0.05$. Then, the alpha level applies to the first test only. In extreme cases, the conditional error probability of the second test can assume the value of $\alpha = 1$. Krauth and Lienert's (1973a) example of such an extreme case is a data set to which Wilcoxon's T-test is first applied. In a second step, results are cross-validated using the Mann-Whitney U-test. Both tests are nonparametric and compare two samples' means. If the Wilcoxon test leads to the rejection of the null hypothesis, it is very unlikely that the Mann-Whitney test will lead to its acceptance. Thus, the null hypothesis does not have a fair chance to survive if both tests are applied to the same data. In CFA testing the problem of mutual dependencies among multiple tests virtually always arises because usually all configurations are tested.

The problem of mutual dependence of multiple tests is closely connected to the well-known problem of *multiple testing*. This problem arises because one admits for each test, even completely independent ones, the error rate alpha. When more than one test is independently performed, there is a relatively high chance that the researcher will "capitalize on chance." With probability alpha, significance tests will falsely suggest significant results. Thus, results are interpreted as significant and null hypotheses are rejected only because a certain alpha risk, in most instances $\alpha = 0.05$, was taken. For example, suppose a researcher analyzes three variables with three categories each. These three variables form a contingency table with $3 \times 3 \times 3 = 27$ cells. Let α be set a priori to 0.05. Then, the chance of committing three alpha errors, that is the chance of committing alpha errors in more than 10% of the cases, is $p = 0.1505$ even if the tests are independent.

In sum, simultaneous CFA testing of more than one configuration entails two interrelated problems. The first is the problem of mutual dependence of multiple tests of the same data set. The second is the problem of multiple testing. Both problems lead to the alpha level, nominally set at an a priori level, becoming, in fact, inflated. The following sections introduce methods that allow the researcher to take into account both problems simultaneously. First, methods are introduced that lead to rather conservative decisions about the rejection of the null hypothesis. Then, more efficient tests for types and antitypes are introduced.

The control of actual alpha in CFA tests can take three forms (see Perli et al. 1987; cf. Westermann and Hager 1986; Hager 1987):

(1) *Tests of local level alpha.* These tests guarantee that for each separate hypothesis on a single configuration the probability of committing a Type I error is not greater than alpha.

(2) *Tests of global level alpha.* These tests guarantee that the probability of a false rejection of at least one type (or antitype) hypothesis is not greater than alpha.

(3) *Tests of multiple level alpha.* These tests guarantee that the probability of committing a Type I error in the evaluation of at least one type (or antitype) hypothesis is not greater than alpha, regardless of which of the other type (or antitype) hypotheses hold true.

Perli, Hommel and Lehmacher (1985; cf. Perli 1985) suggest that the local level alpha be controlled in *exploratory CFA*. In *confirmatory CFA*, that is, when only a priori specified configurations are tested the authors recommend the control of the multiple alpha level. The next sections present methods for controlling the local and the multiple level alphas.

2.4.1 Alpha adjustment using Bonferroni's inequality

Goodman (1965) showed that the researcher can protect the alpha level by using the degrees of freedom of the entire contingency table for each test. Consider for instance, a 3×3 table. In X^2 testing it has four degrees of freedom. In this case, to keep the a priori specified alpha level, one performs each CFA test for types and antitypes under four degrees of freedom. A more efficient method follows from Bonferroni's inequality (see Miller 1966; Krauth and Lienert 1973a; Lienert 1978). For early methods of alpha control see Harter (1980).

Let H_0 be the null hypotheses for r simultaneous tests. These tests may be either mutually dependent or independent. Let α_i be the alpha error of the ith test, for $i = 1, \ldots, r$. Let α^* be the probability that at least one test leads to the rejection of the null hypothesis although all alternative hypotheses H_i hold true. Then, to control the local level alpha, each α_i must be determined such that the sum of all α_i values does not exceed the a priori determined alpha. More formally, the alpha must be

$$\sum_i \alpha_i \overset{!}{\leqslant} \alpha. \tag{2.35}$$

If one requires in addition that

$$\alpha_i = \alpha^* \quad \text{for all } i = 1, \ldots, r, \tag{2.36}$$

that is, that the nominal alpha is the same for all r simultaneous tests, then a conservative solution for α^* is

$$\alpha^* = \alpha/r. \tag{2.37}$$

Alpha adjustment using (2.37) has become known as the *Bonferroni adjustment*. Krauth and Lienert (1973a) showed that the application of (2.37) renders statistical tests only slightly more conservative when all r tests are independent of each other.

For example, suppose CFA is applied to a $2 \times 3 \times 4 \times 2$ matrix. The maximal number r of simultaneous tests is the product of the number of categories of the variables. Here, $r = 48$. Application of (2.37) yields for $\alpha = 0.05$ an $\alpha^* = 0.05/48 = 0.00104$.

2.4.2 Holm's method for alpha adjustment

As with the alpha adjustment using Bonferroni's inequality, Holm's (1979) method attempts to keep the local level alpha for all r tests of hypotheses under control. However, rather than assigning the same α^* to every simultaneous test, Holm suggests taking the number of tests performed before the ith test into account. This suggestion implies successive significance levels rather than one constant level. Here

$$\alpha^* = \alpha/(r - i + 1) \tag{2.38}$$

is the adjusted alpha level at the ith step, for $i = 1, \ldots, r$ (cf. Sonnemann 1982). In more concrete terms, the successive significance levels are

$$\alpha_1^* = \alpha/(r - 1 + 1) = \alpha/r,$$

$$\alpha_2^* = \alpha/(r - 2 + 1) = \alpha/(r - 1), \ldots,$$

$$\alpha_{r-1}^* = \alpha/(r - (r - 1) + 1) = \tfrac{1}{2}\alpha$$

and

$$\alpha_r^* = \alpha/(r - r + 1) = \alpha. \tag{2.39}$$

The equations in (2.39) show that at the first step the Holm adjusted alpha is identical to the Bonferroni adjusted alpha, with $\alpha^* = \alpha/r$. However, application of Holm's procedure yields a less constraining alpha level at the second step and beyond. At the rth step, Holm's procedure yields $\alpha^* = \alpha$. Appendix C gives the Holm adjusted critical alphas for up to 330 tests and a priori alpha levels of 0.05 and 0.01.

As the Newman-Keuls procedure in the analysis of variance, Holm's successive alpha level procedure requires the rank ordering of test statistics before testing. When z, z_L, X^2, or F statistics are evaluated, the largest value is evaluated with respect to α_1^*, the second largest with respect to α_2^*, etc. Accordingly, when tail probabilities are compared with critical alpha levels, the smallest value is compared with α_1^*, the second smallest with α_2^*, etc. A researcher stops applying Holm's test procedure when, for the first time, a null hypothesis cannot be rejected. (Note that the test procedure using Bonferroni adjustment can also be stopped at this point if the test statistics are rank ordered.)

2.4.3 Hommel, Lehmacher, and Perli's modifications of Holm's method

To control the multiple level alpha, Hommel, Lehmacher, and Perli (1985; cf. Perli et al. 1985, 1987) suggested a modification of Holm's method. The modified adjustment procedure is based on the fact that hypotheses on single cells can, under certain conditions, be depicted as intersections of m other cell hypotheses (cf. Marcus, Peritz, and Gabriel 1976). In two-dimensional contingency tables with r cells, it holds that if m cell hypotheses cannot be rejected, the remaining $r-m$ null hypotheses cannot be rejected either and, therefore, the global null hypothesis holds true (for $r > m \geqslant r - 3$). If $m = r - 5$ null hypotheses hold true, at least one additional null hypothesis must also hold true.

It follows from these considerations that within the sequence of tests, a certain number of tests for types and antitypes can be performed at the same alpha level. This level is less restrictive than those given in (2.39). More specifically, in two-dimensional tables in which each variable has at least three categories, one may use instead of (2.39)

$$\alpha_1^* = \alpha/r, \; \alpha_2^* = \cdots = \alpha_5^* = \alpha/(r-4),$$

$$\alpha_6^* = \alpha_7^* = \alpha/(r-6), \; \alpha_8^* = \alpha/(r-7), \ldots,$$

$$\alpha_{r-1}^* = \tfrac{1}{2}\alpha, \; \alpha_r^* = \alpha. \tag{2.40}$$

Again, one must rank order the tail probabilities for all configurations before comparing them with the critical alpha levels given in (2.40).

Hommel et al. (1985) derived a second variant of Holm's method for two-dimensional tables from the following considerations. If one considers that the first $\alpha^* = \alpha/r$ corresponds to a Bonferroni test of the global null hypothesis, then one can explicitly perform a global test before CFA. An example of such a test would be the X^2 contingency test that evaluates the null hypothesis of independence between two variables. If the null hypothesis of the global test cannot be rejected, subsequent CFA tests are unnecessary. If, however, this hypothesis can be rejected, one may use instead of (2.40)

$$\alpha_1^* = \cdots = \alpha_5^* = \alpha/(r-4), \ldots, \alpha_r^* = \alpha. \tag{2.41}$$

In (2.41), already the first test is less restrictive than in the Bonferroni adjustment. After the first step, (2.41) is identical to (2.40).

Perli et al. (1985) describe an extension of (2.40) to three-dimensional tables. Here

$$\alpha_1^* = \alpha/r, \; \alpha_2^* = \cdots = \alpha_5^* = \alpha/(r-4),$$

$$\alpha_m^* = \alpha/(r-m+1), \quad \text{for } m = 6, \ldots, r. \tag{2.42}$$

It might seem plausible to use (2.42) in higher dimensional tables as well. However, Perli et al. (1985) show that in four- or higher-dimensional tables, CFA tests, including the residual tests by Lehmacher (1981) and Haberman (1978), may be strongly nonconservative. Therefore, in higher dimensional tables the more restrictive Holm or Bonferroni methods are more likely to protect the local alpha level. In addition, if one controls the multiple level alpha in confirmatory CFA, tests developed by Perli et al. (1987) should be applied rather than the tests discussed in Sections 2.1–2.3.

Alternative procedures for the adjustment of the nominal alpha in simultaneous testing have been discussed, for example, by Lindner (1979) for CFA, and by Bauer and Hackl (1985) in a more general context. Recent developments in the method of alpha adjustment include Shaffer's (1986) modification of Holm's procedure. This generally applicable method may achieve more power than Holm's (1979) method. In addition, Holland and Copenhaver (1987, 1988) introduced an even more improved sequentially rejective Bonferroni test procedure which may be applied if certain dependence assumptions apply.

2.5 Application and comparison of procedures for alpha adjustment in CFA testing

A sociological data example is used here to compare procedures for alpha adjustment. The example is adapted from Siegel (1956, p. 177). The data describe the frequencies with which $n = 390$ adolescents from four social classes (S) enroll in three different school curricula (C). In Table 2.3 the social classes have the numbers one to four. The highest class is indicated by a 1. The three school curricula are $1 =$ college preparatory, $2 =$ general, and $3 =$ commercial. Together, these two variables form a 3×4 contingency table. This data set was analyzed with CFA under the following specifications. The alpha level was set to 0.05. For significance testing Lehmacher's (1981) test was applied with Küchenhoff's continuity correction. For illustrative purposes the CFA tests were performed as one-sided. Table 2.3 gives the results of CFA along with the alpha levels for the four alpha adjustment procedures. Significant deviations of observed from expected frequencies are labeled with an asterisk. The expected frequencies were estimated under the assumption of independence between social class and school curriculum.

Table 2.3. Comparison of four procedures for alpha adjustment using a sociological data set (n = 390).

Variables SC	Frequencies		Significance tests		Alpha levels[a]				Rank of z value
	o	e	z	p(z)	Bonferroni	Holm	Hom1	Hom2	
11	23	7.27	6.64	1×10^{-11}	0.0042*	0.0042*	0.0042*	0.0063*	1
12	40	30.32	2.36	0.0090	0.0042	0.0071	0.0083	0.0083	6
13	16	38.01	5.37	3×10^{-8}	0.0042*	0.0045*	0.0063*	0.0063*	2
14	2	5.40	1.45	0.0736	0.0042	0.0125	0.0125	0.0125	9
21	11	18.58	2.51	0.0061	0.0042	0.0063*	0.0063*	0.0063*	5
22	75	77.49	0.42	0.3383	0.0042	0.025	0.025	0.025	11
23	107	97.13	1.90	0.0286	0.0042	0.0071	0.0063	0.0063	7
24	14	13.80	0.12	0.4515	0.0042	0.05	0.05	0.05	12
31	1	9.15	3.08	0.0010	0.0042*	0.005*	0.0063*	0.0063*	3
32	31	38.18	1.59	0.0560	0.0042	0.01	0.01	0.01	8
33	60	47.86	2.68	0.0036	0.0042*	0.0056*	0.0063*	0.0063*	4
34	10	6.80	1.25	0.1065	0.0042	0.0167	0.0167	0.0167	10

1. = 81, 2. = 207, 3. = 102
.1 = 35, .2 = 146, .3 = 183, .4 = 26

[a]Abbreviations are explained in text.

Table 2.3 shows that for seven configurations the differences between expected and observed frequencies have probabilities below $p = 0.05$. Again, this probability statement refers to the null hypothesis of independence between social class and choice of curriculum. Using the Bonferroni adjustment, the number of significant deviations is reduced from seven to four. Two of these deviations indicate types and two antitypes.

Reading from the top to the bottom of the table, the first configuration, 11, constitutes a type. Under the assumption of independence, $e = 7.27$ adolescents from the highest social class were expected to enroll in the college preparatory curriculum. However, $o = 23$ did enroll. The one-sided tail probability of this difference between o and e is less than 1×10^{-11}. Configuration 13 constitutes an antitype. The pattern 13 describes adolescents from the third social class who enrolled in the colleage preparatory curriculum. Under the independence assumption $e = 38.01$ students from the third social class were expected to enroll in this curriculum. However, only $o = 16$ did enroll. Considering the number of students from this social class and the number of students enrolled in this curriculum, the probability of this small observed frequency is so low that an antitype appears even under the conservative Bonferroni alpha adjustment. Configuration 31 also forms an antitype. This pattern includes one student from the highest social class enrolled in the commercial curriculum. Under the independence assumption, $e = 9.15$ students from this social class were expected to engage in this track. However, significantly fewer did. In fact, only one did so. Configuration 33 constitutes a type. This pattern includes adolescents from the third social class who chose the commercial curriculum. Over 10 students more than expected from the third social class enrolled in this curriculum.

These CFA results suggest strong local relations between social class and enrollment rates for the three school curricula. More specifically, these local relations can be observed in the first and the third social classes, and in the college preparatory and the commercial curricula. The CFA results suggest that adolescents from the first social class select the college preparatory curriculum more often than expected and choose the commercial track much less than expected. The opposite results were obtained for adolescents from the third social class. These students are more likely than expected to enroll in the commercial curriculum and less likely to choose the college preparatory curriculum. For the second and the fourth social classes and for the general curriculum no clear deviations in the form of types and antitypes result under Bonferroni adjustment.

To perform the Holm alpha adjustment and the two modifications by Hommel et al. (denoted in Table 2.3 by Holm, Hom1, and Hom2), the tail probabilities $p(z)$ of the z statistics were rank ordered, as seen in the last column of Table 2.3. The smallest tail probability was assigned the first rank. The pattern of asterisks shows that Holm's method and its modifications are indeed more efficient than the Bonferroni adjustment, because one additional antitype was identified. This antitype includes adolescents from the first social class who attend the general curriculum. The difference between the observed and the expected frequency indicates that significantly fewer first social class adolescents than expected chose this track.

The comparison between Holm's procedure and its modifications does not reveal any differences in the identified pattern of types and antitypes. However, the columns of critical alpha values show that the second modification suggested by Hommel and collaborators leads to less extreme tail probabilities for the first significance test. The application of the second modification introduced by Hommel and collaborators is justified by a contingency $X^2 = 69.2$. This value is greater than the critical $\chi^2(0.05; 6) = 12.59$. At the second test, Holm's method and modifications are less restrictive than the Bonferroni adjustment. Up to the seventh test the modifications of Holm's method are more efficient. Beginning with the eighth test, Holm's method and modifications require the same minimal tail probability.

It is important to emphasize that CFA does not analyze absolute frequencies (for an exception see Section 4.1). Rather, it compares observed with expected frequencies estimated under some model. In Table 2.3 the highest observed cell frequencies do not indicate types and antitypes because these frequencies differ only marginally from the frequencies expected under the independence model. In CFA, types and antitypes indicate significant *differences* between observed and expected frequencies. Large frequencies can occur for both large and small observed frequencies. The next chapter discusses models under which expected frequencies can be estimated in CFA. These methods are described with reference to log-linear modeling and the general linear model.

3
Models of CFA: concepts and assumptions

This section gives a brief overview of CFA models. A CFA model is characterized by the assumptions the researcher makes when estimating expected frequencies. The second part of this book describes each model in more detail and gives numerical examples.

CFA performs multiple simultaneous or sequential tests to compare observed frequencies, o, with expected ones, e, estimated under some model. Significant differences between o and e indicate local associations beyond the ones assumed when estimating expected frequencies. For the estimation of expected frequencies methods from log-linear modeling can be used (see Bishop et al. 1975; Goodman 1978; Haberman 1978; Agresti 1984). However, the goals of CFA and log-linear modeling are basically different (cf. Krauth 1980a; Lehmacher 1980a, 1984). When applying CFA, the researcher wants to reject null hypotheses concerning single configurations. If null hypotheses can be rejected, types and antitypes may be interpreted. The focus of this interpretation is on the subjects who display patterns of states, or configurations that occurred more or less frequently than expected under some model.

When applying log-linear modeling, the researcher intends to identify the null hypothesis that provides the best fit to the observed frequency distribution. In other words, the researcher attempts to identify a set of relationships that explains the observed frequency distribution. When evaluating fit one refers to such statistical criteria as significance thresholds and to such philosophical criteria as parsimony. (For a more detailed comparison of CFA and log-linear modeling see Chapter 8.)

Both log-linear modeling and CFA involve two steps in data analysis. First, the expected frequency distributions specified in the model of interest are estimated. Closed forms are available for simple models and iterative algorithms are available for complex models to solve this task. These algorithms include iterative proportional fitting (Deming and Stephan 1940; for a proof of convergence see Darroch and Ratcliff 1972) and Newton-Raphson methods (Haberman 1974b). For simple models the expected frequencies can be directly calculated from the univariate marginal sums. The iterative algorithms fulfill the model specifications by performing an iterative sequence of steps until the differences between calculated and expected frequencies are acceptably small.

In the second step, the method of log-linear modeling provides descriptive measures and gives significance tests that allow the researcher to determine whether the assumed model sufficiently reproduces the observed frequency distribution. As discussed in Chapter 2, in its second step CFA performs local tests for types and antitypes instead.

In principle, one may search for types and antitypes under any model. However, the interpretation of significant differences between *o* and *e* can be complicated for certain models. The conclusion that another model might lead to better data description is not always helpful when discussing types and antitypes with respect to the model underlying the estimation of the expected frequencies. Therefore, CFA uses only models for which clear-cut interpretations are possible. These models make assumptions that either apply to all variables in the same manner or allow the researcher to define groups of variables. The former models will be termed *global models*, the latter *regional models*. The following sections briefly and heuristically describe global and regional models of CFA (cf. Lienert and Krauth 1973d, 1974a,b; Krauth and Lienert 1973a; von Eye 1988). Later sections provide more technical descriptions and algorithms to estimate expected frequencies. Also, they describe each CFA model and its application in detail.

3.1 The hierarchy of global CFA models

CFA global models assume that specified relations apply to all variables in the same manner. Therefore, global models of CFA do not allow one to form groups of variables from assumptions that apply to particular subsets of variables only. Emergent types and antitypes indicate relationships beyond the global assumed model. The assumptions made in global CFA models can be hierarchically ordered. The lowest level in this hierarchy makes the least complex, and the highest level makes the most complex assumptions. As in hierarchical log-linear models, assumptions at higher levels imply that all lower level assumptions are also made. Each level of assumption corresponds to a particular log-linear model. The following paragraphs describe the hierarchy of global CFA models. For each CFA model, reference will be made to the corresponding log-linear model.

3.1.1 Zero order CFA (also *configural cluster analysis*; see Lienert and von Eye 1985; von Eye and Lienert, in press)

Zero order CFA is the most basic CFA model. No effects at all are assumed in the matrix under study. Therefore, neither relationships among variables nor main effects of single variables are taken into account in the estimation of expected frequencies. Main effects are present if variable states differ significantly from an assumed univariate, typically uniform, frequency distribution. Associations between two variables are present if for certain states of one variable, certain states of another occur more frequently and the other states occur less frequently than expected from the marginals. Zero order CFA compares the observed frequency distribution with a uniform distribution.

If configural cluster analysis identifies types or antitypes one may conclude that the frequency distribution under study displays main effects or first or higher order variables associations. Main effect types (clusters) indicate that particular states of variables occur more often than expected under the assumption of a uniform distribution. Main effect antitypes (anticlusters) indicate that certain states occurred less often than expected under this assumption. In general, zero order CFA may be viewed as a statistical *omnibus test*, that is a test sensitive to the presence of any kind of effect. Thus, zero order CFA identifies types and antitypes when there are main effects, but also when variables are associated in pairs, triplets, or more complex groupings.

Zero order CFA is best applied when the researcher assumes no main effects and no interactions in the null hypothesis. Examples of such null hypotheses can be found in investigations of differential effects of various kinds of psychotherapy. In such studies, one possible null hypothesis is that the number of successfully treated patients does not depend on the kind of treatment. If the number of successfully treated patients out of a constant number of patients in each group is substantially higher for one kind of therapy, *zero order CFA types* result. If for some therapies, the number of successes is substantially lower, *zero order CFA antitypes* result.

3.1.2 First order CFA

A more complex set of assumptions is made by *first order CFA* (Lienert 1969; Krauth and Lienert 1973a). This version of CFA is the classical form of CFA. Variables under study are assumed totally independent of each other, that is, they are assumed to be not associated in pairs, triplets, or more complex groupings. Main effects, however, may exist.

If first order CFA identifies types and antitypes, one may conclude that relations among variables exist. This conclusion is important, for instance, in clinical research. Type-syndromes, configurations of symptoms that frequently occur together, can be interpreted as resulting from interactions among variables. As such, syndromes contrast with frequently observed combinations of symptoms that are based on main effects rather than interactions of variables. Note that first order CFA does not specify the kind of relation that leads to the identification of types or antitypes. To identify these relations, association structure analysis (Krauth and Lienert

1973a), interaction structure analysis (ISA) (Section 5.1), or log-linear modeling may be applied.

Zero and first order CFA are identical if the marginals of all variables are uniformly distributed. Therefore, zero order CFA, which is computationally easier to perform, may be substituted for first order CFA when main effects can be excluded before data analysis. Main effects can be excluded when marginals are uniform because, for example, the design is orthogonal, or discrete categories result from median or equal-percentile splits. First order CFA is the method of choice if main effects are of no interest.

3.1.3 Second order CFA

Most applications of factor analysis, structural equation models, scaling methods, or cluster analysis start from correlation or covariance matrices depicting pairwise associations in a data set. Therefore, when applying these methods the researcher assumes the relations in the data set can be exhaustively analyzed from *multiple bivariate associations*. However, in many instances higher order relations must be taken into account to obtain a satisfactory description of an observed frequency distribution. Examples include the data in Tables 1.2, 2.1, and 2.2. These tables show frequency distributions that can be described satisfactorily only if the second order relation, that is, the association in the triplet of variables, is considered.

Von Eye and Lienert (1984) suggested a version of CFA, second order CFA, which is based on the assumption that an observed frequency distribution reflects associations between all pairs of variables in addition to all main effects. Thus, second order CFA searches for types and antitypes by comparing observed with expected frequencies which are estimated under the assumption of the existence of all main effects and all pairwise associations. If types or antitypes emerge, higher than second order relations prevail.

Second order CFA is the method of choice if the researcher is interested in that portion of the overall variation in a contingency table not covered by the methods mentioned above. The presence of second order types or antitypes is a strong indicator that these other methods depict only a part of the overall variation. The examples given in Tables 1.2 and 2.2 show that this part may be the smaller one.

When analyzing more than three variables with CFA, one may consider higher than second order versions of CFA. Results obtained with the method of log-linear models suggest there are many instances in which even second order relations may not be sufficient to explain satisfactorily the variation in a contingency table (see, e.g., Fienberg, 1980, Table 5.6 and its interpretation, pp. 85, 98). Examples of *higher order CFA* versions include third order CFA, which estimates expected frequencies under consideration of all main effects and associations in pairs and triplets of variables. Therefore, with third order CFA, types and antitypes emerge only if at least one quadruplet, that is, a group of four variables, shows a substantial interaction.

3.2 Regional CFA models

Regional CFA models make assumptions that differentiate between two or more groups of variables, for instance, between predictors and criteria. Assumptions are selected in regional CFA such that there is only one way to contradict the assumptions. Regional CFA models assume under the null hypothesis that the groups of variables are independent of each other. There may be many ways in which to violate this hypothesis. However, each of these violations is an instance of the only manner in which this hypothesis may be contradicted. For example, interaction structure analysis (see below) assumes there are two groups of variables. Within each of these groups any relations may prevail. Between these groups, however, total independence is assumed. Therefore, only relations between variables from different groups can contradict the null hypothesis. There are many different relations possible between variables from two groups. However, each of them represents an instance of the same type of contradiction. The following sections introduce regional models used in the framework of CFA thus far.

3.2.1 Interaction structure analysis

Krauth and Lienert (1973a, 1974; Lienert 1978) introduced this method of CFA, ISA, as a tool for the analysis of two groups of variables. ISA uses a specific definition of higher order interactions. In information theory (cf. Gokhale and Kullback 1978) or chi-square decomposition approaches (Lancaster 1969), for each set of variables there is only one term that describes the interaction among all variables. For example, for three variables, say A, B, and C, there is only one second order interaction term, $[ABC]$, beyond the three first order interaction terms $[AB]$, $[AC]$, and $[BC]$. In contrast, Krauth and Lienert (1974) term any hypothesis concerning classifications of d variables in two groups such that the hypothesis (1) includes all variables, and (2) contains each variable in only one term

a $(d-1)$st *order interaction hypothesis*. Consider, for instance, the three variables A, B, and C. Then, in addition to the second order term $[ABC]$ this definition admits three other second order interaction terms that meet this definition. These terms are $[A.BC]$, $[B.AC]$, and $[C.AB]$. Each of these terms concerns the classification of variables in two groups that are exhaustive and contain each variable only once. The dots between the symbols in brackets separate groups from each other.

In Krauth and Lienert's scheme the definition of higher order interactions implies (for three variables):

(1) If there are no second order interactions and no first order interactions then the variables are totally independent of each other;

(2) If there are no first order interactions, second order interactions can nevertheless exist;

(3) If first order interactions exist, the respective second order interactions also exist.

If there are more than three variables, the above characteristics apply accordingly. This definition of interactions is advantageous in that maximum likelihood estimators can easily be given in closed forms, and that significant interactions can be interpreted as indicating relations between the two groups. This interpretation is straightforward because within each group any relations may prevail. The null hypothesis restricts the independence assumption to the relation between the two ISA groups.

The major disadvantage of ISA is that in exploratory research the number of possible interaction hypotheses increases exponentially with the number of variables. Therefore, the adjusted α^* moves rapidly toward zero. For $d \geqslant 2$ variables, the number of ISA interaction hypotheses assuming independence between groups of variables is

$$r_d = \tfrac{1}{2}(3^d + 1) - 2^d. \tag{3.1}$$

For instance, for $d = 7$ variables the number of interaction hypotheses is $r_7 = 966$. For $d = 10$ one obtains $r_{10} = 28501$. (Notice that r_d counts only ISA interaction hypotheses. Not included are type and antitype hypotheses which lead to an additional multiplicative increase in the number of tests.)

To the researcher's advantage is the fact that in most applications of ISA the classification of variables into two groups is given a priori. Thus, only one out of r_d interaction hypotheses is of interest. However, if after detection of types and antitypes, ISA is used to determine those variables that contribute little or nothing to the results, the number of tests increases considerably (cf. Lienert and Krauth 1973a).

ISA and first order CFA are formally equivalent if each group contains only one variable, or when there are no interactions among variables within the groups. ISA and second order CFA are formally equivalent if the relations in each group can be exhaustively explained by pairwise associations and all pairwise associations between variables from different groups are equal to zero.

3.2.2 Variations of ISA

The present section briefly describes two variants of ISA. Later sections treat applications and strategical issues of the use of ISA in more detail. The variants introduced here are *prediction*

CFA (PCFA; see Lienert and Krauth 1973a, 1973e; Heilmann, Lienert, and Maly 1979; Lienert and Wolfrum 1979; Hütter, Müller, and Lienert 1981; Heilmann and Lienert 1982; Lienert and Rey 1982; Lienert and Klauer 1983; Funke, Funke and Lienert 1984; Netter and Lienert 1984; Lienert and Bergman 1985) and *generalized ISA* (Lienert and von Eye 1988).

PCFA is formally equivalent to ISA, but adopts a different interpretational perspective. In ISA the two groups of variables have the same status. In PCFA, one group contains predictors and the other criteria. Therefore, in PCFA, types are assumed to reflect local relations between predictors and criteria that lead to an increased occurrence of certain configurations. More specifically, types in PCFA can be interpreted as configurations of predictors that allow the prediction of an increased occurrence of certain criteria configurations. Similarly, antitypes indicate that certain predictor configurations allow one to predict that certain criteria configurations are very unlikely to follow.

3.2.3 *CFA of directed relations*

Von Eye (1985) proposed CFA of directed relations (DCFA) for the analysis of predictions or of assumptions on causal relations. DCFA assumes that the variables under study belong to either the predictor or criteria groups. For the estimation of expected frequencies, DCFA assumes that the predictors totally determine the frequency distribution of the contingency table. Therefore, the criteria are assumed to show no variation beyond what is determined by the predictors. This assumption can be viewed as parallel to the assumptions typically made in applications of regression analysis. In this case, any deviation of criteria scores from the regression line determined by the predictors is said to be error.

In DCFA, any kind of relation may prevail within the group of predictors. The null hypothesis of DCFA assumes that the observed frequency distribution does not differ from the expected frequency distribution estimated under the following assumption. The variation in the entire contingency table can be explained by taking into account only the relations among the predictors. If types or antitypes emerge, then, the assumption that the predictors determine all systematic variation is said to be false. This conclusion holds true for both of the reasons why violations may occur. The first reason is there are particular, local relations between predictors and criteria. These relations are indicated by agglomerations of cases or a lack of cases in certain configurations. The second reason for a rejection of a null hypothesis in DCFA is the presence of interactions or main effects within the group of criteria. Both phenomena may occur simultaneously.

The interpretation of types and antitypes within predictive relationships depends on the manner in which the null hypotheses of DCFA are violated. If no main effects and no interactions in the criteria exist, an interpretation of types or antitypes in terms of directed relations is possible. In this case, types indicate a local relationship between predictors and criteria. Types allow one to predict that certain states are likely subsequent events of certain predictor states. Antitypes allow one to predict that certain criteria states are unlikely subsequent events of certain predictor states. For both types and antitypes the global DCFA null hypothesis assumes the criteria are totally determined by the predictors.

If, however, types or antitypes emerge because main effects and interactions in the group of criteria exist, the interpretation of directed relations between predictors and criteria is no longer justified. Rather, the global null hypothesis of GCFA must be rejected. In this case, the researcher might want to analyze the relations in the data before applying other models of CFA.

DCFA is best applied if the researcher can assume a priori that the criteria do not show main effects or interactions. This is possible, for example in the case of designs with only one criterion, with marginals uniformly distributed. When several criteria are of interest, log-linear modeling or Lancaster's (1969) methods for chi-square decomposition may be used to check the independence of criteria. Only after this assumption is shown to be correct is interpretation of emerging types and antitypes, as reflecting directed relations, clear-cut.

3.2.4 Comparison of DCFA, ISA, and PCFA

If types or antitypes emerge after application of ISA, local relations beyond the interactions assumed to exist within the groups may be assumed to exist between the two groups of variables. A comparison with DCFA shows that ISA basically assumes symmetrical relations between the groups. DCFA assumes asymmetrical relations because interactions are expected only among predictor variables. DCFA and ISA are equivalent if neither main effects nor interactions in the group of criteria exist, or if there is only one criterion, which shows no main effect.

A comparison with PCFA shows that DCFA is more restrictive than PCFA in its assumptions. Therefore, PCFA is the method of choice if there are main effects and interactions within the criteria. In DCFA, types and antitypes may be interpreted with respect to the assumption that the predictors determine the entire frequency distribution in a given contingency table. Based on this assumption one may, therefore, conclude that the observation of certain criteria configurations depends on the presence of certain predictor configurations. In PCFA, however, not the method for the estimation of expected frequencies, but only theoretical reasons justify the interpretation of the two groups as predictors and criteria.

The second variant of ISA introduced here, generalized ISA, does not assume that only two groups of variables are sufficient to explain the covariance structure in a given data set. Rather, with this method, one may use any number of groups of variables, each group containing one or more variables, to identify types and antitypes and to describe the relations among variables. However, although this approach is intuitively attractive, within the framework of CFA it may become difficult to perform because of the exponentially increasing number of significance tests. In addition to the r tests described in Section 3.1 for an ISA with two groups, interaction tests and the respective number of tests for types and antitypes must be performed. Therefore, generalized versions of ISA seem applicable only if one or more of the following conditions apply:

(1) the number of variables is small;
(2) the number of groups of variables is determined a priori;
(3) the researcher applies the generalized ISA in a confirmatory fashion performing only a small number of significance tests.

The following chapters describe CFA and its variants in more detail. For each model a formal introduction and one or more data examples will be given.

Part II:
Applications and Strategies of CFA

The first part of this book introduced concepts of CFA. The second part describes models and applications of CFA. Global models of CFA are presented first, and regional models, second. A special chapter is devoted to the analysis of longitudinal data with CFA. Subsequently, models are discussed that were not included in Chapter 3. These models make special assumptions or require statistical tests other than those discussed in Chapter 2.

Each model and application of CFA is introduced with its underlying assumptions, methods for the estimation of expected frequencies, and with one or more empirical data examples. For most models both maximum likelihood and least squares estimators are given. Most algorithms are described in enough detail to enable the reader to perform the calculations with a pocket calculator. Programs that perform at least some of the calculations, e.g., the estimation of expected frequencies, are also cited.

To define *least squares estimators*, in the following chapters cell frequencies are treated as if they were dependent variables in a linear model (cf. Arminger 1983; von Eye 1988). Let $\mathbf{Y}$ be a vector of observed frequencies, $\mathbf{X}$ a matrix of constants serving as cell indices, β a vector of variable weights in the system of linear equations, and $\mathbf{e}$ a vector of residuals. Then, the general linear model is

$$\mathbf{Y} = \mathbf{X}\beta + \mathbf{e}. \tag{4.1}$$

CFA uses this equation to estimate expected frequencies. The

59

expected frequencies are estimated as

$$\hat{\mathbf{Y}} = \mathbf{X}\boldsymbol{\beta} = \mathbf{Y} - \mathbf{e}. \tag{4.2}$$

To estimate $\mathbf{e}$ we assume that both $\mathbf{Y}$ and $\mathbf{X}$ contain difference scores, that is, the differences between the raw scores and their means. Then, an ordinary least squares solution (OLS) for estimated frequencies can be calculated by first determining the sum of squared differences, SSD, between the observed and the expected frequencies. One obtains

$$\begin{aligned} \mathrm{SSD} &= (\mathbf{Y} - \hat{\mathbf{Y}})'(\mathbf{Y} - \hat{\mathbf{Y}}) \\ &= (\mathbf{Y} - \mathbf{Xb})'(\mathbf{Y} - \mathbf{Xb}) \\ &= \mathbf{Y}'\mathbf{Y} + \mathbf{b}'\mathbf{X}'\mathbf{Xb} - 2\mathbf{b}'\mathbf{X}'\mathbf{Y}. \end{aligned} \tag{4.3}$$

To obtain minimal squared differences (least squares) one solves equation (4.3) with respect to $\mathbf{b}$, the vector with the estimations for $\boldsymbol{\beta}$. One obtains

$$\mathbf{b} = (\mathbf{X}'\mathbf{X})^{-1}\mathbf{X}'\mathbf{Y}, \tag{4.4}$$

The vector of expected cell frequencies is therefore

$$\hat{\mathbf{Y}} = \mathbf{Xb} \tag{4.5}$$

(see (4.2)). Equation (4.5) provides a general least squares solution for expected cell entries in CFA. Notice, however, that in the present context equation (4.5) is valid for qualitative variables only if they have only two categories, or for discretized quantitative variables. Dummy coding enables (4.5) to handle polytomous variables.

Because of violations of equal variance assumptions, the unbounded estimation of p, and other problems OLS solutions are often not valid. Therefore, the use of weighted least squares (WLS) is often recommended. The WLS estimator of $\mathbf{Y}$ is the vector $\mathbf{Y}$ which minimizes the quadratic form

$$(\mathbf{Y} - \hat{\mathbf{Y}})'\mathbf{S}^{-1}(\mathbf{Y} - \hat{\mathbf{Y}}), \tag{4.6}$$

where $\mathbf{S}$ denotes the covariance matrix of $\hat{\mathbf{Y}}$ estimated from the observed frequencies (cf. McCullagh and Nelder 1983; Neter, Wasserman, and Kutner 1985).

Most applications of CFA use maximum likelihood estimators to determine expected frequencies. Suppose a sample has the observed values y_i, with $i = 1, \ldots, n$, and a probability function $f(y_i, \Theta)$ with the parameter Θ. If the probability function is a function of Θ, with the observations y_i given, the likelihood function $L(\Theta)$ for the observed frequencies is

$$L(\Theta) = \prod_{i=1}^{n} f(y_i, \Theta), \tag{4.7}$$

where Π denotes the multiplication operator. If $L(\Theta)$ is maximized with respect to the parameter Θ one obtains the maximum likelihood estimator of Θ. For instance, Neter et al. (1985) give examples of how to derive maximum likelihood estimators. Maximum likelihood estimators are consistent and sufficient. Least squares estimators are unbiased and consistent.

In the following chapters the notation for least squares estimators will be similar to that employed in descriptions of regression or analysis of variance models. If one interprets, for instance, equation (4.1) as a regression model, the vector **Y** represents the observed values of the dependent variable, the matrix **X** the values of independent variables, the vector $\boldsymbol{\beta}$ the weights of independent variables, and the vector **e** the residuals. In scalar notation, (4.1) can be expressed as

$$y_i = x_0 \beta_0 + \sum_j x_j \beta_j + e_i \tag{4.8}$$

and, accordingly, (4.5) can be rewritten as

$$\hat{y}_i = x_0 b_0 + \sum_j x_j b_j. \tag{4.9}$$

Both (4.8) and (4.9) contain only two components. These are the constants $x_0 \beta_0$ and $x_0 b_0$, respectively, and the main effect terms after the sum sign. The matrix **X** in (4.1) and (4.5) can also contain interaction terms. If this is the case, each interaction term is assigned one additional b weight. Suppose, for example, we analyze the main effects and interactions of two independent variables, A and B, with respect to the dependent variable Y. Then, (4.5) becomes

$$\hat{y}_i = x_0 b_0 + x_A b_A + x_B b_B + x_{AB} b_{AB}. \tag{4.10}$$

In the following chapters, equations of the kind given in (4.10) express least squares estimators of expected frequencies. However, as noted above, the y_i are cell frequencies, and the matrix **X** contains descriptions of the configurations.

To express maximum likelihood estimators, log-linear model notation is adopted (see Bishop et al. 1975; Fienberg 1980). In a fashion analogous to equation (4.10), the logarithm of a given cell frequency is expressed as composed of a constant, main effects, and interactions of variables that account for the deviations from the constant. One obtains for a model that considers only main effects

$$\log(y_i) = u_0 + \sum_j u_j, \tag{4.11}$$

where u_0 denotes the constant and the u_j denote the effect of the jth variable. Using (4.11) to express the model in (4.10) one writes

$$\log(y_i) = u_0 + u_A + u_B + u_{AB}. \tag{4.12}$$

In both (4.11) and (4.12), the subscript i indexes the cells. The following chapters use equations of the kind given in (4.12) to express maximum likelihood estimators of expected frequencies. Global, regional, longitudinal, and other models of CFA are discussed.

4

Global models of CFA: applications and examples

4.1 Zero order CFA

Zero order CFA (Lienert and von Eye 1984a, 1985; von Eye and Lienert, in press) is applied to determine if there are effects in a given data set. To answer this question, expected frequencies are estimated under the following assumptions:

(1) There are no main effects; the variables under study are distributed according to a joint uniform sampling distribution.
(2) There are no interactions; the variables under study are totally independent.

In other words, zero order CFA assumes no effects whatsoever in the contingency table under study. Deviations from an overall uniform distribution are assumed random in nature. Therefore, zero order CFA can be viewed as an omnibus test sensitive to any kind of effect. Types in zero order CFA indicate that main effects, interactions, or both have led to agglomerations of cases in certain configurations. These agglomerations are similar to clusters of cases that are identified with, for example, Ward's (1963) method. Both CFA and Ward's method define clusters as spatially close cases. Both methods identify agglomerations of cases without reference to underlying main effects or interactions of variables. Because of this, zero order CFA is also called configural cluster analysis, and zero order types are called clusters. Accordingly, anticlusters indicate relatively sparsely frequented sectors of the data space that are due also to main effects or interactions.

The estimation of expected frequencies in zero order CFA assumes no effects whatsoever. If this assumption is true, the observed frequencies should follow a uniform frequency distribution. Using the notation introduced above, maximum likelihood estimators for cell frequencies in zero order CFA are

$$\log(y) = u_0. \tag{4.12}$$

Least square estimators are

$$\hat{y} = x_0 b_0. \tag{4.13}$$

Computationally, in this special case, these solutions are equivalent, and one obtains as the expected frequency for all cells

$$e = \frac{n}{\Pi_i c_i} \tag{4.14}$$

for $i = 1, \ldots, d$, the number of variables; c_i denotes the number of categories of the ith variable.

Estimations of the sample size required for zero order CFA result from the following considerations. In CFA, variables are completely crossed. Therefore, the number of cells in a contingency table may be found with

$$t = \prod_{i=1}^{d} c_i. \tag{4.15}$$

For each of the t cells in zero order CFA, the expected frequency is the same. In order to estimate the minimum sample size for zero order CFA, the following rules of thumb may be used:

(1) If $e \geqslant 0.5$ and $n \geqslant 8$ (Larntz 1978), the chi-square tests are applicable. The binomial test and the F-test may also be applicable under these conditions.

(2) If $e \geqslant 5$, the standard normal z-test with continuity correction is applicable.

(3) If $e \geqslant 10$, the standard normal z-test is applicable.

Under (1) the minimal sample size for zero order CFA is 0.5t, under (2) 5t, and under (3) 10t. Notice that the figures for minimal sample sizes given here and in later sections constitute basic requirements for the applicability of significance tests. To obtain types and antitypes, one must have much larger samples.

Lehmacher's test is not applicable in zero order CFA because it requires expected frequencies to be estimated under the null hypothesis of total independence. This null hypothesis allows for main effects, and zero order CFA does not. The same applies to Lehmacher's test with Küchenhoff's continuity correction.

The following example, taken from von Eye and Lienert (in press; cf. Lienert and von Kerekjarto 1969; Lienert and von Eye 1985), analyzes four symptoms of depression. The symptoms are I = inhibition, G = feelings of guilt, A = anxiety, and E = excitation. All four symptoms are scaled as either present, 1, or absent, 2. The sample consisted of $n = 339$ depressed inpatients. Table 4.1 gives the results of a zero order CFA. The alpha level was a priori set to 0.05. Holm adjustment was applied with a starting value of $\alpha^* = \alpha/t = 0.05/16 = 0.003125$. Because all $e = 21.19$, the $z = \sqrt{X^2}$ test was used. All significance tests were two-tailed.

Application of zero order CFA reveals three types (clusters) and four antitypes (anticlusters). Reading from the top to the bottom of the table, the first cluster displays the symptom pattern 1122. It describes individuals who are inhibited and feel guilty, but who are neither anxious nor excited. Pattern 1122 therefore combines the two key symptoms of depression, inhibition and feelings of guilt (Lemke and Rennert 1970). More than twice as many cases as expected under the assumptions of zero order CFA display this symptom configuration. The second configuration with an observed frequency significantly different from the expected is the pattern 1212. It also forms a cluster. Pattern 1212 describes patients who are inhibited and anxious without feeling guilty or excited. Here again, the observed frequency exceeds the expected one by a factor of more than two. Configuration 1221

Table 4.1. *Zero order CFA of four symptoms of depression (n = 339).*

Symptom IGAE	Frequencies		Significance tests	Rank	Critical and empirical		Cluster/ anticluster
	o	e	X		Tail	Probability	
1111	30	21.19	1.915				
1112	22	21.19	0.177				
1121	17	21.19	0.910				
1122	59	21.19	8.215	2	0.0032	2×10^{-16}	C
1211	10	21.19	2.430				
1212	57	21.19	7.780	3	0.0033	7×10^{-15}	C
1221	3	21.19	3.951	4	0.0034	0.00008	A
1222	60	21.19	8.432	1	0.0031	3×10^{-17}	C
2111	15	21.19	1.344				
2112	13	21.19	1.779				
2121	6	21.19	3.299	6	0.0037	0.0009	A
2122	6	21.19	3.299	6	0.0037	0.0009	A
2211	14	21.19	1.561				
2212	5	21.19	3.517	5	0.0036	0.0004	A
2221	13	21.19	1.779				
2222	9	21.19	2.648	8	0.004	0.0081	

1... = 258, 2... = 81
.1.. = 168, .2.. = 171
..1. = 166, ..2. = 173
...1 = 108, ...2 = 231

constitutes an anticluster. The present data show that it is very unlikely for depressed inpatients to show feelings of guilt and anxiety only. The observed frequency of three is the smallest in the entire contingency table. It covers only 14% of the expected frequency. This anticluster provides empirical evidence in support of the well-known antinomy of inhibition and excitation in depression.

In addition to the two bisymptomatic clusters, a mono-symptomatic cluster of depression is found. Individuals in the configuration 1222 display only inhibition. The observed frequency of 60 is almost three times as large as expected.

The present data suggest inhibition is a key indicator of depression. The lower panel of Table 4.1, containing patients diagnosed as not inhibited, displays no clusters, but does form three anticlusters. The first of these anticlusters combines the symptoms guilt and excitation. The second and the third anticluster are monosymptomatic. The second contains patients who report only feelings of guilt. The third anticluster contains patients who report only anxiety. Assuming that the diagnoses of these patients as depressed are valid, each of these symptom configurations is highly unlikely.

Zero order CFA is as close to looking at raw frequencies as can be. In examining raw frequencies, the size of cell entries is compared without reference to expectancies that may vary over the contingency table. In zero order CFA, raw frequencies are compared to the average expected frequency which is the same for every cell. Thus, unlike other CFA models, zero order CFA identifies only the largest cell frequencies as types and the smallest as antitypes. For example, in Table 4.1, zero order CFA labeled all observed frequencies that exceeded e by at least 28 as types, and frequencies that were less than e by at least 14, antitypes.

In many instances researchers are interested in reasons for deviations of the observed from the expected frequencies. Since tests in zero order CFA are omnibus tests indicating any significant deviation from the no effect model, main effects, interactions, or both may explain the presence of clusters and anticlusters.

To test for main effects in the present example, the binomial test may be used. Suppose we expect each symptom to have uniformly distributed marginals. We may then use the z-approximation of the binomial test to identify main effects of variables. Taking inhibition as an example, for $n = 339$ and $p = 258/339 = 0.7611$, $q = 1 - p = 0.2389$, $s = (339 \times 0.7611 \times 0.2389)^{\frac{1}{2}} = 7.85$, and $z = (258 - 169.5)/7.85 = 11.272$. The number 169.5 in the numerator of the z-statistic results from the fact that the expectancy of uniform marginals is $e = 1/2$ $339 = 169.5$. The tail probability for z is 8.9×10^{-30}. This value is clearly less than alpha. The z-value for excitation is 7.169, with a corresponding tail probability 3.8×10^{-13}. Thus, inhibition and excitation deviate from the assumption of equal marginals. Notice, however, that the assumption of equally distributed marginals is not necessarily the substantively most meaningful in the present context. Indeed, it is most plausible that symptoms of depression have a high a priori probability in a sample of depressed patients. Therefore, since expected a priori proportions were not specified, the marginal distributions are not discussed further.

The discovery of relationships among variables underlying the zero order types and antitypes seems to be important. One log-linear model for which a good fit was obtained indicates that excitation is associated with anxiety. Inhibition, feelings of guilt, and anxiety form one triplet and inhibition, feelings of guilt, and excitation form another triplet of associated variables. In short, a log-linear model that allows one to reproduce the observed frequency distribution given in Table 4.1 is $[IGA]$, $[IGE]$, $[AE]$ ($df = 3$, $X^2 = 3.79$, $p(X^2) = 0.284$).

4.2 First order CFA

The first form of CFA discussed in the literature was first order CFA (Lienert 1969). This form of CFA assumes that the variables forming the contingency table under study

(1) may show main effects, and
(2) are totally independent of each other.

Types and antitypes that emerge under these assumptions can be traced back to interactions among the variables. Therefore, the explanation that main effects of totally independent variables lead to the detection of pseudotypes or antitypes which are due only to unequal marginals can be ruled out. As in zero order CFA, the estimation of the expected frequencies is relatively simple, and can, in most instances, be performed using calculators. Suppose the ith of d variables has c_i categories, with $i = 1, \ldots, d$. Then, the log-linear model for first order CFA is

$$\log(y_{i,\ldots,l}) = u_0 + u_1 + u_2 + \cdots + u_d. \qquad (4.16)$$

A maximum likelihood estimator for the expected cell frequency is

$$e_{i,\ldots,l} = f_{i\ldots} \times f_{.j\ldots} \times \cdots \times f_{\ldots l}/n^{(d-1)} \qquad (4.17)$$

with $i = 1, \ldots, c_1, j = 1, \ldots, c_2, \ldots$, and $l = 1, \ldots, c_d$. When applied to two-dimensional contingency tables, (4.17) is the same as the well-known formula for the chi-square test. This formula estimates expected frequencies following the algorithm "row sum $\times$ column sum/n." In terms of (4.17) this is equivalent to

$$e_{ij} = f_{i.} \times f_{.j}/n^{(2-1)},$$

with $i = 1, \ldots, c_1$ and $j = 1, \ldots, c_2$.

Within the general linear model, first order CFA corresponds to

$$\hat{y}_{i,\ldots,l} = x_0 b_0 + x_1 b_1 + \cdots + x_d b_d. \qquad (4.18)$$

Equation (4.5) gives a solution for (4.18). When applied to (4.18), matrix $\mathbf{X}$ in (4.5) contains only the indicators of the configurations. Therefore, $\mathbf{X}$ corresponds to an ANOVA model in which there are no interaction terms.

In order to estimate the sample size required for first order CFA, the number of cells must be calculated using (4.15). In a fashion analog to zero order CFA, the following rules of thumb apply:

(1) If $e \geqslant 0.5$ and $n \geqslant 8$, the binomial and F-tests, and the χ^2 approximations are applicable. For these tests the minimal sample size is $0.5t$.

(2) If $e \geqslant 5$, and the es are different from each other, the z-test with continuity correction or its X^2 equivalent is applicable. For these tests the minimal sample size is $5t$.

(3) If $e \geqslant 10$, Lehmacher's z-test (preferably with Küchenhoff's continuity correction) is applicable. For these tests the minimal sample size is $10t$.

The following example from Lienert and Klauer (1983) performs a first order CFA using data from educational psychology. A sample of $n = 554$ students took examinations in education, psychology, and political science. The students' scores were classified into three categories with $+$ = above average, 0 = about average, and $-$ = below average. Table 4.2 summarizes the results of first order CFA. For this analysis, alpha was a priori set to 0.05 and the Bonferroni adjustment was made. Because the matrix under study has $3 \times 3 \times 3 = 27$ cells, the adjusted alpha is $\alpha^* = 0.0037$. A two-tailed z-test from (2.23) was applied.

Application of first order CFA reveals three types and one antitype. Reading from the top to the bottom of the table, the first type displays grade pattern $+ + +$. Under the model of total independence the expected frequency for this pattern is $e = 9.32$. However, $o = 28$ students were observed. The $+ + +$ pattern depicts students who performed above average in all three social science tests. Also significantly more often observed than expected was the pattern $0 + +$. Students with this pattern obtained average grades in education and above average grades in psychology and political science. Since all patterns with two plus and one 0 signs, that is, $+ + 0$, $+ 0 +$, and $0 + +$, tended to occur more often than expected, we may conclude that students who performed well in two of the social science tests may be expected to obtain at least average grades in the third test. This result is most prominent for patterns $+ + +$ and $0 + +$.

Table 4.2. *First order CFA of three grades in the social sciences ($N = 554$).*

Grade EPS[a]	Frequencies		Significance tests		Type/antitype
	o	e	z	p(z)	
+ + +	28	9.32	6.17	6×10^{-10}	T
+ + 0	15	10.81	1.29	0.20	
+ + −	0	4.22	−2.06	0.04	
+ 0 +	18	12.40	1.61	0.11	
+ 0 0	11	14.39	−0.91	0.37	
+ 0 −	4	5.62	−0.69	0.49	
+ − +	10	14.63	−1.23	0.22	
+ − 0	6	16.98	−2.71	0.007	
+ − −	3	6.63	−1.42	0.16	
0 + +	36	19.91	3.67	0.0002	T
0 + 0	26	23.10	0.62	0.54	
0 + −	4	9.02	−1.68	0.09	
0 0 +	28	26.50	0.30	0.77	
0 0 0	26	30.75	−0.88	0.38	
0 0 −	8	12.00	−1.17	0.24	
0 − +	25	31.27	−1.15	0.25	
0 − 0	36	36.28	−0.05	0.96	
0 − −	14	14.16	−0.04	0.97	
− + +	14	25.11	−2.27	0.02	
− + 0	18	29.14	−2.12	0.03	
− + −	1	11.37	−3.11	0.002	A
− 0 +	27	33.42	−1.15	0.25	
− 0 0	51	38.78	2.03	0.04	
− 0 −	16	15.13	0.23	0.82	
− − +	26	39.43	−2.22	0.02	
− − 0	57	45.76	1.74	0.08	
− − −	46	17.86	6.77	1×10^{-11}	T

+.. = 95,   0.. = 203,   −.. = 256
.+. = 142, .0. = 189, .−. = 223
..+ = 212, ..0 = 246, ..− = 96

[a]E = education, P = psychology, S = political science.

The above conclusion is complemented by the result that it is very unlikely for students to perform well only in psychology and poorly in both education and political science. The pattern that describes this configuration, $- + -$, occurred only once. The expected frequency is $e = 11.37$. This event has such a low probability that it constitutes an antitype of grade patterns in the social sciences.

The third type of grades has pattern $- - -$. These are students who do poorly in all three tests. This last type leads to the conclusion that below average students also tend to perform at similar levels in the three social sciences under study.

In order to determine the structure of associations between grades in education, psychology, and political science, one may fit a log-linear model. In the present data example, the main effect model does not need to be estimated any more. It does not fit. Rather, it leads to the detection of three CFA types and one antitype. The models that took either one or two pairwise associations between grades into account did not fit. The first model that reproduces the observed frequency distribution adequately takes all bivariate associations into account. It is model $[EP]$, $[ES]$, $[PS]$. This model has eight degrees of freedom, and the resulting Pearson chi-square is 5.92 ($p = 0.656$).

Before treating second order CFA in the next section, we compare zero and first order CFA. We will show the effects of taking main effects into account versus assuming they do not exist. The results of zero order CFA applied to the data from Table 4.2 appear in Table 4.3. To make the two versions of CFA comparable, the same alpha level, significance tests, and alpha adjustment procedure were chosen as in Table 4.2.

Application of zero order CFA to the social sciences grades yields six anticlusters and five clusters. Altogether, 14 of the 27 cells showed observed frequencies significantly different from expected. Without interpreting each cluster and anticluster in detail, we use the results presented in Table 4.3 to draw the following two conclusions regarding the relation between zero

Table 4.3. *Zero order CFA of three grades in the social sciences* ($N = 554$).

Grade EPS[a]	Frequencies		Significance tests		Cluster/ anticluster
	o	e	z	p(z)	
+ + +	28	20.52	1.68	0.09	
+ + 0	15	20.52	−1.24	0.21	
+ + −	0	20.52	−4.62	3×10^{-6}	A
+ 0 +	18	20.52	−0.57	0.57	
+ 0 0	11	20.52	−2.14	0.03	
+ 0 −	4	20.52	−3.72	0.0002	A
+ − +	10	20.52	−2.37	0.02	
+ − 0	6	20.52	−3.27	0.001	A
+ − −	3	20.52	−3.94	8×10^{-5}	A
0 + +	36	20.52	3.48	0.0005	C
0 + 0	26	20.52	1.23	0.22	
0 + −	4	20.52	−3.72	0.0002	A
0 0 +	28	20.52	1.68	0.09	
0 0 0	26	20.52	1.23	0.22	
0 0 −	8	20.52	−2.82	0.005	
0 − +	25	20.52	1.01	0.31	
0 − 0	36	20.52	3.48	0.0005	C
0 − −	14	20.52	−1.47	0.14	
− + +	14	20.52	−1.47	0.14	
− + 0	18	20.52	−0.57	0.57	
− + −	1	20.52	−4.39	1×10^{-5}	A
− 0 +	27	20.52	1.46	0.14	
− 0 0	51	20.52	6.86	7×10^{-12}	C
− 0 −	16	20.52	−1.02	0.31	
− − +	26	20.52	1.23	0.22	
− − 0	57	20.52	8.21	2×10^{-16}	C
− − −	46	20.52	5.73	9×10^{-1}	C

$+ .. = 95,$ $0.. = 203,$ $- .. = 256$
$. + . = 142,$ $.0. = 189,$ $. - . = 223$
$.. + = 212,$ $..0 = 246,$ $.. - = 96$

[a]E = education, P = psychology, S = political science.

and first order CFA results:

(1) Because first order CFA takes one more class of effects into account – main effects – than zero order CFA, the possible number of deviations from the model is smaller than in zero order CFA. Therefore, the number of types and antitypes detected by first order CFA is usually smaller than the number detected by zero order CFA.

(2) Deviations detected by first order CFA usually are not the same as those detected by zero order CFA. For example, of the four types and antitypes found in Table 4.2, only three also appeared in Table 4.3. (For additional examples see von Eye and Lienert, in press; Lienert and von Eye 1984a, 1985; Krampen, von Eye, and Brandstädter 1987).

The first order model of CFA is the most widely used. Example fields of application include educational psychology (Lösel 1979), political science (Zerges 1982), psychiatry (Krauth and Lienert 1973), medicine (Görtelmeyer 1988), and psychology (Krampen et al. 1987).

4.3 Second and higher order CFA

First order CFA defines types and antitypes as local associations of any order among d variables. Types and antitypes emerge because of first order interactions between two variables, second order interactions among three variables, up to $(d-1)$st order interactions between all t variables. Introductions to log-linear models often give examples of joint frequency distributions that cannot be explained by taking into account only pairwise interactions (e.g., Fienberg 1980, Chapter 5). Variables displaying these kinds of complex relationships may be analyzed with factor analysis or scaling methods only if second and higher order interactions are considered negligible. When analyzed with first order CFA, first and higher order interactions may lead to the presence of types and antitypes. However, since first order CFA may be viewed as an omnibus test against all kinds of interactions, first order types and antitypes cannot be traced back to a particular interaction pattern without further analysis, usually by log-linear analysis.

One way to determine if significant differences between observed and expected frequencies are due only to first order interactions is to perform second order CFA (von Eye and Lienert 1984; Lienert, Netter, and von Eye 1987; von Eye 1988). This variant of CFA estimates expected frequencies under the assumptions that the d variables

(1) show main effects,
(2) show first order interactions, that is, are associated in pairs, and
(3) do not show any second or higher order interactions.

Under these assumptions discrepancies between observed and expected frequencies occur only if second or higher order interactions prevail. Let d variables be given the ith of which has c_i categories, with $i = 1, \ldots, d$. The log-linear model for second order CFA is

$$\log(y_{i,\ldots,l}) = u_0 + \sum_{i=1}^{d} u_i + u_{12} + u_{13} + \cdots + u_{d-1,d}. \qquad (4.19)$$

Closed forms for maximum likelihood estimators of (4.19) are difficult to give in general form. For three variables Lienert, Reynolds, and Wall (1979; cf. von Eye and Lienert 1984) give a closed form that solves a cubic equation using Cardani's formula. This solution appears in Appendix B. For applications of second order CFA, all major program packages (e.g., BMDP, SPSSX, SAS, SYSTAT) provide modules that allow one to estimate expected frequencies according to the above assumptions.

Within the general linear model, second order CFA corresponds to

$$\hat{y}_{i,\ldots,l} = \sum_{i=0}^{d} x_i b_i + x_{12} b_{d+1} + x_{13} b_{d+2} + \cdots + x_{d-1,d} b_{d'}, \qquad (4.20)$$

where $d' = d + \binom{d}{2}$. Equation (4.5) gives a solution for (4.20). When applied to (4.20), matrix **X** in (4.5) contains the indicators of the configurations and coding variables for the first order interactions. Therefore, (4.20) describes an ANOVA-like model in which there are only main effects and first order interactions.

Estimations of the sample size required for second order CFA can be made using the rules applied for first order CFA. In general, three sources of information help determine required sample sizes. First, the selection of significance test determines sample sizes. For instance, the chi-square test can be performed with sample sizes as small as $n = 8$ and expected frequencies as low as $e = 0.5$ (Larntz 1978). Second, if expected frequencies differ greatly from each other, required sample sizes increase. Third, the required sample size depends on the number of cells of the contingency table. To calculate the number of cells in second order CFA, (4.15) can again be applied. It is important to note, again, that these minimal expected cell frequencies provide only the basis for the tests' proper functioning. To obtain types and antitypes, much larger samples sizes are needed.

When selecting significance tests for second order CFA one must remember that expected frequencies are estimated under the additional constraint that first order interactions are allowed to exist. Therefore, Lehmacher's original z-test and Küchenhoff's variant cannot be applied. All other tests are applicable.

The following first example of second order CFA analyzes the data used to compare eight CFA tests in Table 2.2 (see von Eye and Lienert 1984; von Eye and Rovine 1988). The variables under study are C = narrowed consciousness, T = thought disturbance, and A = affective disturbance. These variables were observed after 65 students had been treated with LSD 50. Table 4.4 summarizes results from both first and second order CFA. Both analyses were performed under the same specifications. The exact one-tailed binomial test was used. (To obtain two-tailed tail probabilities one-sided tail probabilities from Table 2.2 must be doubled.) The

Table 4.4. *First and second order CFA of three LSD symptoms* ($n = 65$).

Symptoms		First order CFA		Second order CFA	
CTA^a	o	e	$p(o)$	e	$p(o)$
111	20	12.506	0.0177	14.2	0.0595
112	1	6.848	0.0062*	6.8	0.0065
121	4	11.402	0.0069	9.8	0.0242
122	12	6.244	0.0199	6.2	0.0190
211	3	9.464	0.0104	8.8	0.0180
212	10	5.182	0.0325	4.2	0.0086
221	15	8.629	0.0214	9.2	0.0357
222	0	4.725	0.0074	5.8	0.0023*

$1.. = 37$, $2.. = 28$
$.1. = 34$, $.2. = 31$
$..1 = 42$, $..2 = 23$

$^a C$ = narrowed consciousness, T = thought disturbance, and A = affective disturbance.

significance level was a priori set to $\alpha = 0.05$. For the eight cells of the $2 \times 2 \times 2$ table, the adjusted $\alpha^* = 0.00625$ results. Bonferroni adjustment was used. Thus, the same α^* applies throughout the table. Expected frequencies for first order CFA were estimated using a CFA program written in BASIC. The expected frequencies for second order CFA were estimated using the algorithm described in Appendix B.

Table 4.4 shows that, on average, second order CFA expected frequencies are closer to the observed frequencies than are first order CFA frequencies. This is because second order CFA estimation takes main effects and first order interactions into account. In the present example, however, this advantage of second order CFA is rather marginal because the three pairwise associations BD, BA, and DA are weak. The present data set is an empirical example of the distributional pattern labeled Meehl's paradox (see Tables 1.2, 1.3, and 2.1). Three variables show this pattern if first order interactions are negligible and if the second order interaction accounts for the joint frequency distribution.

Table 4.4 also shows that although in second order CFA, estimated frequencies are on average closer to the empirical values, for some configurations they can be more distant. Configurations 212 and 222 are examples of this. The difference $o - e$ for configuration 222 even reaches significance, indicating a second order antitype.

This antitype results because the joint frequency distribution cannot be described sufficiently by taking into account only main effects and first order interactions. Rather, the second order interaction, the saturated model, must be considered. Thus, the log-linear model $[BD]$, $[BA]$, $[DA]$ did not provide an acceptable fit ($df = 1$, $X^2 = 37.47$, $p \leqslant 0.0001$).

Substantively, this antitype suggests that even if one considers pairwise associations between LSD 50 symptoms it is highly unlikely that no one would show no LSD symptom. (Note that von Eye and Lienert (1984) identified configuration 212 as a type but did not detect 222 as an antitype. This difference from the present results is due to the use of different significance tests. Von Eye and Lienert used the X^2 test given in (2.24). Here, the exact binomial test was used.)

The second example introduces third order CFA. It uses data from the same experiment. However, to introduce third order CFA in addition to second order CFA a fourth variable, H = hallucinations, was included (see von Eye and Lienert 1984; Lienert et al. 1987). For three variables, second order CFA is the most complex approach one may take in the search for types and antitypes because consideration of the interaction of all three variables – the saturated model – implies that expected and observed frequencies are identical. For four variables third order CFA may be considered. This variant of CFA searches for types and antitypes under the assumption that main effects, interactions in variable pairs, and interactions in variable triplets exist. Interactions beyond those between three variables are assumed not to exist. Thus, types and antitypes emerge only if higher than triplet interactions must be considered to account for the joint frequency distribution. The log-linear model under these assumptions is

$$\log(y_{i,\dots,l}) = u_0 + \sum_i u_i + \sum_{ij} u_{ij} + \sum_{ijk} u_{ijk}. \qquad (4.21)$$

Within the general linear model, third order CFA corresponds to

$$\hat{y}_{i,\dots,l} = \sum_i x_i b_i + \sum_{ij} x_{ij} b_{m1} + \sum_{ijk} x_{ijk} b_{m2}, \qquad (4.22)$$

with $m1 = 1, \dots, \binom{d}{2}$ and $m2 = 1, \dots, \binom{d}{3}$. Equation (4.22) describes an ANOVA model that includes main effects, first, and second order interactions. Higher order interactions are assumed not to exist.

Table 4.5 summarizes results from second and third order CFA for the LSD 50 study. The exact binomial test and Bonferroni alpha adjustment was applied. Thus, $\alpha = 0.05$ was adjusted to be $\alpha^* = 0.05/16 = 0.00313$. The expected frequencies for both analyses were estimated using the BMDP4F program.

Table 4.5 shows that neither second nor third order CFA detect any types or antitypes. The log-linear model given in (4.19), however, did not allow the explanation of the joint frequency distribution of variables C, T, H, and A ($df = 5$, $X^2 = 38.07$, $p < 0.0001$). Therefore, we may conclude there are no pronounced local associations, leading to types or antitypes. Rather, all observed frequencies deviate from expected frequencies by nonsignificant amounts. The middle panel of Table 4.5 shows that the tail probabilities only vary between 0.0078 and 0.3238. None of these values is less than the adjusted alpha.

The right-hand panel of Table 4.5 shows that taking into account all interactions among three variables in third order CFA leads to expected frequencies closer to the observed frequencies than in second order CFA. This result applies in general when higher order versions of CFA are compared with lower order versions. In the present example, all expected frequencies estimated in third order CFA are closer to their

Table 4.5. *Second and third order CFA of four LSD symptoms* ($n = 65$).

Symptoms		Second order CFA		Third order CFA	
CHTA	o	e	p(o)	e	p(o)
1111	12	8.109	0.1053	11.907	0.5384
1112	0	2.834	0.0552	0.093	0.9111
1121	1	4.242	0.0689	1.061	0.7132
1122	4	1.816	0.1085	3.939	0.5604
1211	8	6.105	0.2641	8.082	0.5805
1212	1	3.953	0.0882	0.918	0.6033
1221	3	5.544	0.1843	2.940	0.5682
1222	8	4.389	0.0707	8.060	0.5838
2111	1	3.822	0.0985	1.033	0.7235
2112	3	1.234	0.1263	2.967	0.5745
2121	5	2.826	0.1579	5.000	0.5666
2122	0	1.118	0.3238	0.000	1.000
2211	2	4.971	0.1172	1.965	0.5885
2212	7	2.973	0.0287	7.035	0.5934
2221	10	6.381	0.1015	10.000	0.5833
2222	0	4.675	0.0078	0.000	1.000

$1\ldots = 37$, $2\ldots = 28$
$.1.. = 26$, $.2.. = 39$
$..1. = 34$, $..2. = 31$
$...1 = 42$, $...2 = 23$

respective observed frequency than in second order CFA. (In the example in Table 4.4, higher order expected frequencies were closer to observed frequencies only on average.) Consequently, tail probabilities in type and antitype testing are far from being significant. The smallest probability value is 0.5384.

The last three chapters have introduced zero, first, second, and third order CFA. These versions of CFA differ from each other in the complexity of assumptions made for the estimation of expected frequencies. Zero order CFA assumes no effects whatsoever for the explanation of the observed frequency distribution. First order CFA considers main effects. Second order CFA considers main effects and pairwise interactions, and third order CFA considers, in addition, interactions in triplets of variables. Generalizations of this sequence of assumptions are straightforward. For instance fourth order CFA assumes main effects, pairwise, triplet, and quadruplet interactions for the sufficient reproduction of the observed frequency distribution.

All CFA models from this hierarchy share in common that the interpretation of types and antitypes refers to interactions beyond the ones considered when estimating expected frequencies. For instance, types and antitypes in first order CFA may be explained as due to at least pairwise associations. The kind of relations, however, that led to the presence of types or antitypes remains unspecified. Also, the importance of single variables or groups of variables for the definition of types and antitypes are not indicated. Log-linear modeling enables one to handle these problems.

The next chapter introduces regional models of CFA, which allow comparison of groups of variables. Types and antitypes of regional CFA models contradict the null hypothesis of no relationships between variable groups.

5

Regional models of CFA: applications and examples

The last chapter discussed *global CFA models*. These models assign every variable the same status. For instance, first order CFA considers the main effects of all variables, and second order CFA considers all pairwise associations rather than a subset of them. *Regional CFA models* define groups of variables. Variables belonging to the same group may interact. Variables belonging to different groups are assumed to be independent from each other. If these assumptions are violated, types and antitypes indicate local relationships between the groups. The present chapter introduces the following regional models of CFA: interaction structure analysis (ISA; Krauth and Lienert 1974), *d*-sample CFA (Lienert 1971c), prediction CFA (PCFA; Lienert and Krauth 1973a), conditional CFA (Lienert 1978; Krauth 1980a), and CFA of directed relations (DCFA; von Eye 1985).

5.1 Interaction structure analysis

Most approaches to the analysis of relationships among several categorical variables define one interaction term for each group of three or more variables. For instance, information theory defines an interaction as "a unique dependency from which all relations of a lower ordinality are removed." (Krippendorff 1986, p. 37; cf. von Eye 1985). However, in many instances, special concepts are necessary to meet with substantive assumptions. An example of such a concept is Krauth and Lienert's (1973a) definition of *higher order interactions*.

Higher order interactions can be defined only if there are at least three variables. For two variables, interactions coincide with simple associations that can be measured with, for example, chi-square coefficients. Krauth and Lienert consider a higher order interaction as the relationship between any two nonempty, nonoverlapping sets of variables. In other words, to investigate higher order interactions in the Krauth and Lienert sense, two groups of variables are analyzed. Altogether, these groups must contain $d \geqslant 3$ variables. Let the first group contain d_A variables, with $0 < d_A < d$. Let the second contain d_B variables, with $0 < d_B < d$. For the sum $d_c = d_A + d_B$ the inequality $2 < d_c \leqslant d$ holds. The relationship between the two groups is called $(d_c - 1)$st order interaction. For example, if the two groups together contain three variables, the interaction is a second order interaction.

Suppose we analyze the three variables 1, 2, and 3. Information theory and Lancaster's chi-square decomposition define for these variables one second order interaction term involving all three variables. There is no grouping of 1, 2, and 3. Interaction structure analysis (ISA) distinguishes three second order interaction terms [1.23], [2.13], and [3.12].

ISA interactions among three variables have the following characteristics (Krauth and Lienert 1973a):

(1) If there is no second order interaction and no first order interaction (defined as association), the three variables are totally independent.

(2) If there are no first order interactions, there may be second order interactions nevertheless.

(3) The existence of second order interactions follows from the existence of first order interactions.

To further illustrate the concept of ISA interactions let the four variables 1, 2, 3, and 4 be given. For these variables, Table 5.1 summarizes all possible ISA interactions. Table 5.1 shows that there are two types of third order interactions. The first involves one group with one variable and a second group with three variables. The second type of third order interaction involves two groups, each containing two variables. Alto-

Table 5.1. *ISA interactions for four variables.*

No. of variables in grouping	No. of groupings	Groupings
2	$\binom{4}{2} = 6$	1.2, 1.3, 1.4, 2.3, 2.4, 3.4
3	$\binom{4}{3}\binom{3}{2} = 12$	1.23, 1.24, 1.34, 2.13, 2.14, 2.34, 3.12, 3.14, 3.24, 4.12, 4.13, 4.23
4	$\binom{4}{1} + \binom{4}{1}/2 = 7$	1.234, 2.134, 3.124, 4.123, 12.34, 13.24, 14.23

gether, for $d = 4$ variables there are

$$t = 0.5(3^d + 1) - 2^d \tag{5.1}$$

ISA interactions (see equation (3.1)).

When comparing two groups of variables ISA makes the following two assumptions:

(1) Within each group there may be interactions of any order. (Note that these are interactions of the type analyzed with information theory or log-linear models.) Let the first group, A, contain d_A variables, and the second group, B, d_B variables. Then, the variables in group A may show a $(d_A - 1)$st order association, and variables in group B a $(d_B - 1)$st order association.

(2) Groups A and B are independent of each other.

It follows from these assumptions that types and antitypes emerge only if there is a relationship between the two groups. ISA has been used mainly to investigate relationships between dependent and independent variables. However, ISA is also applicable to groups of variables that have the same status.

5.1.1 Estimation of expected frequencies

To estimate expected frequencies for ISA one may pursue either one of two strategies. The first strategy is useful when ISA is calculated with pocket calculators. It utilizes the fact that ISA implicitly transforms a d-dimensional matrix into a two-dimensional one. The categories of the first dimension are formed by variables in group A. Let group A contain d_A variables. By crossing these variables, the matrix of group A variables has

$$c_A = \prod_{i=1}^{d_A} c_{Ai} \qquad (5.2)$$

cells, where c_{Ai} denotes the number of categories of the ith variable of group A. ISA considers each of the c_A cells a state of the composite variable A. In an analogous fashion, group B variables form the composite variable B, with c_B categories.

To compare group A with group B, ISA forms a two-dimensional matrix with $c_A \times c_B$ categories. Each of the cells of A is a marginal cell of the rows of this complete ISA matrix. Each of the cells of B is a marginal cell of the columns of the complete ISA matrix. The order of the states within A and within B is of no importance because ISA considers both composite variables A and B categorical. Due to this fact, changes of the order of the states or changes of the order of A and B have no effect on ISA results.

The expected frequencies of the two-dimensional ISA matrix may be calculated using the well-known chi-square formula "row-sum $\times$ column-sum/n" (see (4.18)).

The second strategy for estimating expected frequencies in ISA is useful when the investigator is using computer programs, for instance, programs for log-linear modeling. In the model specification, variables from group A are allowed to display interactions (in the log-linear modeling sense) of any order with each other. This is also true for variables from group B. For the sake of simplicity, suppose group A contains variables 1 and 2, and group B variables 3 and 4. Then, the log-linear model under ISA assumptions is

$$\log(y_{i,j,k,l}) = u_0 + u_1 + u_2 + u_3 + u_4 + u_{12} + u_{34}. \qquad (5.4)$$

Accordingly, within the general linear model, ISA corresponds to

$$\hat{y}_{i,j,k,l} = x_0 b_0 + x_1 b_1 + x_2 b_2 + x_3 b_3 + x_4 b_4 + x_{12} b_5 + x_{34} b_6.$$

$$(5.5)$$

5.1.2 Goals of ISA

Krauth and Lienert (1973a, 1974) suggested the use of ISA for two purposes. First, ISA allows the researcher to identify the interaction structure of two groups of variables. ISA leads to a description of variable interactions which takes the a priori classification of variables in two groups into consideration. However, as can be seen from (5.4), each ISA model can equivalently be expressed as a log-linear model. Therefore, this first goal of ISA application does not go beyond log-linear modeling techniques. Therefore, this book focuses on the second goal of ISA application.

The second goal is more germane to CFA. It involves the search for types and antitypes. ISA types may be interpreted with respect to the assumption of independence between groups *A* and *B*. Krauth and Lienert (1973) suggested that group *A* contain independent and group *B* dependent variables. Then, types suggest that configurations of independent variables lead to certain configurations of dependent variables. Therefore, ISA types may provide support for the notion of causal relationships between independent and dependent variables. Accordingly, ISA antitypes suggest that the probability of certain configurations of dependent variables, conditional on configurations of independent variables, is below expectancy.

It should be emphasized that even though ISA results may support assumptions of causal relationships between independent and dependent variables, ISA does not prove causality. The basic reason for this caveat is that in ISA, the variables obtain their status as dependent and independent by definition. ISA itself analyzes the two groups *A* and *B* in a symmetrical fashion. Transposing a two-dimensional ISA matrix or switching the dependent and independent status of the variable groups does not affect those cells identified as types or antitypes.

5.1.3 Models of ISA and data examples

To illustrate the analysis of relationships and the search for types and antitypes with ISA, an example from experimental stress research will be taken (Krauth and Lienert 1973). A sample of $n = 150$ young adults participated in an experiment under one of two conditions. The first group took a cognitive performance test twice under relaxed conditions. The second group took the same test once under the same conditions as the first group, and a second time under stress. In each group, half of the participants had an above-average IQ, the other half a below-average IQ. Two variables were observed: change in quantitative performance (X) and change in qualitative performance (Y). X was measured with categories $1 = $ more items processed and $2 = $ the same number or fewer items processed. Y was measured with categories $1 = $ more items correct, $2 = $ the same number of items correct, and $3 = $ fewer items correct. The experimental conditions (S) were assigned a 1 for the control group and a 2 for the experimental group. Intelligence (I) had categories $1 = $ below average and $2 = $ above average. Crossed, these four variables form a 2 (change in quantitative performance) $\times$ 3 (change in qualitative performance) $\times$ 2 (experimental condition) $\times$ 2 (intelligence) contingency table.

To perform an ISA, each of these four variables must be assigned to one of two groups. Table 5.1 showed that for four variables there are 25 possible partitionings of the variables into two groups, or 25 possible ISA designs. Table 5.2 gives for each of these designs the overall Pearson chi-square, degrees of freedom, and tail probabilities. To compute the ISA models, all 25 two-dimensional tables were formed. The overall Pearson chi-squares were calculated using (4.18). Degrees of freedom were calculated using

(1) for two variables in two groupings
$$df = (c_1 - 1)(c_2 - 1), \tag{5.6}$$

(2) for three variables in two groupings, with the second grouping containing two variables
$$df = (c_1 - 1)(c_2 c_3 - 1), \tag{5.7}$$

(3) for four variables in two groupings, each containing two variables
$$df = (c_1 c_2 - 1)(c_3 c_4 - 1), \tag{5.8}$$

Table 5.2. *ISA interactions for the variables quantitative change (X), quali-tative change (Y), experimental condition (S), and intelligence (I).*

No. of variables in grouping	Grouping	X^2	df	$p(X^2)$
2	[X.Y]	4.10	2	0.129
	[X.S]	23.46	1	<0.001
	[X.I]	0.23	1	0.623
	[Y.S]	67.63	2	<0.001
	[Y.I]	0.52	2	0.772
	[S.I]	0.23	1	0.631
3	[YS.X]	31.47	5	<0.001
	[XS.Y]	79.02	6	<0.001
	[XY.S]	92.10	5	<0.001
	[YI.X]	25.95	5	<0.001
	[XI.Y]	25.41	6	<0.001
	[XY.I]	22.61	5	<0.001
	[SI.X]	37.94	3	<0.001
	[XI.S]	37.86	3	<0.001
	[XS.I]	17.16	3	<0.001
	[SI.Y]	69.55	6	<0.001
	[YI.S]	68.60	5	<0.001
	[YS.I]	2.02	5	0.846
4	[YSI.X]	55.16	11	<0.001
	[XSI.Y]	91.21	14	<0.001
	[XYI.S]	96.10	11	<0.001
	[XYS.I]	28.56	11	0.003
	[XY.SI]	135.01	15	<0.001
	[XS.YI]	126.09	15	<0.001
	[YS.XI]	57.52	15	<0.001

(4) for four variables in two groupings, one containing only one variable

$$df = (c_1 - 1)(c_2 c_3 c_4 - 1), \qquad (5.9)$$

where $c_1 - c_4$ denote the number of cells of groups A and B.

For instance, suppose group A contains three variables with 2, 3, and 2 categories, respectively. Then, the matrix of the crossed group A variables has 12 cells. Let group B contain two variables with 5 and 2 categories, respectively. Then, the matrix of the crossed group B variables has 10 cells. This design has (12-1)(10-1) = 99 degrees of freedom.

Table 5.2 shows that, with one exception, for all models with three or four variables, the null hypothesis of no association between the two ISA groups must be rejected. The ISA models that relate only two variables to one another are equivalent to ordinary chi-square analyses. Therefore, they are of only secondary importance in the present context.

For the present purposes we are interested in models that include one or both of the independent variables experimental condition (S) and intelligence (I) in one group, and one or both of the dependent variables X and Y in the other group. The models that fit this description are $[X.S]$, $[X.I]$, $[Y.S]$, $[Y.I]$, $[X.SI]$, $[Y.SI]$, $[XY.S]$, $[XY.I]$, and $[XY.SI]$.

Table 5.2 shows that all ISA models analyzing the dependent variables X and Y in relation to the experimental variable S, suggest a strong association between independent and dependent variables. However, there is no statistically significant association between the dependent variables and intelligence. Combined, however, X and Y are significantly associated with both S and I. There is also a strong association between X and Y as a group and S and I as a group. A complete exploratory ISA searches all [independent variables] [dependent variables] designs for types and antitypes. However, to illustrate the two-dimensional format and the search for types and antitypes, only the most complex ISA interaction will be analyzed here. This interaction contains both independent and both dependent variables. The two independent variables, experimental condition and intelligence, have two categories each. When these variables are crossed, the resulting contingency table has four cells. ISA treats these four cells as row marginals of the two-dimensional ISA cross-tabulation. The order of the cells is irrelevant.

Table 5.3. *Two-dimensional format of ISA with two independent and two dependent variables.*

Independent variables *SI*		Dependent variables						Sums
	X	1	1	1	2	2	2	
	Y	1	2	3	1	2	3	
11		13	6	2	11	2	0	34
12		17	12	3	3	0	1	36
21		1	2	19	1	12	7	42
22		1	3	3	1	10	20	38
Sums		32	23	27	16	24	28	150

Accordingly, the two dependent variables quantitative change (X, two categories) and qualitative change (Y, three categories) form a table with six cells. Thus, the two-dimensional ISA cross-tabulation has 4×6 cells. Table 5.3 gives this cross-tabulation.

For the search for types and antitypes, expected frequencies can be calculated using (4.18). For instance, the expected frequency for cell 1111 is calculated as $e_{1111} = 34 \times 32/150 = 7.25$. Table 5.4 gives the results of CFA under ISA assumptions.

Table 5.4 shows that application of ISA reveals four types and no antitype. The first type has pattern 14. This pattern indicates that the fourth cell in the first row of Table 5.3 forms a type. In terms of the four variables under study this cell has pattern 1121. The type suggests that more often than expected under the null hypothesis of no association between independent and dependent variables, less intelligent control group subjects process fewer items in the second trial while increasing the number of correct solutions.

Pattern 11 almost forms a type. It shows that less intelligent subjects tend to improve in both quantitative and qualitative performance. However, after alpha-adjustment the difference between $o = 13$ and $e = 7.25$ is no longer significant.

Table 5.4. *ISA of the independent variables (group A), experimental condition and intelligence, and the dependent variables (group B), change in quantitative performance and change in qualitative performance.*

Configuration AB	Frequencies		Significance tests		Type/antitype
	o	e	$\|z\|$	$p(z)$	
11	13	7.25	2.187	0.0287	
12	6	5.21	0.351	0.7258	
13	2	6.12	1.700	0.0890	
14	11	3.63	3.919	0.00009	T
15	2	5.44	1.502	0.1330	
16	0	6.35	2.574	0.0100	
21	17	7.68	3.453	0.0005	T
22	12	5.52	2.810	0.0050	
23	3	6.48	1.398	0.1622	
24	3	3.84	0.434	0.6641	
25	0	5.76	2.447	0.0143	
26	1	6.72	2.258	0.0240	
31	1	8.96	2.742	0.0061	
32	2	6.44	1.788	0.0737	
33	19	7.56	4.270	0.00002	T
34	1	4.48	1.669	0.0951	
35	12	6.72	2.084	0.0372	
36	7	7.84	0.308	0.7580	
41	1	8.11	2.566	0.0103	
42	3	5.83	1.194	0.2323	
43	3	6.84	1.503	0.1329	
44	1	4.05	1.537	0.1242	
45	10	6.08	1.623	0.1046	
46	20	7.09	4.965	6×10^{-7}	T

In the group of above-average intelligent subjects the absence of stress led to an improvement in both quantitative and qualitative performance. Configuration 21 (pattern 1211) was observed 17 times, but was expected only 7.68 times. In this experimental group, subjects also tended to increase the number of items processed without also increasing the number of solutions (pattern 1212). However, after alpha adjustment the probability of $p = 0.005$ for the difference between the 12 observed and 5.52 expected cases is no longer significant. (Note that this is the case even if Holm adjustment is applied.)

Table 5.4 shows that the third type, pattern 33, is configuration 2113 from Table 5.3. This type suggests that below-average intelligent subjects increase their speed at the cost of quality of work when they are exposed to experimental stress. The last type, configuration 46 (pattern 2223), suggests that for above-average intelligent subjects, experimental stress has even worse effects. These subjects process fewer items and provide fewer correct solutions.

Overall, the pattern of results suggests that experimental stress affects qualitative performance. Absence of experimental stress improves qualitative performance. The stratification of subjects in groups of below and above average intelligence shows that experimental stress slows the higher intelligence group's performance. The lower intelligence group reacts to the stress with increased speed. Absence of stress speeds both groups' performance. However, some of the lower intelligence subjects slow their performance while increasing the number of correct solutions.

To explain this complex pattern of types one needs a log-linear model with two three-way interactions. The model links both dependent variables in different interaction terms to the independent variables while assuming the independent variables not associated with each other. This model has a goodness of fit Pearson $X^2 = 7.84$, with $p \geqslant 0.25$ ($df = 6$).

5.2 ISA strategies

As discussed in the last chapter, ISA is a strategy for the detection of types and antitypes due to local associations between two groups of variables. In many instances, however, a partitioning of variables into just two groups may not be enough (Fleischmann and Lienert 1982; Havránek and Lienert 1984, von Eye and Lienert, in press). For instance, when chains of variables are assumed, at least three groupings must be considered. In a chain with three elements, a first group of variables, A, determines a second group, B, which, in turn, determines a third group, C. Each of these groups would contain at least one variable.

Thus, in more general terms ISA can be defined as a CFA strategy used to detect types and antitypes that emerge because of local associations between two or more groups of variables. ISA null hypotheses assume

(1) the $g \geqslant 2$ groups of variables are totally independent of each other, and
(2) within each group of variables, interactions of any order may prevail.

The following example is taken from Lienert and von Eye (in press). Four symptoms of depression in children are analyzed. A sample of $n = 349$ children was observed with respect to the following behavior disorders taken as predictors of depression: does not want to play (P), slow thinking and acting (T), addresses topic of death in conversations with parents (D), and cries without obvious reason (C). Each of the symptoms had categories $1 = $ absent and $2 = $ present. For the purposes of ISA, these four symptoms will be assigned to three groups. The first group consists of symptoms P and T which, together, form the composite symptom *psychosocial inhibition*. This group has categories $1 = $ both P and T absent, $2 = P$ absent and T present, $3 = P$ present and T absent, and $4 = $ both P and T present. The other two groups of variables contain only one symptom each; D and C, respectively. For significance tests alpha was set to 0.05. Bonferroni adjustment led to $\alpha^* = 0.05/16 = 0.003125$. Because of the relatively large sample size, Lehmacher's (1981) powerful test was applied without Küchenhoff's (1986) continuity correction. Table 5.5 summarizes the results of *generalized ISA*, that is, results of ISA with more than two variable groups.

Application of Lehmacher's test revealed two ISA types and one ISA antitype. The X^2 and the z-tests, less powerful tests, did not discover any types or antitypes. Because in the present example independent and dependent variables were not

Table 5.5. *ISA of three groups of symptoms of depression.*

Symptom configuration	Frequencies		Significance tests		Type/antitype
	o	e	$|z_L|$	$p(z)$	
111	66	40.046	3.827	0.00006	T
112	27	30.290	0.821	0.2058	
113	15	25.764	2.863	0.0021	A
114	17	17.408	0.128	0.4490	
121	35	44.086	1.973	0.0242	
122	35	27.793	1.834	0.0333	
123	25	23.640	0.369	0.3561	
124	13	15.973	0.953	0.1703	
211	19	23.920	1.270	0.1020	
212	14	15.080	0.332	0.3699	
213	19	12.827	2.031	0.0211	
214	5	8.667	1.433	0.0759	
221	18	21.948	1.047	0.1474	
222	11	13.837	0.899	0.1843	
223	15	11.769	1.096	0.1365	
224	15	7.952	2.845	0.0022	T
Sums (n)	349	349.00			

$1.. = 233, \quad 2.. = 116$
$.1. = 182, \quad .2. = 167$
$..1 = 138, \quad ..2 = 87, \quad ..3 = 74, \quad ..4 = 50$

explicitly distinguished, interpretation refers to the ISA null hypotheses only.

The first type in Table 5.5 has pattern 111. Here, the last 1 denotes the first category of the composite symptom psychosocial inhibition. This type contains those children who do not suffer any depression symptoms. It is the largest group of children in the present sample. The one antitype has pattern 113. It indicates that these are children who do not want to play but who do not show any other symptoms. Only 15 children displayed this pattern while 25.76 were expected. The second type has pattern 224, representing those children who suffer from all four symptoms under study.

Altogether, generalized ISA shows that the three groups of symptoms have a strong tendency to be either all absent or all present. Single groups of symptoms were observed either less often than expected or as often as expected under the null hypothesis. The present data set is so complex that not only the log-linear model that corresponds to the grouping assumption but also the model that assumed all four three-way interactions do not provide an acceptable fit. Thus, CFA and ISA can be seen as methods that shed light on very complex data sets.

It is important to note that while CFA has thus far been introduced as a predominantly exploratory technique, ISA has a strong explanatory component. In all examples given thus far, the grouping of variables was known a priori. If the grouping of variables is not known, or the researcher does not a priori exclude certain groupings as irrelevant, all groupings may be considered in order not to overlook important findings. Table 5.1 showed that for four variables there are 25 possible variable partitions into two groups. This number increases exponentially with the number of variables. For instance, consider the five variables 1, 2, 3, 4, and 5. The number of possible partitions of these five variables into two groups is 90. In addition, there are 80 partitions into three and 15 into four groups. Table 5.6 gives these partitions.

Altogether, there are 185 ISA designs for four variables. Disregarding tests for types and antitypes, 185 tests on the same sample lead to an adjusted significance threshold of $\alpha^* = 0.05/185 = 0.00027$. Including all type and antitype tests leads to adjusted alphas that virtually cannot be exceeded. Therefore, complete exploratory ISAs can be recommended only for small numbers of variables, small numbers of groups, and large sample sizes.

There have been attempts to define strategies for reducing the number of significance tests. For instance, von Eye (1986) proposed *hierarchical ISA*. This strategy starts with an examination of all bivariate interactions. Only the significant bivariate interactions are used in trivariate interactions, and so forth. Hierarchical ISA is more efficient than systematic inspection of all possible interactions when the number of

Table 5.6. *Partitions of five variables in three and four groups.*

No. of variables involved	No. of groups	Groups
Partitions into three groups		
3	$\binom{5}{3} = 10$	1.2.3, 1.2.4, 1.2.5, 1.3.4, 1.3.5, 1.4.5, 2.3.4, 2.3.5, 2.4.5, 3.4.5
4	$\binom{5}{2}\binom{3}{2} = 30$	12.3.4, 12.3.5, 12.4.5, 13.2.4, 13.2.5, 13.4.5, 14.2.3, 14.2.5, 14.3.5, 15.2.3, 15.2.4, 15.3.4, 23.1.4, 23.1.5, 23.4.5, 24.1.3, 24.1.5, 24.3.5, 25.1.3, 25.1.4, 25.3.4, 34.1.2, 34.1.5, 34.2.5, 35.1.2, 35.1.4, 35.2.4, 45.1.2, 45.1.3, 45.2.3
5	$\binom{5}{3} + \binom{5}{2}\binom{3}{1} = 40$	123.4.5, 124.3.5, 125.3.4, 134.2.5, 135.2.4, 145.2.3, 234.1.5, 235.1.4, 245.1.3, 345.1.2, 12.34.5, 12.35.4, 12.45.3, 13.24.5, 13.25.4, 13.45.2, 14.23.5, 14.25.3, 14.35.2, 15.23.4, 15.24.3, 15.34.2, 23.14.5, 23.15.4, 23.45.1, 24.13.5, 24.15.3, 24.35.1, 25.13.4, 25.14.3, 25.34.1, 34.12.5, 34.15.2, 34.25.1, 35.12.4, 35.14.2, 35.24.1, 45.12.3, 45.13.2, 45.23.1
Partitions into four groups		
4	$\binom{5}{4} = 5$	1.2.3.4, 1.2.3.5, 1.2.4.5, 1.3.4.5, 2.3.4.5
5	$\binom{6}{2} = 10$	12.3.4.5, 13.2.4.5, 14.2.3.5, 15.2.3.4, 23.1.4.5, 24.1.3.5, 25.1.3.4, 34.1.2.5, 35.1.2.4, 45.1.2.3

variables is large, the number of significant interactions at each level of the hierarchy is small, and when the complexity of interactions needed to explain the observed frequency distribution is low. However, the adjusted alpha level may still be prohibitively small. Therefore, ISA still is best applied if the grouping of variables is known a priori.

Another important issue of ISA application concerns the status of variables. In Section 5.1, ISA was introduced as a method of distinguishing between dependent and independent variables. It should be emphasized again that this distinction is purely interpretational in nature. ISA treats groups of variables symmetrically. When the researcher transposes the matrix and reinterprets independent variables as dependent and vice versa, the same configurations constitute types and antitypes. Therefore, ISA cannot prove causal relationships. Rather, it is a method for detecting types and antitypes that suggest local causal relationships. In addition, ISA is applicable even if causal relationships between groups of variables are not assumed. Table 5.5 gives an example of a case in which the three groups of variables have the same status.

Table 5.5 shows also that ISA and first order CFA coincide if each group contains only one variable. ISA coincides with zero order CFA if each group contains only one variable and all marginals are uniformly distributed. Subsequent chapters will show that prediction CFA and k-sample CFA follow the same strategy as ISA. (Table 5.22 gives another example of an ISA with three groups of variables.)

5.3 Special ISA application: independence of factorially defined tests

Fleischmann and Lienert (1982) applied ISA to investigate the independence structure of subtests loading on different factors. A sample of $n = 237$ older adults, aged between 60 and 94 years, took six cognitive performance tests. The tests were assumed to require performance in terms of either speed or power. The tests included the Benton (1974) test (B), the maze test (Chapius 1959) (L), memory span for numbers (N), number symbol test (S), mosaic test (M), and the number series test (Oswald and Roth 1978) (V). Performance in each test was scored as either below median (1) or above median (2).

A varimax rotated two-factor solution revealed that B, N, and M loaded only on the power factor, and L only on the speed factor. S and V showed high loadings on both factors. Therefore, they were excluded from ISA.

If factorial independence implies independence in ISA the null hypothesis of no association between the group of power tests and the speed test cannot be rejected. To test this hypothesis an eight row by two column contingency table was formed. The eight rows result from crossing the three binary power variables B, N, and M. The two columns are the two levels of the speed variable L. Table 5.7 gives this cross-tabulation and the results of ISA. Lehmacher's (1981) test was applied with Küchenhoff's continuity correction. Bonferroni adjustment resulted in an $\alpha^* = 0.05/16 = 0.003125$.

Application of ISA revealed two types and two antitypes. Considering that no causal relationship between the two groups of variables was assumed, this result contradicts the assumption that test scales from different, orthogonal factors are necessarily independent in ISA. More specifically, the first antitype, pattern 11, shows that the number of subjects who perform below the median in all three power tests, as well as in the speed test, is below expectation. In accordance with this antitype, the first type, pattern 12, suggests there are far more old adults than expected who perform below the median in the power tests but above the median in the speed test. We may conclude this is a group of subjects who respond quickly at the cost of accuracy.

The second type-antitype pair shows a corresponding pattern of performance. The type contains subjects who score above the median in the power tests B and M, and below the median in the power test N and the speed test. Accordingly, there are fewer subjects than expected who perform above the median in B, M, and in L. This type-antitype pair suggests there is a larger than expected group of older subjects who sacrifice speed to improve performance in some of the power tests, thus complementing the first type-antitype pair.

Altogether, the pattern of type and antitype pairs suggests that in this sample of older adults there is a systematic pattern of high speed-low power, and low speed-high power perfor-

Table 5.7. *ISA of three power tests and one speed test* ($n = 237$).

Tests[a]	Frequencies		Significance tests		
PL	o	e	$|z'_L|$	$p(z)$	Type/antitype
11	16	28.380	3.603	0.0002	A
12	41	28.620	3.603	0.0002	T
21	11	8.464	1.023	0.1532	
22	6	8.536	1.023	0.1532	
31	5	5.975	0.281	0.3895	
32	7	6.025	0.281	0.3895	
41	14	11.949	0.666	0.2526	
42	10	12.051	0.666	0.2526	
51	12	16.928	1.638	0.0507	
52	22	17.072	1.638	0.0507	
61	26	16.928	3.170	0.0008	T
62	8	17.072	3.170	0.0008	A
71	8	9.460	0.458	0.3234	
72	11	9.540	0.458	0.3234	
81	26	19.916	1.933	0.0267	
82	14	20.084	1.933	0.0267	

$1. = 57,$ $2. = 17,$ $3. = 12,$ $4. = 24,$
$5. = 34,$ $6. = 34,$ $7. = 19,$ $8. = 40,$
$.1 = 118,$ $.2 = 119$

[a]P denotes the composite variable "power tests"; for explanation see text.

mance. This pattern contradicts the assumption that tests loading on different orthogonal simple structure factors are necessarily independent when analyzed with ISA.

5.4 Prediction CFA

Sections 5.1–5.3 presented ISA as a method for the investigation of local relationships between two or more groups of variables. ISA typically includes independent and dependent variables. However, Sections 5.2 and 5.3 showed that variable groups with the same status may also be analyzed with ISA. Essentially, interpretations of relationships as causal or symmetrical depend on the researcher's perception of the status of variables. In and of itself, ISA is symmetrical.

The same principle applies to *prediction CFA* (PCFA) (Lienert and Krauth 1973a; Lienert and Wolfrum 1979; Heilmann, Lienert and Maly 1979; Hütter, Müller, and Lienert 1981; Lienert and Rey 1982; Havránek, Kohnen, and Lienert 1984). This approach uses the same rationale as ISA. It assigns variables to one of two groups. One is the group of predictors, the other the group of criteria. Predictors combined form a composite variable, as do criteria. The assumptions PCFA makes for the estimation of expected frequencies parallel the assumptions of ISA:

(1) Predictors are totally independent from criteria.
(2) Within the predictors and within the criteria, interactions of any order may prevail.

The following example of PCFA application analyzes suicide frequencies in Germany during and after World War II (Krauth and Lienert 1973a; cf. Chipuer and von Eye 1989). PCFA analyzes the three variables sex (1 = male, 2 = female), year of observation (1 = 1952, 2 = 1944), and method of suicide (1 = gas, 2 = hanging, 3 = soporific, 4 = drowning, 5 = cutting veins, 6 = shooting, and 7 = jumping). For the present purposes, sex and year of observation serve as predictors and method of suicide as the criterion. Together, the two predictors form a composite variable with the four categories 1 = male in 1952, 2 = male in 1944, 3 = female in 1952, and 4 = female in 1944. Table 5.8 presents the results of PCFA. Bonferroni adjustment resulted in an adjusted $\alpha^* = 0.05/28 = 0.00179$. The standard normal z-approximation of the binomial test was applied.

Table 5.8 shows that PCFA identified five types and six antitypes of suicide. The first level of the composite predictor forms a type. It is pattern 51, which indicates that more males than expected for 1952 commit suicide by cutting their veins. The second level of the composite predictor forms two types and two antitypes. The types suggest that during World War

Table 5.8. *PCFA of the predictors sex and year of occurrence and criterion method of suicide.*

Configurations[a]	Frequencies		Significance tests		Type/ antitype
	o	e	$\|z\|$	$p(z)$	
11	52	43.624	1.310	0.1904	
12	16	44.376	4.401	0.00001	A
13	47	43.875	0.487	0.6260	
14	61	44.125	2.624	0.0087	
21	31	38.667	1.268	0.2047	
22	76	39.333	6.017	1.7×10^{-9}	T
23	14	38.889	4.106	0.00004	A
24	35	39.111	0.676	0.4987	
31	44	38.915	0.839	0.4016	
32	7	39.585	5.332	9.8×10^{-8}	A
33	97	39.138	9.518	1.8×10^{-21}	T
34	9	39.362	4.981	6.3×10^{-7}	A
41	20	25.530	1.115	0.2649	
42	19	25.970	1.394	0.1634	
43	10	25.677	3.152	0.0002	A
44	54	25.823	5.650	1.6×10^{-8}	T
51	22	11.402	3.165	0.0016	T
52	15	11.598	1.007	0.3138	
53	5	11.467	1.926	0.0542	
54	4	11.533	2.237	0.0253	
61	3	12.145	2.647	0.0081	
62	35	12.355	6.500	8.1×10^{-11}	T
63	0	12.215	3.526	0.0004	A
64	11	12.285	0.370	0.7115	
71	2	3.718	0.893	0.3717	
72	9	3.782	2.690	0.0071	
73	2	3.739	0.902	0.3671	
74	2	3.761	0.910	0.3626	

1. = 176, 2. = 156, 3. = 157, 4. = 103, 5. = 46, 6. = 49, 7. = 15
.1 = 174, .2 = 177, .3 = 175, .4 = 176

[a]Predictor is composite (sex and year of suicide); criterion is method of suicide.

II males committed suicide by hanging (pattern 22) or shooting themselves (pattern 62). The antitypes suggest that during World War II males did not commit suicide using gas or soporifics.

The third level of the composite predictor forms one type and three antitypes. The type suggests that in 1952 women committed suicide using soporifics (pattern 33). The antitypes indicate that in 1952 women less often than expected committed suicide by hanging, drowning, or shooting themselves (patterns 23, 43, and 63). The fourth level of the composite predictor forms one antitype, indicating that women in 1944 far less often than expected used soporifics for suicide (pattern 34). This predictor level also forms a type, indicating that women during that period more often than expected drowned themselves (pattern 44).

The large number of types and antitypes leads one to the conclusion that the model for the estimation of expected frequencies, assuming there are no local associations between predictors and criteria, is untenable. Log-linear analyses, conducted to identify the structure of interactions between the three variables sex, year of observation, and method of suicide did not lead to a parsimonious description of the observed joint frequency distribution. Rather, all (unconditional) models less complex than the saturated model had to be rejected.

Depending on the number of predictors and criteria the following *classification of PCFA* models can be introduced:

(1) uni-univariate PCFA: one predictor – one criterion
(2) multi-univariate PCFA: two or more predictors – one criterion
(3) uni-multivariate PCFA: one predictor – two or more criteria
(4) multi-multivariate PCFA: two or more predictors – two or more criteria.

Several times it has been claimed in the literature (e.g., Lienert and Krauth 1973e; Lienert and Wolfrum 1979; Heilmann et al. 1979), that PCFA is a nonparametric analog of parametric

Table 5.9 *Characteristics of ISA and PCFA in comparison to ANOVA and regression.*

Characteristics[a]	ISA/PCFA	ANOVA	Regression
Measurement level			
(a) Predictors	Discrete	Discrete	Discrete or continuous
(b) Criteria	Discrete	Continuous	Continuous
Nature of variables			
(a) Predictors	Random or constant	Constant	Constant
(b) Criteria	Random or constant	Random	Random
Nature of relationship	Symmetrical	Asymmetrical	Asymmetrical
Basic equation	$e = [P][C]$	$\hat{y} = $ grand mean $ + f(P)$[b]	
Typical research strategy	Exploratory	Explanatory	Explanatory

[a]For the purposes of this table the notion of predictors includes independent variables and "variables in group *A*", and criteria includes dependent variables and "variables in group *B*."
[b]*P* denotes predictors, *C* denotes criteria.

regression analysis. However, an inspection of the algorithms for estimating expectancies shows that regression analysis is basically an asymmetric approach. Regression explains a criterion by the weighted sum of predictor contributions. The well-known equation for simple regression is

$$y = a_0 + a_1 x + e. \tag{5.10}$$

Even though PCFA uses a similar equation for calculating expected frequencies (see (5.4) and (5.5)), there is a basic difference. In regression analysis the criterion is explained as a function of the predictors. In PCFA, main effects and interactions of both predictors and criteria contribute to the explanation of the joint frequency distribution. Thus, PCFA is essentially a symmetrical approach.

Transposing the two-dimensional matrix of PFCA and exchanging predictors and criteria leads to the same results. In contrast, exchanging x and y in (5.10) may lead to different results. Because $p(x \mid y) \geqslant p(x) \rightarrow p(y \mid x) \geqslant p(y)$, it is rarely the case that the equation $y = a_0 + a_1 x + e$ leads to significant regression coefficients while the equation $x = a_2 + a_3 y + e$ leads to nonsignificant coefficients. However, one of the estimated parameters may very well be more impressive.

When comparing ISA and ANOVA we obtain the same results. ANOVA explains dependent variables as a function of independent constants. ISA explains a frequency distribution as a function of two groups of variables assumed independent of one another. However, both ISA and ANOVA contribute to the explanation of the observed frequency distribution. Table 5.9 summarizes characteristics of ISA/PCFA and ANOVA/regression.

5.5 Application of PCFA: special issues

This section introduces three special PCFA applications. The first is conditional PCFA, a technique that applies PCFA separately to different strata of subjects (Lienert and Krauth 1973e). The second is biprediction PCFA. This allows the researcher to test predictions of the kind "if a then b and if non a then non b" (Lienert and Netter 1987). The third involves the calculation of prediction coefficients measuring the practical significance of predictor-criterion combinations (Funke et al. 1984).

5.5.1 Conditional prediction CFA: stratifying on a variable

Thus far, PCFA has been applied mainly to differential, educational, sociological, and psychological data. For instance, Lienert and Krauth (1973a) predicted performance in elementary school from gender, socioeconomic status (SES), and performance in reading, vocabulary, and spelling tests. Lienert and Wolfrum (1979) used PCFA to predict success of psychotherapy techniques. Hütter et al. (1981) predicted psychiatric diagnoses from the treating hospital, SES, and family status. Krauth and Lienert (1973b) predicted dyslexia from performance in reading, vocabulary, and reading tests.

All these applications included stratification variables, e.g., SES and gender. Wermuth (1976) discussed the possibility that types and antitypes may emerge even if variables are independent at certain levels of the stratification variables. To control for this effect, Krauth and Lienert (1982a) suggested to apply *conditional CFA* (CCFA) (cf. Lienert 1978; Krauth 1980a). Conditional CFA searches for types and antitypes separately for each category of the stratification variables. For these analyses, expected frequencies are estimated separately. In contrast to pooling over categories of a variable, essentially eliminating that variable, CCFA "slices" the data analysis. For each stratum a separate analysis is performed (cf. conditional log-linear models) (Fienberg 1980).

Krauth and Lienert (1982a) suggest the use of conditional CFA if

(1) one of the variables is a stratification variable, and
(2) the association between other predictors and the criteria differs across the levels of the stratification variable.

The authors strongly recommend the use of CCFA in the analysis of clinical data when, for instance, symptoms can be observed in inpatients but not in outpatients. For these groups the assumption of proportionally distributed symptom configurations may be hard to justify and thus, types and antitypes may result as artifacts rather than indicators of local associations.

CCFA may be applied also in the context of PCFA. Conditional PCFA investigates if, for certain levels of the stratification variable, separate analyses yield the same picture of predictor-criteria relationships as the analysis of the entire sample. For instance, one may wonder if the relationship between method of suicide and year is the same when analyzed separately for men and women. Table 5.10 gives the results of conditional PCFA for both subsamples. Both analyses applied Bonferroni alpha adjustment, resulting in an $\alpha^* = 0.05/14 = 0.00357$. The standard normal approximation of the binomial test was applied. Since in the present example conditional PCFA computes separate results for each of the two gender categories, only one predictor is left. Therefore, each panel's PCFA is equivalent to a conditional simple first order CFA.

The upper panel of Table 5.10 displays results for males. It shows four types and four antitypes. Reading from the top to the bottom of the table, the types indicate:

(1) In 1952, males committed suicide mostly using gas or soporifics (configurations 11 and 13).
(2) In 1944, males committed suicide mostly by hanging or shooting themselves (configurations 22 and 26).

The antitypes suggest

(1) In 1952, hanging and shooting were relatively infrequent means of committing suicide (configurations 12 and 16).
(2) In 1944, gas and soporifics were relatively infrequent means of committing suicide (configurations 21 and 23).

These results differ from the ones shown in Table 5.8 in that the first two types and the first two antitypes are new.

The lower panel of Table 5.10 displays results for females. It contains only two types and two antitypes. The types suggest that in 1952 females used soporifics more often than was expected as means of suicide, and in 1944 drowning occurred more often than was expected. The antitypes suggest that in 1952, drowning, and in 1944, the use of soporifics, occurred less often than was expected. These results are also different from the ones shown in Table 5.8.

Table 5.10. *Conditional prediction CFA of the variables, year of occurrence and method of suicide by sex.*

Configuration ym	Frequencies		Significance tests		Type/ antitype
	o	e	|z|	p(z)	
Males					
11	52	33.709	3.313	0.0009	T
12	31	53.043	3.285	0.0010	A
13	44	25.282	3.864	0.0001	T
14	20	19.333	0.156	0.8761	
15	22	18.342	0.877	0.3803	
16	3	18.838	3.751	0.0002	A
17	2	5.453	1.490	0.1361	
21	16	34.291	3.288	0.0010	A
22	76	53.957	3.262	0.0011	T
23	7	25.718	3.834	0.0001	A
24	19	19.667	0.155	0.8770	
25	15	18.658	0.870	0.3841	
26	35	19.162	3.721	0.0002	T
27	9	5.547	1.478	0.1395	
Females					
11	47	53.846	1.014	0.3106	
12	14	24.430	2.188	0.0287	
13	97	52.849	6.590	4.4×10^{-11}	T
14	10	31.909	4.068	4.7×10^{-5}	A
15	5	4.487	0.244	0.8075	
16	0	5.484	2.360	0.0183	
17	2	1.994	0.004	0.9968	
21	61	54.154	1.012	0.3117	
22	35	24.570	2.182	0.0291	
23	9	53.151	6.574	4.9×10^{-11}	A
24	54	32.091	4.057	4.9×10^{-5}	T
25	4	4.513	0.243	0.8080	
26	11	5.516	2.354	0.0186	
27	2	2.006	0.004	0.9968	

5.5.2 Biprediction CFA

Section 5.4 introduced PCFA as an exploratory method for the investigation of predictor-criterion relationships. The only explanatory component involved was the distinction between predictors and criteria. An additional explanatory component is the conditional PCFA's assumption that predictor-criterion relationships may vary across the levels of one or more stratification variables. This assumption may be tested, for instance, using conditional log-linear models or conditional CFA. The present section introduces biprediction CFA (BCFA) (Lienert and Netter 1987). This method allows the researcher to test the following two predictions simultaneously:

(1) Predictor level A leads to outcome a.
(2) Predictor level B leads to outcome b, with $A \neq B$ and $a \neq b$.

BCFA is derived from an approach by Havránek and Lienert (1984) designed to analyze parts of contingency tables, and from two-cell outlier testing as discussed by Kotze and Hawkins (1984). For example, let a drug be applied in the three doses 1, 2, and 3. Let the response be measured as positive ($+$), neutral (0), or negative ($-$). Then, a 3×3 contingency table may be formed as shown in the upper panel of Table 5.11.

To test these hypotheses from the 3×3 table, a subtable must be extracted that allows one to depict the two simultaneous predictions. For the present purposes suppose

(1) dose 1 leads to positive responses, and
(2) dose 3 leads to negative responses.

Here, a 2×2 subtable must be examined including only cells 11, 13, 31, and 33 from the original table. This subtable is given in the lower panel of Table 5.11. Marginals not included in the prediction are labeled with an $\times$. To test the biprediction hypothesis for this table the following formula from Kimball (1954) may be used.

$$X^2 = \frac{(A(Ba - Cb) - B(Dc - Cd))^2}{ABCD(A + B)(C + D)/N} \tag{5.11}$$

Table 5.11. *Scheme for a* 3 × 3 *table and subtable for BCFA.*

Predictor levels	Criterion levels				
	1	2	3		
Complete table					
1	11	12	13		
2	21	22	23		
3	31	32	33		
BCFA subtable					
1	$11 = a$	12	$13 = b$	$a + b = A$	
2	21	22	23	×	
3	$31 = c$	32	$33 = d$	$c + d = B$	
	$a + c + 21 = C$		$b + d + 23 = D$	$A + B + x = n$	

This test statistic is distributed approximately as chi-square with $df = 1$. For a table with just two predictor levels and two criterion levels (5.11) simplifies to

$$X^2 = \frac{N(ad - bc)^2}{ABCD/N} \tag{5.12}$$

This test statistic is also distributed approximately as chi-square with $df = 1$. It is useful especially in designs that compare two treatments supposed to have divergent outcomes.

The following example, taken from Lienert and Netter (1987), applies (5.11) to data from an experiment on the effects of nicotine. A sample of $n = 48$ young males (m) and females (f) took in balanced order at one week intervals a placebo (P), 0.5 mg (H), and 1 mg (F) of nicotine. The responses to each of the doses were measured as an increase (1) or decrease (2) in finger pulse volume. Thus, each of the variables P, H, and F had categories 1 and 2. Participants were either smokers (S) or nonsmokers (N). Table 5.12 gives the observed frequency distribution. Doses were predictors, and the responses in the subject groups were the criteria. Table 5.12 shows the results of

Table 5.12. *PCFA of the predictors placebo (P), 0.5 mg (H), and 1 mg (F) nicotine, and the criteria sex (G) and smoking habits (S) (n = 48).*

Configurations PHFGS	Frequencies o	e	Binomial test B(o)
111mS	4	2.333	0.4079
111mN	3	1.313	0.2871
111fS	0	2.042	0.2483
111fN	0	1.313	0.5285
112mS	3	1.667	0.4648
112mN	1	0.938	0.7760
112fS	1	1.458	0.8611
112fN	0	0.938	0.7760
121mS	1	1.000	0.7280
121mN	0	0.563	0.8642
121fS	2	0.875	0.4359
121fN	0	0.563	0.8642
122mS	1	3.000	0.3792
122mN	1	1.688	0.9866
122fS	0	2.625	0.1345
122fN	7	1.688	0.0027
211mS	3	2.333	0.8299
211mN	1	1.313	0.5286
211fS	3	2.042	0.6696
211fN	0	1.313	0.5285
212mS	2	1.667	0.9999
212mN	0	0.938	0.7760
212fS	3	1.458	0.3573
212fN	0	0.938	0.7760
221mS	1	1.667	0.9999
221mN	2	0.938	0.4820
221fS	2	1.458	0.8610
221fN	0	0.938	0.7760
222mS	1	2.333	0.6315
222mN	1	1.313	0.7582
222fS	3	2.042	0.6696
222fN	2	1.313	0.7582

1.... = 24,   2... = 24
.1... = 24,   .2... = 24
..1.. = 22,   ..2.. = 26
...m. = 25,   ...f. = 23
....S = 30, ...N = 18

Table 5.13. *Biprediction CFA of the predictors placebo (P), 0.5 mg (H) and 1 mg (F) nicotine and the criterion sex (n = 48).*

Configurations PHF	Strata m	f	
111	$a = 7$	$b = 0$	$A = 7$
112	4	1	
121	1	2	
122	$c = 2$	$d = 7$	$B = 9$
211	4	3	
212	2	3	
221	3	2	
222	2	5	
	$C = 25$	$D = 23$	

exploratory PCFA. The Bonferroni adjusted alpha was $\alpha^* = 0.05/32 = 0.00156$. The binomial test was applied.

Application of exploratory PCFA reveals no single cell for which the local null hypothesis must be rejected. To illustrate BCFA, we analyze the following bipredictive type hypothesis: In the group of subjects who take the placebo

(1) males will respond to nicotine with an increase in pulse rate,
(2) females will respond with a decrease.

This prediction does not involve the variable smoking habit. Therefore, the BCFA contingency table pools over the categories of this variable. Table 5.13 gives the resulting contingency table in two-dimensional format.

Application of (5.11) to Table 5.13 yields a $X^2 = 9.032$. For $df = 1$ the tail probability of this value is 0.00265, a value smaller than the Bonferroni adjusted $\alpha^* = 0.05/16 = 0.00313$. Thus, we may conclude the expected bipredictive type $111 \mid m$ vs. $122 \mid f$ does exist, suggesting that in the group of subjects who took the placebo, males responded with an increase in pulse rate and females with a decrease (Table 6.12 gives a second example of biprediction CFA).

5.5.3 Prediction coefficients

So far, types and antitypes have been evaluated with respect to the null hypothesis which states there are only random differences between observed and expected frequencies. Significant differences, however, do not necessarily coincide with large portions of accounted variability. It is well known from analysis of variance that significant effects sometimes explain no more than 1/1000 of the overall variance.

To estimate portions of variance accounted for by single or combined effects, measures such as omega squared have been developed (see Hays 1981). Some of these measures can be used in an analogous fashion in CFA (Funke et al. 1984). This section introduces three of these measures. All of them are applicable to PCFA. All measures are derived from Pearson's phi. As given in equation (1.3) the *point-fourfold phi coefficient* is

$$\Phi = (ad - bc)/((a + b)(c + d)(a + c)(b + d))^{1/2},$$

$[-1 \leqslant \Phi \leqslant +1]$, where a, b, c, and d denote the cell frequencies in a 2×2 table, read clockwise starting from the upper left. Under the null hypothesis $\Phi = 0$, the following relation holds

$$z = \sqrt{n\Phi}, \tag{5.13}$$

where n denotes the sample size, or

$$\chi^2 = \Phi_n^2 \tag{5.14}$$

with $df = 1$. Because $p(z, \alpha/2) = p(\chi, \alpha)$, the tail probability for z must be multiplied by two for two-tailed testing.

The phi coefficient in CFA, derived from X^2 components, is

$$\Phi = (o - e)/(ne)^{1/2}. \tag{5.15}$$

If binomial tests rather than X^2 component tests have been performed, phi may be calculated by

$$\Phi = (o - e)/(ne - e^2)^{1/2}. \tag{5.16}$$

Coefficients (5.15) and (5.16) are called *phi prediction coefficients* (Funke et al. 1984). Both coefficients can be tested against $\Phi = 0$ using either (5.13) or (5.14).

The square of phi coefficients may be interpreted as that portion of the variability of the criterion that is accounted for by the predictors. For example, in Table 5.12 the observed frequency for configuration $122fN$ is $o = 7$ and the expected is $e = 1.68$.

Application of (5.15) yields for $n = 48$, a phi $= 0.5903$ and a phi-squared $= 0.3484$. Application of (5.16) yields phi $= 0.6009$ and phi-squared $= 0.3611$. These values indicate that about 35% of the variability of the target configuration is accounted for by the predictor configuration. The tail probability for both coefficients is $p < 1 \times 10^{-8}$.

Phi prediction coefficients are best applied in the search for types and antitypes with prediction CFA. They can be interpreted as measures of practical relevance, for instance, clinical relevance.

The second coefficient, introduced by Funke et al. (1984), is the *phi discriminant coefficient*. It is best applied when the criterion is dichotomous and only one configuration of the predictors is of interest. For example, if the researcher assumes a particular pattern of test scores that allows one to discriminate between alcoholics and nonalcoholics, the phi discriminant would be the measure of choice. To test this assumption, a 2×2 table must be created in which one row represents the configuration under study and the other row combines all other configurations. The two columns are formed by the two target groups. If there is a significant association in this 2×2 table, the phi discriminant may be applied to estimate the amount of variation covered by the predictor-criterion relation. The coefficient is

$$\Phi = (ad - bc)/(ABCD), \tag{5.17}$$

where, as before, a, b, c, and d denote the cell frequencies, and A and B are the row, and C and D the column marginals. Equation (5.17) is applicable if the predictor and the criterion have two categories each. If the criterion has more than two

Table 5.14. *Scheme for the estimation of practical significance of a biprediction hypothesis.*

Predictor configurations	Outcome		
	1	2	
Critical 1	a	b	$a+b=A$
Critical 2	c	d	$c+d=B$
Rest	$x1$	$x2$	$x1+x2=n-A-B$
	$a+c=C$	$b+d=D$	$n=A+B+x1+x2$

categories, (5.17) becomes

$$\Phi = (ad - bc)/(ABCD(C + D)/n)^{1/2}. \tag{5.18}$$

For example, let $a = 112$, $b = 0$, $c = 125$, and $d = 215$. Then, application of (5.17) yields $\Phi = 0.5467$ and $\Phi^2 = 0.2988$. We may conclude from these figures that about 30% of the entire variability in this 2×2 table is accounted for by Φ. The tail probability of is $p < 8 \times 10^{-11}$. If the target configuration and the critical predictor pattern form cell 11, this result would support the following interpretation: The target configuration is linked to the critical predictor pattern, and there is no relation between any other observed response and the critical predictor pattern.

When the researcher wants to predict that a critical predictor pattern leads to a particular response and the complementary pattern leads to the opposite response, still a third phi coefficient may be applied. Complementary patterns can occur only in dichotomous variables. Two patterns are complementary if the second pattern displays for all variables the categories opposite to the first pattern. For example, patterns $+ - +$ and $- + -$ are complementary. If one investigates a multi-univariate design with PCFA and is interested in the practical significance of the bipredictive relationship, the contingency table under study must be condensed to form a 3×2 cross-tabulation. The schema for this cross-tabulation is given in Table 5.14.

Table 5.15. *Cross-tabulation of alcohol consumption and general alcoholism score.*

Pattern of alcohol consumption	General alcoholism score			
	$+$	$+/-$	$-$	
$+++-$	$a = 13$	24	$b = 4$	$A = 41$
$---+$	$c = 1$	12	$d = 15$	$B = 28$
Rest	223	205	195	
Sums	$C = 237$	241	$D = 214$	$n = 692$

Table 5.14 may be viewed as a condensed form of Table 5.13 (cf. Table 5.12). The bipredictive hypothesis for this table assumes

(1) critical predictor configuration 1 leads to outcome 1, and
(2) critical predictor configuration 2 leads to outcome 2.

The coefficient that measures the practical significance of this relationship is the *phi association coefficient*. It is

$$\Phi = (B(Da - Cb) - A(Dc - Cd))/(ABCD(A + B)(C + D))^{1/2}.$$

(5.19)

Obviously, (5.19) is derived from (5.11). The square of (5.19) gives the amount of variability convered by the partial association between critical configuration 1 and outcome 1 on the one hand side and critical configuration 2 and outcome 2 on the other. For example, suppose a researcher is interested in the discrimination between alcoholic and nonalcoholic people. Suppose a hypothesis is that the pattern $+++-$ of a four scale alcohol consumption test allows one to predict high scores $(+)$ on a general alcoholism scale, and that the complementary pattern, $---+$, predicts low scores. Then, the frequency table shown in Table 5.15 may result (from Funke et al. 1984).

Application of (5.19) yields 0.1399 for the phi association coefficient. When squared, this coefficient shows that only 2%

of the variability are accounted for by the partial association between $+++-$ and high scores, and $---+$ and low scores. The tail probability for this value is $p = 0.0002$. Thus, we find another example of a significant association covering only a tiny fraction of the variation.

5.6 Comparison of k samples

So far, the presentation of strategies and applications of CFA has emphasized the analysis of one sample designs only. Only Section 5.5.1 on conditional prediction CFA has discussed the use of organismic or stratification variables. This section introduces CFA methods for the comparison of k groups of subjects. The basic assumption behind these comparisons is that all groups were drawn from the same parent population. Therefore, the groups should have the same parameters; differences should be random in nature.

This section first discusses two-sample CFA. Comparisons of more than two groups and special applications are then presented.

5.6.1 Two-sample CFA

Two-sample CFA is used to compare two samples with respect to a series of configurations of states of random variables (Lienert 1971c; Krauth and Lienert 1973a). The basic question asked by two sample CFA is: Are the frequency distributions of the configurations homogeneous when compared across the two samples? The null hypothesis of no differences is locally tested for each configuration.

To test the null hypothesis of no differences between the two frequency distributions, two-sample CFA estimates expected frequencies under the following model:

(1) the variables with respect to which the two samples are compared may show interactions of any order, and

(2) there is independence between the two groups and the variables.

If these two assumptions are violated, association between the two groups and the variables must exist. An association of this kind suggests that the frequency distributions of the two groups differ in at least one configuration. A type in two-sample CFA suggests that in one of the samples, for a particular configuration, more cases were observed than expected under the assumption of homogeneity of frequency distributions. An antitype suggests that in one of the samples, for a particular configuration, fewer cases were observed than expected.

To calculate expected frequencies for two-sample ISA either one of the two methods of ISA may be used. The first of these methods forms a two-dimensional cross-tabulation. The configurations of variables form the rows and the two samples form the two columns of the table. The number of rows may be calculated by (5.2). This equation gives the number of configurations when a group of variables is crossed. For the two-dimensional cross-tabulation, expected frequencies may be calculated using the "row sum by column sum over n"-rule.

The second way of estimating expected frequencies for two-sample CFA is, again, to apply log-linear models or the general linear model. For example, suppose two samples (s) are compared with respect to the three variables 1, 2, and 3. Then, the log-linear model for a two-sample CFA is

$$\log(y_{i,j,k,s}) = u_0 + u_1 + u_2 + u_3 + u_s + u_{12} + u_{13} + u_{23} + u_{123}.$$

$$(5.20)$$

Accordingly, within the general linear model, this example of two-sample CFA corresponds to

$$y_{i,j,k,s} = x_0 b_0 + x_1 b_1 + x_2 b_2 + x_3 b_3 + x_s b_4$$
$$+ x_{12} b_5 + x_{13} b_6 + x_{23} b_7 + x_{123} b_8. \qquad (5.21)$$

If one defines the variables 1, 2, and 3 as members of group A and sample membership as group B, (5.20) corresponds to (5.4) and (5.21) corresponds to (5.5).

The following explanation of significance tests for two-sample CFA uses the two-dimensional format of the cross-

Table 5.16. *Two-dimensional format of two-sample CFA for three dichotomous variables.*

| Configurations 123 | Samples | | |
	A	B	Marginals
111	A111	B111	f111
112	A112	B112	f112
121	A121	B121	f121
122	A122	B122	f122
211	A211	B211	f211
212	A212	B212	f212
221	A221	B221	f221
222	A222	B222	f222
Sums	n_A	b_B	n

tabulation. To illustrate this format, Table 5.16 gives an example of a scheme for three dichotomous variables.

One-sample CFA examines every configuration to determine how close the observed frequencies are to the expected ones. The models given in (5.20) and (5.21) may be used for this purpose. Types and antitypes resulting from this approach, however, do not explicitly compare the two samples. Therefore, two-sample CFA compares, for each configuration, two frequencies to determine if sample *A* differs from sample *B*. For the local comparison of two frequencies two-sample CFA uses *fourfold tests of homogeneity*. Each fourfold test examines a table of the form given in Table 5.17.

One of the best known tests for homogeneity in 2 × 2 tables is Fisher's exact test. This test calculates all fourfold tables possible when the marginals are fixed, and assigns a probability to each table. If the sum of the probabilities of the observed and all more extreme tables is less than the adjusted alpha, the assumption of homogeneity is rejected. Since we assume the marginal frequencies are fixed, or determined a priori, the frequencies in the fourfold table follow a hypergeometric distribution.

Table 5.17. *Fourfold table for the examination of configuration ijk in two-sample CFA.*

Configurations 123	Samples		Marginals
	A	*B*	
ijk	$a = Aijk$	$b = Bijk$	$fijk$
All others combined	$c = n_A - Aijk$	$d = n_B - Bijk$	$n - fijk$
Sums	n_A	n_B	n

Fisher's exact test calculates the point probability for the homogeneity of the fourfold table under the null hypothesis of no differences between the two samples. This results in

$$p(a) = \frac{\binom{a+c}{a}\binom{b+d}{b}}{\binom{n}{a+b}}, \tag{5.22}$$

where a, b, c, and d denote the observed frequencies in cells a, b, c, and d, respectively (see Table 5.17). Replacing the expressions in (5.22) with the explicit factorial terms, the equation for Fisher's exact test may be rewritten in the following equivalent forms:

$$p(a) = \frac{\dfrac{(a+c)!\,(b+d)!}{a!\,c!\quad b!\,c!}}{\dfrac{n!}{(a+b)!(n-a-b)!}} \tag{5.23a}$$

or

$$p(a) = \frac{A!\,B!\,C!\,D!}{N!\,a!\,b!\,c!\,d!} \tag{5.23b}$$

where $A = a + b$, $B = c + d$, $C = a + c$, and $D = b + d$.

In either form, Fisher's exact test is tedious to calculate when cell frequencies are high (see the discussion of the binomial test in Chapter 2). For small sample sizes, tables are available (e.g., Krüger, Lehmacher, and Wall 1980; Krause and Metzler 1984). Some statistical program packages for microcomputers include the test as an option for the analysis of two-dimensional tables. For example, SYSTAT (1986) provides Fisher's exact test for $n < 50$ as an option in the TABLES module. Suppose, for example, the cells in a four-fold table have values $a = 4$, $b = 1$, $c = 2$, and $d = 2$. Then, the lower tail of the hypergeometric distribution has probability $p(a = 4) = 0.9524$. The upper tail has probability $p(a = 4) = 0.4048$. Note that these two values do not add up to $p = 1$ because both contain the case $a = 4$.

For larger samples the calculation of the exact Fisher test is tedious and there are no tabulated tail probabilities. The researcher has at least the following three alternatives: the X^2-test, the approximation of the binomial distribution with the standard normal distribution, and a standard normal z-test.

The X^2-*test* for 2×2-tables may be calculated by

$$X^2 = n(ad - bc)^2/(a + b)(c + d)(a + c)(b + d).$$

(5.24)

With continuity correction, recommended when sample sizes are small, (5.24) becomes

$$X^2 = n(|ad - bc| - 1/2n)^2/(a + b)(c + d)(a + c)(b + d).$$

(5.25)

X^2 is approximately distributed as chi-square with $df = 1$. The X^2-test is recommended for two-sided hypotheses.

For the approximation of the binomial distributions of groups A and B, respectively, one calculates first the relative frequencies

$$p_1 = a/n_A \quad \text{and} \quad p_2 = b/n_B,$$

where n_A and n_B denote the samples sizes of groups A and B, respectively. As a test statistic one obtains the standard normally distributed

$$z = (p_1 - p_2)/(h(1 - h)(1/n_A + 1/n_B))^{1/2}, \qquad (5.26)$$

where $h = (a + c)/n$ (Krause and Metzler 1984). This approximation is recommended if $(a + b)/n > 0.1$ and $n \geq 60$, and can be applied for both one- and two-sided hypotheses.

If $(a + b)n_A/n \geq 4$ the following standard normally distributed test statistic may be used

$$z = (a - (a+b)n_A/n)/(((a+b)(n-(a+b))n_A n_B)/n^2(n-1))^{1/2}.$$
$$(5.27)$$

For example, suppose the following cell frequencies of a fourfold table are given: $a = 9$, $b = 46$, $c = 152$, $d = 155$ (see Krauth and Lienert 1973a, p. 91). Then, we obtain

(1) for the lower tail of the exact Fisher test, $p = 2.116 \times 10^{-6}$,
(2) for the X^2-test given in (5.24), $X^2 = 20.754$, $p = 5.223 \times 10^{-6}$,
(3) for the X^2-test given in (5.25), $X^2 = 19.433$, $p = 1.042 \times 10^{-5}$,
(4) for the z-test given in (5.26), $z = -3.291$, $p = 0.0005$,
(5) for the z-test given in (5.27), $z = -4.549$, $p = 2.695 \times 10^{-6}$.

Considering that, for $df = 1$, $z(\alpha/2) = \chi^2(\alpha)$, it is obvious that the two X^2-tests in the present example are more powerful than the two standard normal approximations. The most powerful test of the five, however, is the exact Fisher test. However, simulations have shown that X^2 without continuity correction can be more powerful than the exact test. Heilmann and Lienert (1982) propose researchers use Berchtold's (1972) test for 2×2 tables. This test is most efficient if the tables contain three small and one large cell frequency.

Configurations for which the null hypothesis can be rejected are called *discrimination types*. These types discriminate locally between the two frequency distributions. In the interpretation of discrimination types in two-sample CFA one must remember that a rejection of the null hypothesis suggests only that there are local differences. Only if the researcher assumes a priori that, in one of the samples the observed frequency is greater, is an interpretation in terms of greater or less than justified. If such an assumption does exist before data inspection, a one-sided test must be performed.

The following example uses the suicide data again (see Tables 5.8 and 5.10). For the illustration of two-sample CFA the three variables year of suicide (y), method of suicide (m), and sex of person committing suicide are arranged in a two-dimensional format. The rows of this cross-tabulation result from the 2×7 configurations of year and method of suicide. The two columns contain the frequencies of the two sexes. Table 5.18 gives the results of two-sample CFA. Bonferroni-adjustment led to $\alpha^* = 0.05/14 = 0.00357$ as a significance threshold. The X^2-test without continuity correction (5.24) was applied.

Two-sample CFA identified five discrimination types. Reading from the top to the bottom of the table, the first configuration in which males and females differ is 13. This suggests that in 1952 women used soporifics more, and men used soporifics less often than expected. In 1945, women used gas more, and men used gas less often than expected. Men, on the other hand hung themselves more often, and women hung themselves less often than expected. In 1945 drowning was observed more often than expected for women and less often than expected for men. Shooting was observed more often for men and less often for women.

Applications of two-sample CFA have focused on clinical and educational research. For example, Lienert (1971c) compared depressive patients after treatment. He identified configurations of items of a temperament scale which allowed him to discriminate between successful and unsuccessful treatments. Netter (1981) compared two interview methods in epidemiological research. The author observed that the relative frequency of certain answer patterns varied with the interview method. In educational research, Lösel (1978) used two-sample CFA to compare male adolescents who underwent compensatory education programs with a control

Table 5.18. Two-sample CFA of suicide data ($n(males) = 351$, $n(females) = 351$).

Configuration ym	Observed frequencies		Expected frequencies		Significance tests	
	Males	Females	Males	Females	X^2	$p(X^2)$
11	52	47	49.5	49.5	0.376	0.5399
12	31	14	22.5	22.5	7.547	0.0060
13	44	97	70.5	70.5	37.369	0.00001
14	20	10	15.0	15.0	3.701	0.0544
15	22	5	13.5	13.5	11.755	0.0006
16	3	0	1.5	1.5	3.030	0.0817
17	2	2	2.0	2.0	0	1.0
21	16	61	38.5	38.5	35.299	3×10^{-9}
22	76	35	55.5	55.5	23.945	1×10^{-7}
23	7	9	8.0	8.0	0.264	0.6074
24	19	54	36.5	36.5	22.130	3×10^{-6}
25	15	4	9.5	9.5	6.796	0.0091
26	35	11	23.0	23.0	14.772	0.0001
27	9	2	5.5	5.5	4.623	0.0315

sample with respect to family characteristics. He found that configurations of family climate scales discriminated between the two groups.

5.6.2 k-sample CFA

The two-sample CFA is easily extended to the k-sample CFA. k-sample CFA, with $k \geqslant 2$, follows the same scheme as described in Section 5.6.1. Two options exist. One option is to form a two-dimensional cross-tabulation, with rows formed from the configurations of the crossed variables, and columns formed by the k groups. For this format, expected frequencies may be calculated as for a chi-square test. The second, equivalent option is to use programs for log-linear modeling, and to estimate expected frequencies under the following assumptions:

(1) There may be interactions of any order among the variables used to compare the k samples.
(2) The k samples and the variables are independent of each other.

These assumptions can be violated only when the configurations of variables allow the prediction of sample membership.

The assumption for the calculation of expected frequencies carry over from two- to k-sample CFA, as one might expect. Statistical testing of these assumptions, however, is not exactly the same. Each test in two-sample CFA basically compares only two frequencies. If one frequency exceeds expectancy, the other must necessarily be below expectancy. In k-sample CFA this rule does not apply. An above-expectancy frequency in one sample does not necessarily determine where there are below-expectancy frequencies. Therefore, a two-stage testing procedure for k-sample CFA is proposed (Krauth and Lienert 1973a).

The first stage involves a $2 \times k$ chi-square test for each of the configurations. The contingency table for this test is set up in a fashion analogous to Table 5.17. The first row contains the

Table 5.19. 2 × k *contingency table to examine configuration ijk in k-sample* CFA.

Configurations 123	Samples				Marginals
	A	B	$\cdots$	K	
ijk	$Aijk$	$Bijk$	$\cdots$	$Kijk$	$fijk$
All others combined	$n_A - Aijk$	$n_B - Bijk$	$\cdots$	$n_K - Kijk$	$n - fijk$
Sums	n_A	n_B	$\cdots$	n_K	n

frequencies of all groups for the configuration under study. The second row contains, for each group, the sum of all other frequencies. Suppose, as for Table 5.17, the three variables 1, 2, and 2 are given. Then, the table for the test of the *ijk*th configuration adopts the format given in Table 5.19.

For each configuration a 2 × k chi-square test is calculated to determine if there are differences between the k samples. However, this test does not show where the differences are located. Therefore, the second stage of k-sample testing identifies those samples that differ from each other in certain configurations. The basic strategy of the second stage is to reduce the k-sample problem to a series of two-sample CFA tests for each 2 × k-table shown to be heterogeneous.

Each of the k × 2 tables has k columns, one for each of the k samples. To analyze each pair of samples a total of $\binom{k}{2}$ pairs can be formed. For each of these pairs, a test as schematized in Table 5.17 must be performed. If sample sizes are equal, a strategy analogous to the comparison of means with the Newman-Keuls test helps to keep the number of CFA tests small. This procedure calculates all differences between observed frequencies for a given configuration. In this case, the following iteration is performed:

(1) Form a 2 × 2 table with those two samples whose observed differences are the largest not yet tested.

(2) Apply a test of homogeneity to this table.
(3) If the null hypothesis can be rejected, reiterate; otherwise stop.

Since one usually does not know for which of the $2 \times k$ tables the null hypothesis does not hold true, one must adjust alpha to the maximum number of tests. The two-stage procedure of k-sample CFA involves

(1) t tests of $2 \times k$ tables for the t configurations, and
(2) $t\binom{k}{2}$ tests for pairs of samples.

Thus, the adjusted alpha in k-sample CFA is

$$\alpha^* = \alpha/(t + t\binom{k}{2}). \tag{5.28}$$

In a Bonferroni procedure, α^* is constant for each test. In a Holm procedure, α^* is the starting value for the changing adjusted alphas.

The following example, taken from Krauth and Lienert (1973a) (see Maxwell 1961), analyzes a psychiatric data set. A sample of $n = 380$ inpatients was observed for the symptoms depression (D), feelings of unsecurity (U), and mood swings (S). The patients had been diagnosed as either cyclothymics (C), anxiety neurotics (A), or neurotic depressed (N). The symptoms were scaled as either present (1) or absent (2). Table 5.20 shows the results of three-sample CFA. Bonferroni alpha adjustment lead to $\alpha^* = 0.05/(8 + 8 \times 3) = 0.00156$.

Table 5.20 shows three configurations in which the three groups differ. These configurations are 111, 121, and 122. For each of these configurations, three fourfold tables are analyzed to identify the pattern of group differences. Table 5.21 gives the results of these analyses. It gives, for the three configurations 111, 121, and 122, the observed frequencies and the X^2 values for the fourfold test. The X^2-test was applied without continuity correction. The adjusted significance level is $\alpha^* = 0.00156$.

The fourfold tests revealed that anxiety neurotics show the symptom pattern 111 far more often than the neurotic depressed. The group of patients who felt insecure does not differ from either of the other two. Anxiety neurotics also

Table 5.20. Three-sample CFA of psychiatric patients ($n_C = 148$, $n_A = 100$, $n_N = 132$).

Configurations DUS	Observed frequencies o_C	o_A	o_N	Expected frequencies e_C	e_A	e_N	Significance tests X^2	$p(X^2)$
111	11	19	3	12.85	8.68	11.46	20.554	3×10^{-5}
112	13	9	6	10.91	7.37	9.28	2.366	0.3064
121	3	13	0	6.23	4.21	5.56	26.706	2×10^{-6}
122	4	12	1	6.62	4.47	5.91	18.607	9×10^{-5}
211	30	14	44	34.27	23.16	30.57	13.087	0.0014
212	38	11	23	28.04	18.95	25.01	8.675	0.0131
221	18	9	23	19.47	13.16	17.37	3.744	0.1538
222	31	13	32	29.60	20.00	26.40	4.630	0.0988

1.. = 94, 2.. = 286
.1. = 221, .2. = 159
..1 = 187, ..2 = 193

Table 5.21. *Comparison of three psychiatric groups in three configurations of symptoms.*

Configurations DUS	Observed frequencies			Comparison X^2		
	o_C	o_A	o_N	C-A	C-N	A-N
111	11	19	3	7.51	3.91	18.55*
121	3	13	0	11.91*	2.71	18.18*
122	4	12	1	8.55	1.51	13.60*

showed pattern 121 more often than both other groups, and pattern 122 more often than the neurotic depressed.

5.6.3. Combination of ISA and k-sample CFA

ISA was introduced as a method for investigating relationships between two groups of variables. k-sample CFA investigates the relationships between classification variables and one grouping variable. As a straightforward combination of both approaches, *k-sample ISA* allows the examination of relationships between two groups of variables differentially in k samples (Netter and Lienert 1984; cf. Kohnen and Rudolf 1981). For example, suppose a first group of variables contains variables 1 and 2, and a second group contains variables 3 and 4. Then, ISA analyzes the relationships between 1 and 2 on the one hand side, and 3 and 4 on the other hand, under the following assumptions: (1) 1 and 2 are associated, (2) 3 and 4 are associated, and (3) the first pair of variables is independent of the second. k-sample ISA makes one additional assumption: (4) these relationships do not vary across the k samples.

In more general terms, when comparing k groups of subjects, k-sample ISA analyzes the relationships among three groups of variables. Two of these groups, A and B, contain variables as in ISA. In ISA, variables are either dependent or independent, or belong to groups that have the same status. The third group, C, contains only one variable. This variable, G, has group membership of subjects as categories.

Netter and Lienert (1984) discuss several approaches to the analysis of local hypotheses in the $A \times B \times C$-design. Each of the approaches involves either the reduction of the design via pooling over variable groups or the construction of subtables that allow the researcher to compare the subject groups as in k-sample CFA or in biprediction CFA.

To test the general assumption of total independence among the three groups of variables one estimates expected frequencies such that

(1) interactions of any order in variable group A are considered,
(2) interactions of any order in variable group B are considered, and
(3) there is total independence among the three groups of variables.

For the sake of simplicity of notation, suppose three groups of variables are given as above. Group A contains variables 1 and 2, group B contains variables 3 and 4, and group C contains the variable group membership, 5. Then, the log-linear model that tests the above assumptions is

$$\log(y_{i,j,k,l,s}) = u_0 + u_1 + u_2 + u_3 + u_4 + u_5 + u_{12} + u_{34}.$$
$$(5.29)$$

Within the general linear model, this example of k-sample ISA corresponds to

$$\hat{y}_{i,j,k,l,s} = x_0 b_0 + x_1 b_1 + x_2 b_2 + x_3 b_3 + x_4 b_4$$
$$+ x_5 b_5 + x_{12} b_6 + x_{34} b_7. \qquad (5.30)$$

An ordinary CFA with expectancies estimated under either one of these models may lead to types and antitypes that suggest an interaction between the variable groups either in pairs or as a triplet. This approach was adopted by generalized ISA (see Section 5.2). However, k-sample ISA compares k samples with respect to their frequency distributions in an ISA design. Such comparisons are not performed by generalized ISA. Rather, one either pools over certain variables, or forms subtables of the type given in Tables 5.17 and 5.19, respectively.

The following paragraphs introduce three approaches to comparing k samples in an ISA design. The approaches will be introduced using an example from physiological psychology (Netter 1982; Netter and Lienert 1984). In an experiment on stress responses two stress conditions were set. A sample of $n = 162$ participated for ten minutes in a response time task and for three minutes in a verbal fluency task. The sequence of the two tasks was balanced. Under each condition samples of blood plasma were taken to measure the levels of adrenalin and noradrenalin. Thus, the four observables were adrenalin and noradrenalin, both measured under the response time and the verbal test condition. Each of these four variables had categories $1 =$ level increased and $2 =$ level not increased. Two groups of subjects participated in the experiment. The first was a group of hypertonics, the second a control sample of normals.

Before presenting methods for the detailed comparison, we will analyze this data set with generalized ISA under the above assumptions. In this analysis the two variables adrenalin and noradrenalin, observed under the first stress condition, were combined to the composite variable catecholamines with the four categories $1 = 22$, $2 = 21$, $3 = 12$, and $4 = 11$. Also, adrenalin and noradrenalin were combined to a composite variable for the variable test condition. Again, the four categories $1 = 22$, $2 = 21$, $3 = 12$, and $4 = 11$ resulted. The third group of variables was formed by group membership. Table 5.22 summarizes the results of the generalized ISA. In the significance tests, the z-approximation of the binomial test was applied. The Bonferroni-adjusted significance level was $\alpha^* = 0.05/32 = 0.0015625$.

In spite of the low critical α^*, generalized ISA detected four types of stress responses. Reading from the top to the bottom of Table 5.22, the first type has pattern $11n$, or, in terms of the individual variables, $2222n$, where n denotes normals. It suggests that more normals than expected show no strong reaction to any of the stress conditions. The second type has

Table 5.22. *Generalized ISA of three variable groups.*

Configurations 123[a]	Frequencies		Significance tests		Type/ antitype
	o	e	$|z|$	$p(z)$	
11h	6	3.468	1.375	0.1693	
11n	11	3.643	3.898	0.00009	T
12h	3	4.118	0.558	0.5768	
12n	2	4.326	1.134	0.2569	
13h	4	5.960	0.818	0.4133	
13n	8	6.262	0.708	0.4787	
14h	1	4.010	1.522	0.1280	
14n	1	4.213	1.586	0.1127	
21h	4	4.335	0.163	0.8706	
21n	1	4.554	1.689	0.0911	
22h	9	5.147	1.726	0.0844	
22n	14	5.408	3.758	0.0002	T
23h	4	7.450	1.294	0.1956	
23n	1	7.828	2.502	0.0124	
24h	5	5.012	0.005	0.9957	
24n	7	5.266	0.768	0.4423	
31h	4	4.431	0.208	0.8355	
31n	5	4.655	0.162	0.8713	
32h	2	5.262	1.446	0.1483	
32n	0	5.528	2.392	0.0167	
33h	14	7.616	2.370	0.0178	
33n	17	8.001	3.262	0.0011	T
34h	1	5.123	1.851	0.0641	
34n	3	5.383	1.045	0.2962	
41h	0	3.371	1.856	0.0635	
41n	1	3.542	1.366	0.1720	
42h	7	4.004	1.516	0.1294	
42n	1	4.206	1.584	0.1132	
43h	2	5.795	1.605	0.1084	
43n	5	6.088	0.450	0.6531	
44h	13	3.898	4.666	3×10^{-6}	T
44n	6	4.096	0.953	0.3405	

Table 5.22 (*Cont.*)
Marginal frequencies of original variables

1.... = 81,	2.... = 81
.1... = 82,	.2... = 80
..1.. = 70,	..2.. = 92
...1. = 87,	...2. = 75
....1 = 79,	....2 = 83, n = 162

Marginal frequencies of the two composite variables

1. = 36,	2. = 45,	3. = 46,	4. = 35
.1 = 32,	.2 = 38,	.3 = 55,	.4 = 37

[a]For explanation of composite variables, see text.

pattern 22*n* or 2121*n*, respectively. It suggests that more hypertonics than expected show increased adrenalin levels under both stress conditions, but no increment in noradrenalin. The third type has pattern 33*n* or 1212*n*. It includes normals who, under both conditions show only increases in their noradrenalin levels. The last type has pattern 44*h* or 1111*h*, where *h* denotes the group of hypertonics. This type describes hypertonics who react with an increased level of both adrenalin and noradrenalin under both stress conditions.

Altogether, these results suggest normals and hypertonics respond differently to the two stress conditions. However, a conclusive interpretation in terms of differences between the two subject groups is not possible. Therefore, three methods for a comparison of the two groups in the present ISA design will be introduced.

The first method of comparing two samples in the present example focuses on the marginal frequencies of single responses. For instance, pooled over the reactions to the verbal task, 14 hypertonics and 22 normals showed pattern 22, that is, no strong physiological reaction to the response time condition. In a manner analogous to that shown in Table 5.17, these frequencies can be inserted into a 2 × 2 table. The following example compares normo- and hypertonics with

Table 5.23. *Analysis of two stress patterns in the comparison of normals and hypertonics* ($n_h = 79$, $n_n = 83$, $N = 162$).

	Subject group	
Configuration	*h*	*n*
22	14	22
Others	65	61
11	22	13
Others	57	70

respect to response patterns 11 and 22 under the response time condition. Table 5.23 summarizes the results for both patterns. The upper panel of the table contains the table for pattern 11, the lower for pattern 22. The exact Fisher test, given in equation (5.22), was applied.

Fisher's exact test yielded a lower tail probability of $p = 0.1238$ for configuration 22, and $p = 0.0450$ for configuration 11. The first value does not allow one to reject the null hypothesis of marginal homogeneity. The second, slightly less than the usual $\alpha = 0.05$ allows one to reject the null hypothesis only if it was determined a priori to be the only two-sample ISA test. Since this is not the case, the null hypothesis cannot be rejected.

None of the other differences between the observed marginal frequencies of the normals and the hypertonics is greater than the ones tested. Therefore, we refrain from further marginal testing. A complete exploratory analysis would test all four response configurations under each of the experimental conditions.

The first method of comparing the two samples in an ISA design reduces the problem of two-sample ISA to one of two-sample CFA. It pools over the categories of either the response time or the verbal task conditions. The second method of comparing the two samples conserves the three groups of variables. It still simplifies the problem by looking at one variable only, rather than considering the data multivariate. More specifically, the second method takes one variable from each group and forms a $c1 \times c2 \times c3$ cross-tabulation, where $c1$, $c2$, and $c3$ denote the number of categories of the variables. All variables in the present example are dichotomous. Thus, the table under study has eight cells.

For example, suppose the researcher is interested in adrenalin reaction differences between normals and hypertonics under both experimental conditions. Then, the table has 2(experimental conditions) × 2(response level) × 2(groups of subjects) cells. The upper panel of Table 5.24 gives this cross-tabulation. It shows that the two groups of subjects differ most in configuration 12. While 13 hypertonics show an increased adrenalin level under response time stress and no increase when they tackle the verbal task, only seven normals do so. To compare these two frequencies one may, again, form a fourfold table as shown in Table 5.17. The lower panel of Table 5.24 gives this cross-tabulation.

Fisher's exact test shows that the difference between 13 hypertonics and 7 normals is not significant. The upper tail probability for the difference is $p = 0.0944$. Thus we may, again, not conclude that the two groups of subjects differ in their physiological reactions to the experimental conditions.

The third method of analyzing k-sample ISA designs provides the most thorough approach. It analyzes all variables simultaneously by forming pairs of configurations. The terms of the pairs are selected from the variable groups. In the present example the first term describes a configuration of adrenalin-noradrenalin reactions to response time task. The second term describes a configuration of adrenalin-noradrenalin reactions to the verbal task condition. The method of pairs of configurations compares the two samples in such pairs.

Table 5.22 shows that seven hypertonics and one normal displayed response pattern pair 22/12. This pattern may be compared with reference to either the first or the second term of the pair. Holding 12 constant, one obtains as the cells of a

Table 5.24. *Cross-tabulation of adrenalin reactions to two stress conditions ($n_h = 79$, $n_n = 83$).*

Configurations[a] 12	Samples h	n
11	30	31
12	13	7
21	14	17
21	22	28
Subtable		
12	13	7
Others	66	76

[a]The first variable denotes adrenalin reaction under response time condition; the second variable denotes adrenalin under verbal test condition.

2×2 table, $a = 7$, $b = 1$, $c = 14$, and $d = 16$. The upper tail of the distribution of Fisher's exact test for this table is $p = 0.0446$. This value suggests a marginally significant deviation from homogeneity. If there are no other tests to perform, one might conclude that the null hypothesis of homogeneity of distributions for configuration 22/12 is untenable.

Holding term 22 constant, one obtains cell frequencies $a = 7$, $b = 1$, $c = 15$, and $d = 12$. For this table, the exact Fisher test yields $p = 0.1078$. Holding neither 22 nor 12 constant one obtains cell frequencies $a = 7$, $b = 1$, $c = 72$, and $d = 82$. Fisher's exact test yields an upper tail probability of $p = 0.0270$ for this table.

These results suggest that hypertonics display more often than normals reaction pattern 22 under response time stress and pattern 12 under verbal performance task stress. However, this conclusion applies only if one takes the relative frequency of pattern 12 as a reference.

Altogether, the method of k-sample ISA offers four options. The first is to perform a generalized ISA, preserving both the identity of the groups of variables and sample membership of subjects. Types and antitypes resulting from this approach suggest an interaction among the groups of variables. However, this approach is not sensitive to the question of how the samples compare. The second approach pools over the groups of variables, preserving the identity of only one group of variables and sample membership of subjects. It then performs an ordinary k-sample CFA. Even though this approach compares groups, it simplifies the design, assuming no interaction between the collapsed and any other group of variables. The third approach both preserves the identity of the groups of variables and sample memberships and compares samples with each other. It, however, simplifies the multivariate design by focusing on single variables, assuming no information is gained by a multivariate procedure. The fourth approach selects pairs of configurations–single cells in the complete, not the reduced contingency table – and compares them across the samples. These comparisons either use one of the terms in the pair as reference or the entire table.

When the researcher chooses this last approach, the number of sample comparisons to perform equals the number of cells in the contingency table, disregarding the k samples. Suppose the first group of variables has $c1$ configurations and the second $c2$. Then, the number of sample comparisons is $t = c1 \times c2$. If there are only two samples, alpha must be adjusted only to t. For $k > 2$ samples alpha must be adjusted to

$$t = c1 \times c2 \binom{k}{2}. \tag{5.31}$$

5.7 CFA of directed relationships

The present section describes CFA of directed relationships (DCFA) (von Eye 1985). DCFA is a special case of ISA. ISA assumes that there are two or more groups of variables that are independent of each other. Variables within the same group may show interactions of any order. Sections 5.1 and 5.2 explained that the interpretation of one ISA group of variables determining or predicting another one is based solely on researcher a priori knowledge (see Table 5.9). ISA treats the groups of variables symmetrically. DCFA takes an approach closer to regression. As was explained in Section 5.2, the regression equation is asymmetrical in that it explains the variability of one dependent variable in terms of one or more independent variables. DCFA makes the following assumptions.

(1) There are two groups of variables, A and B. These groups are independent of each other.
(2) In the group of independent variables, A, interactions of any order may prevail.
(3) In the group of dependent variables, B, interactions may not exist. Variables in B

    – do not show any main effects
    – do not show any interactions with each other.

Recent discussions include models that allow the dependent variables to have main effects. Such models bring DCFA closer to PCFA. This chapter, however, makes the above assumptions.

If, under these assumptions, types or antitypes emerge, three possible reasons for the rejection of the null hypothesis may be considered. The first is that the independence assumption is violated. If this is the case and assumption (3) still holds, we may conclude that deviations from the expected frequency distribution are due to the independent variables' determining the dependent ones. The second reason is that the dependent variables show main effects. If this is the case it is not easy to determine whether types and antitypes are due to these main effects or to interactions with the independent variables. One way of analyzing this question is to recompute the CFA under consideration of main effects of dependent variables. The third reason is that the dependent variables interact with each other.

Main effects and interactions of the dependent variables contradict the basic assumptions of DCFA. Therefore, types and antitypes emerging for these reasons cannot be interpreted as due to the effects of independent on dependent variables. Rather, they indicate that the DCFA assumptions must be rejected. Only types and antitypes that emerge because assumption (1) is violated indicate directed relationships between dependent and independent variables, or between predictors and criteria.

Suppose the group of independent variables, A, contains variables 1, 2, and 3, and the group of dependent variables contains variables 4 and 5. Then, the above listed DCFA assumptions imply the estimation of expected frequencies under the following log-linear model:

$$\log(x_{i,j,k,l,m}) = u_0 + u_1 + u_2 + u_3 + u_{12} + u_{13} + u_{23} + u_{123},$$

$$(5.32)$$

or the following regression model

$$y_{i,j,k,l,m} = x_0 b_0 + x_1 b_1 + x_2 b_2 + x_3 b_3$$
$$+ x_{12} b_4 + x_{13} b_5 + x_{23} b_6 + x_{123} b_7. \quad (5.33)$$

To make sure types and antitypes are not due to main effects and interactions among dependent variables one can fit a log-linear model including only the dependent variables. The model must be a no-effect model, assuming there are no effects whatsoever in the cross-tabulation of the independent variables (cf. the assumptions of zero order CFA). If the null hypothesis of no effects cannot be rejected, there are neither main effects nor interactions in the dependent variables. If the null hypothesis can be rejected, the basic assumptions of DCFA are not met and the researcher might want to apply another model of CFA, for instance ISA.

DCFA makes stronger assumptions than ISA because the dependent variables are not assumed to show any variation by themselves. However, in contrast to ISA, DCFA assumes an asymmetrical relationship between predictors and criteria. DCFA and ISA coincide if both criteria are completely independent of each other and have no main effects.

The following example analyzes data from a sample of 162 patients who suffered from aphasia (Krauth and Lienert 1973a; von Eye 1985). The patients were observed on the three variables O = naming of objects, A = forming of alliterations, and E = number of phonemic and verbalization errors made while solving the first two tasks. All three variables were dichotomized at their medians with 1 indicating pathological and 2 indicating rather rather normal performance. For the present purposes we assume that variable A allows one to predict the other two.

Before searching for types and antitypes with CFA one must make sure that the third of the above DCFA assumptions holds true. This is a precondition for the interpretability of types and antitypes in terms of directed relationships between A on the one hand and O and E on the other. Under the assumption of no effects the expected frequencies in the 2×2 table of O and E are all $e = 162/4 = 40.5$. The Pearson X^2 for this assumption is 0.86, a value that is not significant for $df = 3$. Thus, we may conclude that types and antitypes resulting from DCFA will not be due to main effects or interactions of the dependent variables O and E. Table 5.25 presents the results of DCFA. Expected frequencies were estimated under the following two assumptions. (1) Variable A determines the joint frequency distribution of all three variables. (2) Variables O and E show neither main effects nor interactions. Bonferroni-adjustment led to an adjusted $\alpha^* = 0.05/8 = 0.00625$. The X^2 component test was applied.

Application of DCFA revealed one type and two antitypes. The type 112 indicates that pathologically weak performance in alliterations allows one to predict weak performance in naming objects and a rather normal number of errors in these two tasks. The first antitype, 111, shows that there is only weak evidence in support of the prediction from weak performance in alliterations to weak performance in the other two variables. The observed frequency is only about a third of the expected. Only about 4% of the expected number of patients was observed for configuration 122, the second antitype. This indicates that weak performance in naming objects and a

Table 5.25. *DCFA of three variables measuring aphasia.*

Variables[a] $O\underline{A}E$	o	e	X^2	$p(X^2)$	Type/ antitype
111	6	17.0	7.12	0.0075	A
112	43	17.0	39.77	3×10^{-10}	T
121	30	23.5	1.80	0.1797	
122	1	23.5	21.54	3×10^{-6}	A
211	7	17.0	5.88	0.0153	
212	12	17.0	1.47	0.2253	
221	35	23.5	5.63	0.0176	
222	28	23.5	0.86	0.3537	

$1.. = 80, \quad 2.. = 82$
$.1. = 68, \quad .2. = 94$
$..1 = 78, \quad ..2 = 84, \quad N = 162$

[a]Variable A is underlined to indicate its status as independent variable in DCFA.

normal number of phonemic and verbal mistakes cannot be predicted from normal performance in forming alliterations.

5.8 Aggregation of types and antitypes

Often in the analysis of dichotomous variables, types or antitypes differ on only one characteristic. Suppose in an investigation of three symptoms of schizophrenia two types, 110 and 111, emerged. Because the three symptoms were scaled as either present (1) or absent (0) one can say the first two symptoms go together, regardless of whether the third symptom is present or not.

In CFA of dichotomous variables, such types and antitypes can be aggregated using a theorem by Quine and McCluskey (see Hoernes and Heilweil 1964; von Eye and Brandtstädter 1982). Suppose two dichotomous variables are given, where both can take either state A or B, and a statement includes the two configurations AA and AB. Then, the theorem is

$$AA + AB = A., \qquad (5.34)$$

where the period indicates that the second variable disappears by aggregation. In other words, the second variable is redundant for the description of the results because state A for the first variable occurs across all states of the second variable.

The theorem may be used to aggregate types or antitypes. It can be applied in CFA under the following rules:

(1) Only one variable at a time can be aggregated. For example, AA and BB cannot be aggregated to ..

(2) The position of the aggregated variable is irrelevant. For example, all three aggregations $AA + BA = .A$, $AA + AB = A.$, and $AAA + ABA = A.A$ are correct.

(3) Aggregations combine only types or antitypes. Types must not be combined with antitypes.

(4) Aggregating configurations before significance testing is not acceptable, because the overall X-square is no longer distributed as chi-square.

(5) Each configuration may be aggregated with any number of other configurations in the same table.

The following example takes the results of zero order CFA of data representing the four symptoms of depression inhibition (I), feelings of guilt (G), anxiety (A), and excitation (E) (see Table 4.1). The analysis revealed the following clusters and anticlusters:

> Cluster: 1122, 1212, 1222;
> Anticluster: 1221, 2121, 2122, 2212.

Application of (5.34) to the clusters shows that the following aggregations are possible: 1.22 as the result of aggregating 1122 and 1222, and 12.2 as the result of aggregating 1212 and 1222. The two aggregated clusters differ in two variables and can, therefore, not be further aggregated. Only one aggregated anticluster, 212., results from the aggregation of 2121 and 2122.

The first aggregated cluster contains individuals who are inhibited, regardless of whether or not they feel guilty, and are neither anxious nor excited. The second aggregated cluster contains individuals who are inhibited regardless of their anxiety level, but feel neither guilty nor excited. The aggregated anticluster contains the few cases who are not inhibited, do feel guilty, and are not anxious across both levels of excitation.

In the analysis of polytomous data, on extended version of Quine and McCluskey's theorem can be applied. It follows the same principle as (5.34). If a state of a variable occurs under every state of another variable to form either only types or antitypes, the second variable may be considered redundant. For example, a variable with the three states A, B, and C can be aggregated following the rule

$$AA + AB + AC = A .,\tag{5.35}$$

where the period indicates that the second variable disappeared. Accordingly, for a variable with the four states A, B, C, and D the theorem becomes

$$AA + AB + AC + AD = A .,$$

and so forth. The same rules for theorem use as for dichotomous variables must be observed.

Part III:
Methods of Longitudinal CFA

The following chapters introduce methods of longitudinal CFA. Simple longitudinal designs involve two observation points for one variable. In complex designs several variables are observed for several samples over many points in time. CFA enables one to analyze contingency tables displaying patterns of constancy and change in a unique way. Rather than identifying models of interrelationships among variables across time, CFA identifies cases with patterns that remain stable or show specific changes in behavior. CFA shows which patterns occur more often than expected by chance and what other patterns are very unlikely.

Longitudinal CFA deals with several types of change. For instance, systematic shifts in means may be described as trends, and systematic changes in variability may be described as examples of the "Law of Initial Values" (cf. Wall 1977). The following sections pay special attention to specifying the particular type of change under study, and to the model under which the expected frequencies are estimated.

Most of the models discussed in the above chapters assume independent samples. In longitudinal CFA, samples are no longer independent. Therefore, repeated observations cannot be analyzed with, for instance, k-sample CFA. This approach assumes the k samples to be independent. Treating repeated observations as independent would lead to an artificial increase of the sample size and, therefore, to grossly nonconservative statistical decisions. Thus, the following chapters present methods for the investigation of longitudinal data that avoid these problems.

143

6

CFA of change over time

In longitudinal research one or more samples of n subjects are observed t times on d variables. Each variable may either be constant or change across time. Parameters that systematically vary display a trend (cf. Anderson 1971; Metzler and Nickel 1986). For instance, time series have a trend in location if the mean of the observed variable systematically varies over the t observation points. Examples of trends in location include monotone linear trends, that is, constant increases or decreases in the mean. Other time series may have a quadratic trend, that is, they look either U-shaped or inversely U-shaped. Still other time series may have a trend in dispersion. For instance, it has been hypothesized that the dispersion of intelligence increases during childhood and adolescence and decreases during senescence.

If we analyze ordinal or continuous variables, we are interested chiefly in trends in location. If we analyze nominal variables, on the other hand, we are interested in shifts from one configuration to another. Trends in location at the ordinal level can be identified by cases that, t later points in time, show higher or lower scores than those observed at earlier points in time. For example, suppose a psychotherapist uses a seven point scale to measure patient anxiety, with higher scores indicating more anxiety. An example of a trend would be a monotonous decrease in scores on the scale, across time.

The following sections present CFA methods for the analysis of trends in location. The question asked with CFA is: Are there sequences of locations or changes in location that

145

contradict the assumption of random shifts over time? The next section introduces methods for the analysis of change patterns. Later sections introduce methods that allow one to analyze the location of subjects at different points in time.

6.1 CFA of differences

Suppose, a sample of n subjects has been observed twice on $d = 3$ variables, all three at the ordinal level. One possible research question concerns the subjects' change in locations over the two points in time. As was mentioned above, two-sample CFA might be a suitable method of analysis. This approach would compare the $\Pi_i c_{1i}$ configurations from the first point in time with the $\Pi_i c_{2i}$ configurations from the second point in time. The resulting table has the format given in Table 5.16. However, two-sample CFA assumes the two samples are independent. This would obviously not be the case in a repeated measurement design. Therefore, the following approach was proposed (Lienert and Krauth 1973b, c).

For each variable measured at the rank level the difference $y_i - y_{i+1}$ between a single subjects' two measures is set to

$$
\Delta = \begin{cases} + & \text{if } y_1 > y_2 \\ = & \text{if } y_1 = y_2 \\ - & \text{if } y_1 < y_2. \end{cases} \tag{6.1}
$$

Application of (6.1) to each of d variables yields d difference scores that may be analyzed with standard CFA. The null hypothesis for such an analysis assumes for instance that all difference score patterns are equally likely (zero order CFA) or that there is total independence between difference scores from different variables (first order CFA). Types and antitypes emerging from zero order CFA of differences indicate there are either main effects in difference scores, in other words, certain differences occur more often than others, or that there are interactions between difference scores. Types and antitypes from first order CFA indicate only interactions, that is, differences in one group of variables allow one to predict differences in other variables.

The transformation given in (6.1) solves the problem of dependent measures in a straightforward way. Rather than analyzing each case twice, only one change value is examined. Section 6.3 shows how multiple observation points can be considered.

Suppose d variables have been observed twice and transformed using (6.1). Then, the log-linear model for the estimation of expected frequencies for first order CFA is

$$\log(\Delta) = u_0 + \sum_{i=1}^{d} u_i. \tag{6.2}$$

Accordingly, within the general linear model, one obtains

$$\hat{\Delta}_i = x_0 b_0 + \sum_{i=1}^{d} x_i b_i. \tag{6.3}$$

The first example of CFA of difference scores presented here analyses shifts in scores on three symptoms of experimental psychosis (cf. Table 2.2) (Krauth and Lienert 1973a; Lienert and Krauth 1973b). A sample of $n = 72$ subjects was administered a barbiturate. Before and after taking the drug, subjects were observed for emotional oversensitivity (E), daydreaming (D), and feelings of loneliness (L). Each symptom was measured on an ordinal scale with five levels. Differences were determined using (6.1). Thus, three difference scales resulted, each with the three states $+$, $=$, and $-$. Together, these three scales form a $3 \times 3 \times 3$ cross-tabulation. Table 6.1 summarizes first order CFA results for this data set. The significance level after Bonferroni-adjustment was $\alpha^* = 0.001852$ (0.05/27).

Table 6.1 shows that CFA of differences revealed two types and no antitypes. The first type has pattern $- + =$ and contains individuals whose emotional oversensitivity decreases, day dreaming increases, and feelings of loneliness remain unchanged when given a barbiturate. Because barbiturates are posited to provide the individual with a protection screen against external stimuli, this response was expected. Accordingly, the second type, $= + -$, also contains individuals who report more intense day dreaming after taking

Table 6.1. *First order CFA of differences in three scales of psychosis, observed before and after administration of a drug (n = 72).*

Configurations E D L	Frequencies o	e	Binomial test B(o)	Type/antitype
− − −	2	4.933	0.2428	
− − =	0	2.705	0.1269	
− − +	1	3.819	0.1988	
− = −	0	1.345	0.5142	
− = =	0	0.738	0.9527	
− = +	1	1.042	0.5593	
− + −	3	4.485	0.6735	
− + =	12	2.459	3.6×10^{-6}	T
− + +	6	3.472	0.2675	
= − −	2	2.565	0.9509	
= − =	0	1.407	0.4831	
= − +	0	1.986	0.2669	
= = −	0	0.670	0.6387	
= = =	0	0.384	0.9901	
= = +	2	0.542	0.2051	
= + −	9	2.332	0.0010	T
= + =	0	1.279	0.5503	
= + +	0	1.806	0.3213	
+ − −	13	6.709	0.0300	
+ − =	5	3.679	0.6142	
+ − +	10	5.194	0.0672	
+ = −	2	1.830	0.9078	
+ = =	0	1.003	0.7281	
+ = +	4	1.417	0.1076	
+ + −	0	6.100	0.0034	
+ + =	0	3.345	0.0651	
+ + +	0	4.722	0.0151	

$- .. = 25,$ $\quad = .. = 13,$ $\quad + .. = 34$
$. - . = 33,$ $\quad . = . = 9,$ $\quad . + . = 30$
$.. - = 31,$ $\quad .. = = 17,$ $\quad .. + = 24$

the barbiturate. However, their emotional oversensitivity remains constant and their feelings of loneliness are reduced.

In a second example, CFA of differences will be applied to data from a repeated observation study of caffeine effects (Lienert and Krauth 1973b). A sample of $n = 238$ subjects participated in an experiment where they were randomly assigned to the levels of the two experimental factors caffeine treatment (C) and suggestion of treatment (S). Factor C had the levels caffeine (1) and placebo (2). At the first level of factor S, subjects were told they had received caffeine (1). At the second level of S, subjects were told they had participated in the placebo group (2). Subjects were first administered the drug or placebo and given information according to their assigned level of factor S. Half an hour later they were presented with drawings. Immediately after this presentation subjects were asked to reproduce the drawings. A second reproduction took place one week later. The number of drawings correctly reproduced in the first session was subtracted from the number reproduced in the second session. Since none of the subjects reproduced the same number of drawings in both trials, a difference score resulted that assumed only the two values

$$\Delta = \begin{cases} + & \text{if } R2 > R1 \\ - & \text{if } R2 < R1, \end{cases} \tag{6.4}$$

where $R2$ and $R1$ denote scores obtained at the second and first session, respectively.

Together, the variables C, S, and Δ form a $2 \times 2 \times 2$ contingency table. The results obtained with first order CFA appear in Table 6.2. Because of the relatively large sample size, Lehmacher's (1980) test was applied without continuity correction. The significance level was adjusted using the method of Perli et al. (1987).

First order CFA of differences revealed one type and one antitype. Reading from the top to the bottom of the table, the type has pattern $12+$. It contains subjects who received caffeine but who were told they were in the placebo group. These subjects reproduced more drawings one week later than

Table 6.2. *First order CFA of differences in memory performance in a caffeine experiment (n = 238).*

Configurations CSR	Frequencies		Significance tests		Critical alpha	Rank	Type/ antitype
	o	e	z	p(z)			
11 +	19	19.124	0.037	0.4852			
11 −	48	47.809	0.046	0.4817			
12 +	24	14.591	3.068	0.0011	0.00625	1	T
12 −	27	36.477	2.392	0.0084	0.0125	2	A
21 +	12	19.448	2.231	0.0128	0.0125	3	
21 −	56	48.619	1.767	0.0386			
22 +	13	14.838	0.596	0.2755			
22 −	39	37.095	0.479	0.3158			

1.. = 118,   2.. = 120

.1. = 135,   .2. = 103

.. + = 68,   .. − = 170

in the first experimental session that is under the influence of caffeine. The antitype (pattern 12 −) complements this type. It shows that fewer subjects than expected showed an increase in drawing performance if they received caffeine.

It should be emphasized again, that these statements compare observed with expected frequencies. In absolute terms the number of subjects who perform less well in the second session is larger than the number of those who perform better in the second session. However, first order CFA does not compare absolute frequencies with each other. Rather, it compares observed with expected frequencies calculated from the assumption of total independence among variables. Here, this assumption means independence between the experimental variables and the differences in the recall rates. For the evaluation of raw frequencies with respect to a common mean, zero order CFA is the method of choice.

Equations (6.1) and (6.4) transform ordinal, interval, or ratio scale data into discrete difference scores. While in many instances such transformations may not be necessary, as when time series or analysis of variance methods are directly applied to the data, other times such transformations are useful. In particular, transformations are useful under the following conditions (see von Eye and Nesselroade, in press):

(1) When measures are taken at the ordinal level, the number of possible values is often unknown. Examples of such rank measures include self reports of patients undergoing therapy who say they "feel better" and responses from students who say they "like school this year much better than last year." The number of times these patients say they feel better and, therefore, the number of states of this scale is unknown. For this type of measures, transformations (6.1) and (6.4) establish a metric for the change process. CFA allows one to form a classification of individuals when this kind of weak data is given.

(2) When a researcher is interested only in change that takes place between two adjacent observation points.

(3) When conditions for the application of parametric tests are violated. For instance, to apply repeated measurement analysis of variance independent, identically distributed variables are required (for an overview see Hertzog and Rovine 1985). Often, either these conditions are not met or the tests to check whether they are met are not conclusive.

It is important to note that the transformations (6.1) and (6.4) eliminate mean differences. For instance, both the differences $15 - 12$ and $25 - 22$ yield a difference score of $+$. Also, differences in variation are eliminated. Therefore, CFA of differences conserves only ordinal change information. Furthermore, both (6.1) and (6.4) conserve only the direction of changes. The size of the change is not considered. For example, both the differences $1000 - 900$ and $1.4 - 1.3$ yield a difference score of $+$. Later sections will present CFA strategies that also consider the level from which the change started, and the size of the change.

CFA of differences reduces the t observations for each individual to t-1 differences. Therefore, the contingency table that results from crossing difference variables has

$$c = \prod_{i=1}^{d} c_i^{(t-1)} \tag{6.5}$$

cells where c_i denotes the number of categories of the ith difference score. Suppose all difference scales were formed using (6.4). Then, the number of cells is

$$c = 2^{(t-1)}2^{(t-1)}\ldots 2^{(t-1)} = 2^{d(t-1)}.$$

Suppose $d = 3$ and $t = 3$. Then, one obtains

$$c = 2^{3 \times 2} = 2^6 = 64$$

cells. In the example in Table 6.1 we had $d = 3$ and $t = 2$, and (6.1) was applied. Thus, a matrix resulted with

$$c = 3^{3 \times 1} = 27$$

cells. Accordingly, in the example in Table 6.2, the number of cells was $c = 2 \times 2 \times 2 = 8$.

Generalizations of CFA of differences to more than two observations are straightforward (see Keuchel and Lienert 1985; von Eye and Lienert 1985). Section 6.3.1 discusses examples with three and four observation points.

6.2 CFA of shifts in location

The last section used the direction of change, that is, signs of differences as the only information. This section will use the location of an individual relative to an a priori determined anchor. This anchor can be the median of the sample (as an example of group-based scaling; see von Eye and Lienert 1985), the median of each individual's own scores (as an example of individual-based scaling; see Keuchel and Lienert 1985), or some reference value. Again, the scoring of a position relative to an anchor or reference requires that variables be measured at least at the ordinal level. Nominal variables can be compared with an anchor only with respect to whether they are identical. Therefore, evaluation of shifts in location in terms of "higher vs. lower" are possible only for variables at least at the ordinal level.

Suppose d variables have been observed t times. Then, for each value, a transformation can be performed such that

$$\delta_{ij} = \begin{cases} + & \text{if } x_{ij} > \text{md } x_i \\ 0 & \text{if } x_{ij} = \text{md } x_i \\ - & \text{if } x_{ij} < \text{md } x_i \end{cases} \tag{6.6}$$

describes the position of individual i at point in time j, relative to the median of the ith variable, where $i = 1, \ldots, d$, $j = 1, \ldots, t$, and md x_i denotes the median of the ith variable.

If the resolution level of a variable is fine enough to exclude median ties, on obtains instead of (6.6)

$$\delta_{ij} = \begin{cases} + & \text{if } x_{ij} > \text{md } x_i \\ - & \text{if } x_{ij} < \text{md } x_i \end{cases} \tag{6.7}$$

(cf. Bierschenk and Lienert 1977). Transformations (6.6) and (6.7) are performed for each variable at each point in time.

Therefore, the resulting contingency table contains

$$c = \prod_{i=1}^{d} c_i^t \tag{6.8}$$

cells, and the same problem, analyzed with CFA of shifts in location, requires t times more cases than when analyzed with CFA of differences.

Relative to the anchor, and dependent upon the number of variable categories, a time series can have different forms (cf. Ferguson 1965; Lienert and Krauth 1973c):

(1) *Monotonic trends* either only increase $(-0+)$ or decrease $(+0-)$ in location. One needs at least two observations for the analysis of a monotonic trend $(+-, -+)$.

(2) *Bitonic trends* are either U-shaped $(+0+$ or $0-0)$ or inversely U-shaped $(-0-$ or $0+0)$. One needs at least three observations for the analysis of a bitonic trend.

(3) *Tritonic trends* look either like a horizontal S (e.g., $0-+0$) or like an inverted horizontal S (e.g., $0+-0$). At least four observations are required for the observation of a tritonic trend.

(4) *Polytomous trends* can result from more than four observation points.

The basic question of CFA of shifts in location is whether certain patterns of location occur more or less often than expected under a certain CFA model. For instance, one CFA model tests the independence of scores across the observation points (first order CFA of shifts in location). If, for this model, types and antitypes emerge, the null hypothesis of independence can be rejected and systematic shifts in location have occurred. Suppose variable X has been observed three times. Then, the log-linear model for the estimation of expected frequencies for univariate first order CFA of shifts in location is

$$\log(\delta_i) = u_0 + u_1 + u_2 + u_3, \tag{6.9}$$

for $i = 1, \ldots, 3$. Accordingly, within the general linear model, CFA of shifts in location corresponds to

$$\hat{\delta}_i = x_0 b_0 + x_1 b_1 + x_2 b_2 + x_3 b_3. \tag{6.10}$$

The following univariate example of CFA of shifts in location analyzes shifts in mood (Krauth and Lienert 1973a). In this experiment, subjects performed seven trials of mathematical calculations. A total of 60 subjects rated their mood after the first, third, fifth, and seventh trial of calculations on a five point Likert scale. For the present purposes ratings were transformed using (6.6). A scale with three values resulted. Rating levels 1 and 2 were assigned a $+$, 3 was assigned a 0, and 4 and 5 were assigned a $-$, where $+$ denotes good mood. A complete contingency table, including all four observation points would have 81 cells and, therefore, many very small expected frequencies. The last two ratings were, therefore, pooled. A three-dimensional table with 27 cells resulted. Table 6.3 gives this cross-tabulation. The data were analyzed with first order CFA using the standard normal $z = \sqrt{X^2}$ statistic and Bonferroni alpha adjustment ($\alpha^* = 0.05/27 = 0.001852$).

Table 6.3 shows three types and no antitypes. The first type has pattern $+ + 0$ and includes subjects who keep their good mood during the first two trials of number crunching. Only in the second half of the experiment do they lose their good mood.

The pattern one would have expected from an experiment of this kind was observed for a fourth of the sample. These subjects started calculating in a good mood. However, already after the third trial their mood was no longer positive, and towards the end of the experiment they were in a rather bad mood. The second type contains these subjects.

A third group of subjects (pattern $0 + +$), also far more than expected, seemed to respond in a counterintuitive manner. In a neutral mood at the beginning of the experiment, they responded as if continuing calculations improved their mood.

Most instances of social science research involve more than one variable. Therefore, the next example of CFA of shifts in

Table 6.3. *First order univariate CFA of shifts in mood* ($n = 60$).

Trial 357	Frequencies		Significance tests		Type/antitype
	o	e	z	$p(z)$	
+ + +	0	3.045	1.745	0.0810	
+ + 0	12	4.350	3.668	0.0003	T
+ + −	0	5.655	2.378	0.0174	
+ 0 +	0	2.030	1.425	0.1542	
+ 0 0	1	2.900	1.116	0.2645	
+ 0 −	15	3.770	5.784	7×10^{-1}	T
+ − +	0	1.692	1.301	0.1934	
+ − 0	0	2.417	1.555	0.1201	
+ − −	1	3.142	1.208	0.2269	
0 + +	13	2.205	7.270	3×10^{-12}	T
0 + 0	0	3.150	1.775	0.0759	
0 + −	0	4.095	2.024	0.0430	
0 0 +	0	1.470	1.212	0.2253	
0 0 0	0	2.100	1.449	0.1473	
0 0 −	1	2.730	1.047	0.2951	
0 − +	0	1.225	1.107	0.2684	
0 − 0	2	1.750	0.190	0.8501	
0 − −	5	2.275	1.807	0.0708	
− + +	0	1.050	1.025	0.3055	
− + 0	1	1.500	0.408	0.6831	
− + −	1	1.950	0.680	0.4963	
− 0 +	0	0.700	0.837	0.4028	
− 0 0	1	0.999	0	1	
− 0 −	0	1.300	1.140	0.2542	
− − +	1	0.583	0.546	0.5854	
− − 0	3	0.833	2.373	0.0176	
− − −	3	1.083	1.841	0.0655	

$+ .. = 29$, $0 .. = 21$, $− .. = 10$
$. + . = 27$, $. 0 . = 18$, $. − . = 15$
$.. + = 14$, $.. 0 = 20$, $.. − = 26$

location illustrates the multivariate approach using two variables, each observed twice. While in univariate CFA of shifts in location the selection of the model for the estimation of expected frequencies is obvious (there is only one variable), in multivariate designs several models might be considered. Suppose first order CFA is performed assuming total independence. This assumption can be violated if

(1) variables are autocorrelated, that is, if the location at earlier points in time allow one to predict scores at later points in time,
(2) variables are correlated with one another, or
(3) both (1) and (2) apply.

In either case the simplicity of the independence model is, to a certain extent, outweighed by the problem that types and antitypes indicate solely time related interactions only if the variables are independent of each other. Therefore, a model might be considered that assumes no autocorrelations and the variables may display interactions of any order.

The following example uses data from the same experiment as above. Sixty subjects participated in a seven trial experiment in which they had to do calculations. In addition to the mood variable analyzed above, the flicker fusion threshold (F) and performance in calculations (R) were observed after the first and the seventh trial of calculations. Each of the variables was dichotomized at the group median. For the present analyses, four variables were used on which subjects scored either above (1) or below (2) the median: flicker threshold after the first ($R1$) and the seventh ($R7$) trial, and performance in calculating after the first ($R1$) and the seventh ($R7$) trial. Crossed, these four variables form a contingency table with 16 cells. Table 6.4 gives the results of first order CFA of this data set. Alpha was adjusted using Bonferroni's procedure ($\alpha^* = 0.05/16 = 0.003125$). The z-approximation of the binomial test was applied. Two types and no antitype emerged. The first type, at the top of Table 6.4, has pattern 1111. It contains participants who score above average in both F and R on both observation points. These subjects were

Table 6.4. *First order multivariate CFA of shifts in location (n = 60).*

Configurations				Frequencies		Significance tests		Type/
R1	R7	F1	F7	o	e	z	p(z)	antitype
1	1	1	1	11	3.718	3.899	0.0001	T
1	1	1	2	2	5.577	−1.590	0.1117	
1	1	2	1	1	2.002	−0.720	0.4713	
1	1	2	2	0	3.003	−1.778	0.0754	
1	2	1	1	3	4.682	−0.881	0.3784	
1	2	1	2	12	7.293	1.860	0.0629	
1	2	2	1	0	2.618	−1.654	0.0980	
1	2	2	2	4	3.927	0.038	0.9700	
2	1	1	1	1	3.042	−1.202	0.2295	
2	1	1	2	4	4.563	−0.274	0.7839	
2	1	2	1	7	1.638	4.248	2×10^{-5}	T
2	1	2	2	0	2.457	−1.601	0.1095	
2	2	1	1	0	3.978	−2.064	0.0390	
2	2	1	2	6	5.967	0.014	0.9886	
2	2	2	1	1	2.142	−0.795	0.4268	
2	2	2	2	8	3.213	2.745	0.0060	

$1... = 33$, $2... = 27$
$.1.. = 26$, $.2.. = 34$
$..1. = 39$, $..2. = 21$
$...1 = 24$, $...2 = 36$

highly activated both at the beginning and at the end of the experiment. Thus, the first type can be interpreted as a type of subjects stable in location. Somewhat surprising is the pattern of the second type. Rather than getting tired, the subjects of this type started in both variables below average and ended up with above average scores. One can assume that these subjects needed a relatively long training phase before showing practice effects.

With respect to the above discussion of the selection of multivariate CFA models for shifts in location, one might wonder what variable interactions led to the emergence of these two types. Exact Fisher tests show that the autocorrelations of both F and R are very low. The upper tail probability for the association between $R1$ and $R7$ is 0.66, and for $F1/F7$, 0.73. However, the associations between R and F are strong. After one trial for the association between $R1$ and $F1$ shows an upper tail probability of 0.0004. After the seventh trial the probability is 3×10^{-7}. Thus, we may conclude that the two types reflect stable relationships between F and R. The types are local contradictions of the assumption that locations within trials are independent.

6.3 CFA of first, second, and higher differences

Section 6.1 introduced CFA of differences between two observations. This section generalizes this approach in two ways. First, the number of observation points is increased (cf. Krauth 1973; Bartoszyk and Lienert 1978). Second, higher order differences are considered. CFA can be applied to differences of differences (CFA of second differences) and higher order differences, rather than only to differences between observed scores (first differences). Each approach allows one to answer specific questions concerning the form of trends in location.

6.3.1 CFA of first differences between t observation points

Suppose a sample of n subjects was observed t times on one variable. We can, then, ask if groups of homogeneous time series have the same pattern, or slope, of increasing and decreasing values. If, as in Section 6.1, the level from which the change started is of no particular interest, the method of differences between adjacent values can be applied. The vector of t raw scores from variables at the ordinal or higher levels can be transformed into a vector of t-1 differences Δ or δ using (6.1) or (6.6), respectively. This vector describes the up-and-down pattern of a subject's time series. If (6.1) is applied, zero differences, or periods of no change, are included. Transformation (6.4) is sensible in particular for variables with very high resolution levels making "no change" scores close to impossible.

If (6.1) is used to describe the shape of a time series, a total of 3^{t-1} possible slopes results. With (6.4) the number of different slopes is 2^{t-1}. To determine whether certain shapes occur more often and other shapes occur less often than expected by chance, the researcher may apply, for instance, zero or first order CFA.

First order CFA assumes total independence between all difference variables. In other words, it assumes that shape values cannot be predicted in pairs of values, nor in triplets of values, and so forth. The log-linear model for this approach is

$$\log(\Delta_i) = u_0 + \sum_{i=1}^{t-1} u_i. \tag{6.11}$$

Obviously, (6.11) is parallel to (6.2). The difference between these two equations is that (6.2) estimates expected frequencies under the assumption of total independence between d variables, while (6.11) treats the t-1 Δ values as realizations of t-1 variables. As in (6.2), these variables are assumed independent of each other.

Accordingly, one obtains within the general linear model

$$\hat{\Delta}_i = x_0 b_0 + \sum_{i=1}^{t-1} x_i b_i. \tag{6.12}$$

The relationship between (6.12) and (6.3) is the same as that between (6.11) and (6.2).

A second approach in CFA for the analysis of the up-and-down patterning of time series is parallel to zero order CFA. It assumes all patterns are equally likely. Thus, the expected frequency for each of the possible slope patterns is

$$e = np^{t-1}. \tag{6.13}$$

The transformation given in (6.1) leads to $p = 1/3$. Equation (6.4) leads to $p = 0.5$.

The following paragraph shows that the assumption of equally likely first differences is problematic. Suppose a researcher observes a characteristic three times. Then, the three measures 1, 2, and 3 result. For these measures, the following sequences are possible: 123, 132, 213, 231, 312, and 321. The first differences for these sequences are $++$, $+-$, $-+$, $+-$, $-+$, and $--$, The a priori probabilities for these difference patterns are $p(++) = 0.167$, $p(+-) = 0.333$, $p(-+) = 0.333$, and $p(--) = 0.167$. Therefore, application of (6.13) may lead to wrong conclusions. For longer time series, these considerations apply in an analogous fashion.

With respect to the assumptions made by zero order CFA, we see that the first differences cannot be equally likely. Rather, one can assume that the values 123 are equally likely. From this assumption a priori probabilities for the first differences follow that can be calculated using combinatorics.

A comparison between these two approaches shows that first order CFA allows the relative frequencies of $+$, $=$, and $-$ changes to differ for every Δ. This approach is useful when one analyzes one sample of subjects to find differences in trends due to associations among Δ-variables. The second approach assumes $+$, $=$, and $-$ probabilities are derived from equally likely raw scores. This approach might be considered when CFA of first differences is used to compare k groups as to their relative frequencies of $+$, $=$, and $-$ changes.

The first example of CFA of first differences between t observation points analyzes a sample of $n = 30$ subjects who took an intelligence test (Bartoszyk and Lienert 1978). Pulse rate of the subjects was measured before, during, and after administration of the test. Application of (6.4) leads to two difference scores for each subject, yielding $2^{3-1} = 4$ possible patterns of differences Δ: $++$, $+-$, $-+$, and $--$. The pattern $++$ indicates that the pulse rate increased from the measurement before the administration of the intelligence test to the measurement during the administration of the test. The pulse rate kept increasing until after the test was taken. Table 6.5 summarizes the results of both CFA strategies for this data set. The binomial test was applied. Alpha was Bonferroni adjusted ($\alpha^* = 0.05/4 = 0.00125$).

Table 6.5. *First and zero order CFA of first differences between three pulse rate measurements (n = 30).*

Configurations	First order CFA			Zero order CFA	
	o	e	B(o)	e	B(o)
+ +	5	7.367	0.4371	5	0.7671
+ −	8	5.633	0.3757	10	0.5721
− +	12	9.633	0.4591	10	0.5522
− −	5	7.367	0.4371	5	0.7671
+ . = 13, − . = 17					
. + = 17, . − = 13					

Table 6.5 shows that first order CFA of first differences reveals no types or antitypes. There are no local deviations from stationarity that can be identified as homogeneous change patterns. Therefore, the null hypothesis of stationarity cannot be rejected. To test the assumption that the change patterns follow their a priori probabilities, zero order CFA of first differences was performed. The last two columns in Table 6.5 show that no tail probability comes even close to the critical α^*. Therefore, the null hypotheses of no local deviations from the assumption cannot be rejected either.

The second example of CFA of first differences combines trend analysis with a comparison of two groups. Two fictitious samples have been observed three times in one hour time intervals. Difference scores were calculated using transformation (6.4). Table 6.6 gives the results of two sample CFA of the change patterns in the two samples. Pearson's X^2 test was applied. Alpha was Bonferroni adjusted ($\alpha^* = 0.05/4 = 0.0125$). The expected frequencies were calculated under the assumptions of first order CFA. Because of the equal marginal frequencies, the expected frequencies are the same for both groups.

Of the four patterns of first differences, only + + discriminates sufficiently between the two samples. It shows that a monotonous increase occurs far more often in the first sample than in the second.

Table 6.6. *Two-sample CFA of first differences.*

Configurations	Frequencies					Significance tests			
	o			e		X^2-Components			p
+ +	11	1	12	6	6	4.167	4.167	8.333	0.0039
+ −	2	10	12	6	6	2.667	2.667	5.333	0.0209
− +	5	7	12	6	6	0.167	0.167	0.333	0.5637
− −	0	0	0	0	0	0	0	0	
	18	18	36	18	18			14.000	

6.3.2 CFA of second and higher differences between t observation points

To describe trends, CFA uses the differences between adjacent measures. Such differences can be calculated

(1) between raw scores (first differences),
(2) between differences between raw scores (second differences),
(3) between second differences (third differences), and so forth.

The method of calculating differences is well known in time series analysis. Differencing requires at least interval data. Differences of a series of numbers have certain characteristics analogous to derivatives of a function. The characteristic most important for the present context is that differences of a certain order become constants if a function of the same order perfectly describes the time series. For example, the differences between the values $x = 2, 3, 4, 5, \ldots$ are $3 - 2 = 1, 4 - 3 = 1, 5 - 4 = 1$, and so forth. Because the first differences of this time series are constant, this time series can be described as a linear function. Similarly, the first differences between the values $x = 1, 4, 9, 16, 25, \ldots$ are $3, 5, 7, 9, \ldots$, and the second differences are $2, 2, 2, \ldots$. In this example the second differences are constant. Therefore, a quadratic function describes this time series perfectly. The method of differences uses this result. Differences can be used to estimate the degree of a polynomial that sufficiently reproduces a time series, and to estimate the coefficients of this polynomial.

CFA uses the method of differences to determine whether the linear, quadratic, cubic, or higher components of time series are homogeneous. These components are heterogeneous when there are subgroups that differ in their slope parameters. Typically, CFA uses either only the signs of the differences, that is transformation (6.4), or distinguishes between negative, positive, and zero differences, that is, applies transformation (6.1). However, more refined differences scales are conceivable.

The signs of first differences have an obvious interpretation. Positive differences indicate a positive trend; an increase in values. Similarly, negative signs indicate a negative trend, that is, a decrease in values. The signs of second differences have the following interpretation:

(1) positive signs indicate positive acceleration, that is, the curve is U- or J-shaped;
(2) negative signs indicate negative acceleration, that is, the curve is inversely U- or J-shaped.

Switches from positive to negative signs of second differences occur at inflection points, that is, when U- or J-shaped slopes turn into inversely U- or inversely J-shaped ones. Similarly, switches from negative to positive signs occur when inversely U-shaped curves turn into U-shaped ones. Generally, switches in signs of second differences indicate that at least cubic functions are needed to describe the time series perfectly. This interpretation of signs of differences applies to higher order functions accordingly.

The following example, taken from Bartoszyk and Lienert (1978), analyzes time series from $n = 48$ subjects who participated in an investigation on vigilance. Four measures per subject were transformed into sign patterns of first and second differences using (6.4). From four measures, three first differences result from which, in turn, two second differences result. The signs of the two second differences can have patterns $++$, $+-$, $-+$, and $--$.

The present analysis uses only the second differences. When analyzing patterns of second differences CFA can calculate expected frequencies under, for instance, the following two assumptions. The first assumption uses the main effect model from first order CFA. It posits that

(1) negative, positive, and (if calculated) zero differences may occur at different rates, and
(2) the accelerations, decelerations (and no changes in slope) at later points in time are independent from those at earlier points in time.

The second assumption is based on a zero order CFA-model, applied to the first differences. This model assumes every first order difference pattern is equally likely. If this assumption holds, second differences are no longer equally likely. Rather, the same considerations as for first differences from equally likely raw scores apply. Suppose, as is the case in the present data example, the three first differences 1, 2, and 3 are given. Here the numbers describe the ordinal relationship between adjacent values rather than the exact numerical value of the differences, with $1 < 2 < 3$. Then, the second differences pattern $+ +$ can result only from the first differences pattern 1, 2, 3. However, second differences pattern $+ -$ can result from 1, 3, 2, and from 2, 3, 1. Accordingly, $- +$ can result from 2, 1, 3 and 3, 1, 2, and $- -$ can result only from 3, 2, 1. It follows that patterns $+ -$ and $- +$ have a higher a priori rate if all first differences are considered equally likely. For longer time series and higher than second differences similar considerations apply.

Table 6.2 gives the results of CFA of second differences under assumptions of zero and first order CFA. The binomial test was applied, and alpha was adjusted using the procedure of Hommel et al. (1985) for two-dimensional tables. Applied to the present example for each CFA test $\alpha^* = \alpha$ if the global contingency X^2 is significant. We obtain $X^2 = 18.89$ ($p = 1 \times 10^{-5}$) for first order CFA of second differences and $X^2 = 5.9375$ ($p = 0.0148$) for CFA under the assumption of equally likely first differences. Both values are significant, the first one even under an adjusted $\alpha^* = 0.05/5 = 0.01$.

The results given in Table 6.7 show that first order CFA of second differences identified two types and two antitypes. The antitypes $+ +$ and $- -$ indicate that consistent positive and consistent negative acceleration of vigilance occur less often than expected. Rather, positive accelerations of vigilance, counterbalanced by negative accelerations (pattern $+ -$), and negative accelerations, counterbalanced by positive accelerations (pattern $- +$), occurred more often than expected under the assumption that the first sign of second differences does not allow the prediction of the second one.

The assumption that sign patterns of second differences are observed as often as expected under the assumption of equally

Table 6.7. *Two approaches to CFA of second differences* ($n = 48$).

Configuration	o	e	B(o)	T/A	e	B(o)	T/A
+ +	6	13.417	0.0183	A	8	0.5819	
+ −	22	14.583	0.0345	T	16	0.0969	
− +	17	9.583	0.0183	T	16	0.8654	
− −	3	10.417	0.0074	A	8	0.0307	A

$+ . = 28, \quad - . = 20$
$. + = 23, \quad . - = 25$

distributed first differences allows one to describe the observed frequency distribution much better than the above first order CFA assumption. Even though the overall X^2 is significant, only one antitype was identified. It is pattern $- -$ which indicates that the vigilance of far fewer subjects than expected went increasingly down.

In many instances, the a priori probabilities of second differences depend on the a priori probabilities of the first differences. The following example illustrates this dependency. Suppose a researcher observes a characteristic four times. Suppose also, this characteristic can assume only the values 1, 2, 3, and 4. If one disregards the cases that show no changes from one occasion to another, these four values can assume the 24 sequences ranging from 1234 to 4321. The first of these sequences has first differences $1, 1, 1$ and, thus, the first differences pattern $+ + +$. The second sequence, 1243, has first differences $1, -2, -1$ and, thus, the first differences pattern $+ - -$. The resulting 24 first differences patterns fall into eight groups. These groups have a priori probabilities $p(+ + +) = 1/24$, $p(+ + -) = 3/24$, $p(+ - +) = 5/24$, $p(+ - -) = 3/24$, $p(- + +) = 3/24$, $p(- + -) = 5/24$, $p(- - +) = 3/24$, and $p(- - -) = 1/24$.

From the 24 first differences, 24 second differences result. For instance, the second differences pattern resulting from the first differences pattern $1, 1, 1$ is 00. The second differences pattern resulting from first differences pattern $1, -2, -1$ is

$-+$. Including the no change patterns, a total of nine different second differences patterns results. These have a priori probabilities $p(00) = 2/24$, $p(-+) = 8/24$, $p(--) = 2/24$, $p(-0) = 1/24$, $p(+-) = 6/24$, $p(0-) = 1/24$, $p(++) = 2/24$, $p(0+) = 1/24$, $p(+0) = 1/24$. These considerations apply accordingly to third and higher differences.

6.4 Considering both level and trend information

When analyzing first differences (Section 6.1) or second and higher differences (Section 6.3), trend parameters were the focus and means were disregarded. Researchers interested in level as well as trend information can adopt one of three approaches. The first approach describes the position of an individual relative to an anchor. Examples of anchors include the mean of an individual, a learning criterion, or the mean of the group. In Section 6.2 shifts in location were expressed relative to the group median for each variable.

The second approach of considering both level and trend information treats the level as a separate variable. Usually level is expressed in terms of the location of individuals relative to the group mean of the time series. The location of individuals may also be considered based on their status at the beginning of the time series, at the end of the time series, or at some other critical point in time. The third approach approximates and smoothes time series with exponential, logistic, or polynomial functions. If orthogonal polynomials are used, the coefficients can be interpreted in a fashion analogous to regression coefficients. CFA analyzes these coefficients after categorizing them.

Section 6.4.1 introduces the approach that analyzes categorized scores of variables observed several times. Sections 6.4.2 and 6.4.3 present CFA of orthogonal polynomials.

6.4.1 CFA of categories of trend and location

This section discusses the analysis of categorized scores of variables observed at several times (Lienert and von Eye 1984b; von Eye and Nesselroade, in press). Suppose a continuous variable is observed t times. For analysis with longitudinal CFA this variable is discretized at $c - 1$ percentile points to have c categories. Then, univariate CFA of the location of subjects on this variable over t points in time crosses the t observations with each other. The resulting matrix has

$$c = \prod_{i=1}^{t} c_i = c_i^t \qquad (6.14)$$

cells.

This matrix can be modeled under two sets of assumptions. The first assumes total independence between the measures at the t observation points. Under this model any kind of autocorrelation is a violation and can lead to the presence of types or antitypes. The second model allows first, second, and higher order autocorrelations or combinations of these. This model, therefore, is violated only if autocorrelations prevail that were not considered in the null hypotheses. For example, if first order autocorrelations, that is, correlations between values adjacent in time, are taken into account in the estimation of expected frequencies, second or higher order autocorrelations between values more distant in time can lead to types and antitypes.

Model considerations for the third approach of CFA to trend analysis become more complex if multivariate repeated measurement designs are investigated. Suppose d variables are observed, the ith of which has c_i categories. The cross-tabulation of these variables has

$$c = c_1 \times c_2 \times \cdots \times c_d = \prod_{i=1}^{d} c_i \qquad (6.15)$$

possible categories at the first observation point. There are two ways to analyze the time series of these c cells with CFA (see von Eye and Nesselroade, in press). The first considers t, the observation points, an additional variable, crossed with the d observed variables. A matrix with

$$c = t \prod_i c_i \qquad (6.16)$$

cells results. This matrix can be analyzed using the usual CFA models, for instance, first order CFA. However, this matrix can also be analyzed under the assumption that the d variables show interactions of any order, but are independent of t. This approach can be considered parallel to prediction CFA, ISA, or t-sample CFA. Under these assumptions violations and, therefore, types and antitypes can occur only if the joint frequency distribution is not homogeneous over time. In other words, types and antitypes will emerge only if the frequency of configurations of the d variables can be predicted from the observation points.

The main characteristic of this approach is that time series are viewed from a static perspective. Rather than analyzing the change characteristics of trends, only the locations of individuals on the variables at each point in time are considered. The moves individuals make from level to level are disregarded. Therefore, a second approach that allows one to investigate such moves in addition to the locations might be considered. This approach crosses the matrices described in (6.15). A cross-tabulation with

$$c = \left(\prod_{i=1}^{d} c_i \right)^t \tag{6.17}$$

cells results. Obviously, this approach allows one to do time series analysis with CFA in a most detailed manner. However, the number of cells increases rapidly with each additional variable and additional point in time. Therefore, one needs very large samples to apply CFA with chances of identifying types and antitypes under the prohibitively small adjusted alpha.

The following example analyzes one continuous variable, observed three times (Lienert and von Eye 1984b; von Eye and Nesselroade, in press). In an experiment on problem solving behavior, a sample of $n = 118$ third, fifth, and seventh graders played the "master mind" game on a microcomputer (Funke and Hussy 1979). The students played a variant of the game in which six symbols were placed on four positions. The maximum number of trials was eight. Students were allowed to proceed at their own pace. The time needed to propose a solution at each step of the master mind game was categorized into the three levels 1 (0–10 s), 2 (10–20 s), and 3 (> 20 s). The following analyses include only those students who needed all eight trials. Therefore, the cell frequencies in Table 6.8 add up only to $n = 98$. Twenty students had solved the problem before the last trial.

The following CFA includes the problem solving times from trials 6, 7, and 8. The measured time categories were crossed to form a $3 \times 3 \times 3$ contingency table (see (6.14)). This table was analyzed under first and modified second order CFA assumptions.

The modifications of second order CFA assumptions concern the interactions assumed present. In ordinary second order CFA, all variables are allowed to demonstrate pairwise interactions. In the present example only first order autocorrelations were allowed. Thus, only the interaction between trials 6 and 7 and between 7 and 8 were considered. The interaction between trials 6 and 8 was not considered. The log-linear model for the estimation of expected frequencies was, therefore,

$$\log(y_{ijk}) = u_0 + u_{ij} + u_{jk} \qquad (6.18)$$

rather than

$$\log(y_{ijk}) = u_0 + u_{ij} + u_{ik} + u_{jk} \qquad (6.19)$$

as in ordinary second order CFA.

Both first and second order CFA applied the binomial test and Bonferroni alpha adjustment. The adjusted alpha was $\alpha^* = 0.001852$. Table 6.8 gives the results of both analyses. First order CFA revealed one type and one antitype. The type, pattern 111, contains those students who consistently responded in 10 s or less. It is, therefore, a stability type. The antitype has pattern 211. This is the pattern of medium response times in trial 6 and short times in trials 7 and 8. About seven students were expected to show this pattern, but none were observed.

Table 6.8. *First and second order CFA of problem solving times* ($n = 98$).

Configuration	First order CFA				Second order CFA		
	o	e	p	T/A	e	p	T/A
111	18	3.90	1×10^{-18}	T	12.74	0.0809	
112	4	3.09	0.7501		5.21	0.3983	
113	0	4.25	0.0261		4.05	0.0160	
121	0	2.77	0.1202		0.44	0.6482	
122	1	2.20	0.7019		0.89	0.5917	
123	2	3.02	0.8319		1.67	0.4979	
131	1	3.39	0.2869		0.97	0.6228	
132	0	2.69	0.1307		1.21	0.2973	
133	3	3.69	0.9883		1.82	0.2750	
211	0	7.00	0.0014	A	5.79	0.0026	
212	4	5.56	0.6840		2.37	0.2137	
213	6	7.61	0.7083		1.84	0.0107	
221	3	4.97	0.5239		2.81	0.5364	
222	3	3.95	0.8800		5.63	0.1797	
223	13	5.41	0.0058		10.56	0.2559	
231	6	6.07	0.8122		5.58	0.4870	
232	6	4.82	0.7048		6.97	0.4492	
233	11	6.61	0.1325		10.45	0.4758	
311	4	2.29	0.3926		3.47	0.4585	
312	1	1.82	0.9116		1.42	0.5835	
313	1	2.49	0.5713		1.11	0.6961	
321	1	1.62	0.9695		0.74	0.5171	
322	4	1.29	0.0820		1.48	0.0617	
323	0	1.77	0.3358		2.78	0.0594	
331	1	1.99	0.8141		1.45	0.5734	
332	4	1.58	0.1483		1.82	0.1106	
333	1	2.16	0.7218		2.73	0.2382	

$1.. = 29, \quad 2.. = 52, \quad 3.. = 17$
$.1. = 38, \quad .2. = 27, \quad .3. = 33$
$..1 = 34, \quad ..2 = 27, \quad ..3 = 37$

Modified second order CFA revealed no types or antitypes. Even though the Pearson X^2 for the log-linear model under which the expected frequencies were estimated did not provide an acceptable fit ($X^2 = 38.53$, $df = 12$, $p = 0.00013$; the respective figures for the first order CFA model are $X^2 = 101.44$, $df = 20$, $p < 0.00001$), no observed frequencies deviated from their expected values dramatically enough to justify their interpretation as types or antitypes.

6.4.2 CFA of orthogonal polynomial coefficients for equidistant time points

The present section introduces CFA of coefficients of orthogonal polynomials. This method allows one to consider level and slope information simultaneously (Krauth 1973, 1980b; Krauth and Lienert 1975, 1978; Lienert 1980; von Eye and Hussy 1980, von Eye and Nesselroade, in press). Two variants of the method are discussed. The first method estimates polynomial coefficients for equidistant observation points, that is, observation points separated by time intervals of equal length. Whereas many methods of time series analysis, including Box-Jenkins models, require equidistant points on the x-axis, in social science research this desideratum is rarely met. For instance, if a therapist calls a patient in twice a week, observation points are not equidistant. Therefore, polynomial approximation for nonequidistant observation points are also covered (Section 6.4.3).

Univariate time series of $t > 1$ measures can be approximated by polynomials. Using a general regression approach the observed value y can be approximated using the polynomial

$$\hat{y} = b_0 x^0 + b_1 x^1 + b_2 x^2 + \cdots = \sum_{i=0}^{j} b_i x^i, \qquad (6.20)$$

where x are the observation points, and the b_i are the estimators of regression coefficients, with $i = 0, 1, \ldots, t - 1$. The value j is called the degree of the polynomial. For instance, if $j = 2$, (6.20) becomes

$$\hat{y} = x_0 b^0 + x_1 b^1 + x_2 b^2,$$

which is a quadratic curve or a second degree polynomial. As long as $j < t - 1$ the polynomial does not necessarily hit the y-values. Rather, the polynomial smoothes the curve and flattens the peaks. Only for $j = t - 1$ does the polynomial hit the observed values exactly. For reasons of scientific parsimony, polynomial models usually are fit with less than $t - 1$ coefficients. For instance, in regression analysis, one typically fits linear curves, that is, first degree polynomials.

There are many methods for determining the polynomial coefficients b. Examples include ordinary least squares methods as in standard regression models, and the method of differences used in Sections 6.1 and 6.3. The advantages of both these methods are well known. They are easy to calculate and computer programs are readily available, in particular for regression analysis. Disadvantages are twofold. First, lower degree coefficients can be dependent on higher degree coefficients if ordinary nonlinear polynomial regression is calculated. Therefore, the researcher must recalculate the entire analysis if he/she decides to use a polynomial of a higher degree. The second problem is that coefficients of ordinary polynomials do not allow substantive interpretation.

▼

Because of these problems Krauth (1973), Krauth and Lienert (1975, 1978) (cf. Bliss 1970; von Eye and Hussy 1980), and Lienert (1980) have proposed the use of orthogonal polynomials. To describe orthogonal polynomial models a reformulation of (6.20) seems useful. One obtains

$$\hat{y} = a_0 \beta_0 + a_1 \beta_1 + a_2 \beta_2 + \cdots, \tag{6.21}$$

where β_i denotes orthogonal polynomials of the ith degree, with $i = 0, 1, \ldots$, and the a_i are the polynomial coefficients. For instance, β_1 is a first degree polynomial, that is, a straight line as a simple regression line of the form

$$y = ax + b.$$

β_2 denotes a second degree or quadratic polynomial of the form

$$y = ax^2 + bx + c.$$

A system of polynomials $f^n(x)$ of degree j is called orthogonal on the interval $a \leqslant x \leqslant b$ with respect to the weight function $w(x)$ if

$$\int_a^b w(x) f^n(x) f^m(x)\, dx = 0 \qquad (6.22)$$

with $n \neq m$ and $n, m = 0, 1, 2, \ldots$ (see Abramowitz and Stegun 1970). To check whether or not a system of polynomials is orthogonal one calculates, for instance,

$$\sum_x \beta_1 = 0, \quad \sum_x \beta_2 = 0, \ldots,$$

$$\sum_x \beta_1 \beta_2 = 0, \quad \sum_x \beta_1 \beta_3 = 0, \ldots. \qquad (6.23)$$

▲

Again, there are many ways to determine the coefficients of orthogonal polynomials, and there are many forms of such polynomials. The following sections use polynomials with easy to determine coefficients and with the following desirable characteristics. First, their coefficients can be interpreted in a fashion similar to regression coefficients. Specifically, a_0 is the arithmetic mean of the time series, a_1 describes the linear trend and, thus, is the linear regression coefficient. Coefficient a_2 describes the quadratic trend as explained in Section 6.3.2, a_3 the cubic trend, and so on.

The second characteristic follows from the definition of orthogonality given in (6.22) and (6.23). The polynomial coefficients of lower degree polynomials are independent of the coefficients of higher degree polynomials. Therefore, decisions to increase or decrease the degree of the polynomial used to describe a time series will not require that the calculations be redone from scratch. Rather, one can simply pick those polynomials which seem interesting, important, or significant.

▼

Polynomial coefficients are most easily calculated if the observation points are equidistant, that is, if $x_2 - x_1 = x_3 - x_2 = x_4 - x_3 = \cdots = $ constant. For such designs one sets

$$\hat{y} = a_0\beta'_0 + a_1\beta'_1 + a_2\beta'_2 + \cdots + a_j\beta'_j, \qquad (6.24)$$

where $\beta'_0 = 1$, $a_0 = \bar{y}$, and $\beta'_i = \lambda_i\beta_i$ for $i = 1, \ldots, j$. The values for the polynomials β_i and the λ_i are given, for instance, in standard textbooks of analysis of variance (e.g., Kirk 1982, Table E12) or in standard volumes containing statistical tables (e.g., Fisher and Yates 1948).

The following example shows how a time series can be approximated using orthogonal polynomials. A least squares solution will be presented. Suppose a time series is given with the following six values: $y_1 = 2$, $y_2 = 12$, $y_3 = 24$, $y_4 = 10$, $y_5 = 8$, $y_6 = 11$. The x-values are equidistant between 1 and 6. This time series will be approximated by a second and a third order polynomial. First, a table can be set up as in Table 6.9 (values of polynomials are taken from Kirk 1982). Before we calculate the polynomial coefficients, we check whether the polynomial values given in Table 6.9 meet the orthogonality conditions given in (6.23). We obtain, for instance,

$$\sum_x \beta_1 = -5 - 3 - 1 + 1 + 3 + 5 = 0,$$

and

$$\sum \beta_1\beta_2 = (-5 \times 5) + (-3 \times -1) + (-1 \times -4)$$
$$+ (1 \times -4) + (3 \times -1) + (5 \times 5) = 0.$$

The reader is invited to check that $\Sigma_x\beta_i$, $\Sigma_x\beta_3$, $\Sigma_x\beta_1\beta_3$, and $\Sigma_x\beta_2\beta_3$ are also equal to zero.

To calculate the polynomial coefficients one uses the following:

$$a_0 = \bar{y}, \qquad (6.25)$$

$$a_j = \frac{\sum_{i=1}^{t} (y_i\beta'_{ji})}{\sum_{i=1}^{t} (\beta'^2_{ji})}. \qquad (6.26)$$

Table 6.9. *Numerical example of approximation with orthogonal polynomials.*

Observed point	x	y	β_1	β_2	β_3
1	-2.5	2	-5	5	-5
2	-1.5	12	-3	-1	7
3	-0.5	24	-1	-4	4
4	0.5	10	1	-4	-4
5	1.5	8	3	-1	-7
6	2.5	11	5	5	5
$(\beta_i')^2$			70	84	180
λ			2	3/2	5/3

Inserting the values from Table 6.9 into (6.25) one obtains $a_0 = 11.17$. We set $\beta_0' = 1$. To calculate a_1, one obtains from (6.26)

$$a_1 = \frac{\sum_{i=1}^{t} (y_i \beta_{1i}')}{\sum_{i=1}^{t} (\beta_{1i}'^2)}. \tag{6.27}$$

Inserting the values from Table 6.9 one obtains $a_1 = (-(5 \times 2) - (3 \times 12) + \cdots + (5 \times 11))/70 = 0.2714$, indicating that the linear trend in the present data is positive, with an average increase of 0.27 in y coinciding with an increase of 1 in x. To calculate a_2 one obtains from (6.26)

$$a_2 = \frac{\sum_{i=1}^{t} (y_i \beta_{2i}')}{\sum_{i=1}^{t} (\beta_{2i}'^2)}. \tag{6.28}$$

In this example, (6.28) yields $a_2 = (-(5 \times 2) - (1 \times 12) + \cdots + (5 \times 11))/84 = -1.0833$. This value indicates a relatively strong quadratic trend in the present data. The negative sign indicates that the quadratic trend describes an inversely U-shaped curve. To calculate a_3, one obtains from (6.26)

$$a_3 = \frac{\sum_{i=1}^{t} (y_i \beta_{3i}')}{\sum_{i=1}^{t} (\beta_{3i}'^2)}, \tag{6.29}$$

and $a_3 = (-(5 \times 2) + (7 \times 12) + \cdots + (5 \times 11))/180 = 0.7167$.

This value indicates that the last direction of the curve is upwards (positive sign of a_3).

The values for a_0, a_1, a_2, and a_3 can be used to calculate the values the second and the third degree polynomial give us as estimates of y. For instance, the observed value $y = 2$ is estimated to be $\hat{y} = (11.17 - (5 \times 0.2714) - (5 \times 1.0833) - (5 \times 0.7167) = 0.8130$. For $y = 12$ one obtains as an estimate $\hat{y} = 11.17 - (3 \times 0.2714) + 1.0833 + (7 \times 0.7167) = 16.4560$, and so forth.

To determine the polynomials explicitly one uses the relationship $\beta_i' = \lambda_i \beta_i$. The β_i can be determined by the recursive formula

$$\beta_{i+1} = \beta_1 \beta_i - \frac{i^2(t^2 - i^2)}{4(4i^2 - 1)} \beta_{i-1}, \tag{6.30}$$

with $\beta_1 = x$. For reasons of comparability the equidistant x-values are transformed to be difference scores of natural numbers. For $i = 1$ one obtains

$$\beta_2 = \beta_1 \beta_1 - \frac{1(6^2 - 1)}{4(4 - 1)} = x^2 - \frac{t^2 - 1}{12}, \tag{6.31}$$

and for $i = 2$

$$\beta_3 = x^3 - \frac{x(3t^2 - 7)}{20},$$

and so forth (see Snedecor and Cochran 1967).

The resulting second degree polynomial for the present example is

$$\hat{y} = 11.17 + 0.2714 \times 2x - 1.0833 \times 1/2(x^2 - (t^2 - 1)/12),$$

or, inserting $t = 6$

$$\hat{y} = 15.9096 + 0.5428x - 1.625x^2,$$

and the third degree polynomial is

$$\hat{y} = 11.17 + 0.2714 \times 2x - 1.0833 \times 3/2(x^2 - (t^2 - 1)/12$$
$$+ 0.7167 \times 5/13(x^3 - x(3t^2 - 7)/20),$$

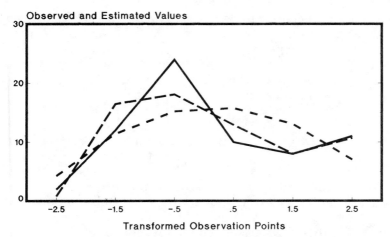

Fig. 6.1. Approximation of empirical y-values (solid line) by second (dashed line) and third (interrupted line) degree polynomials.

or

$$\hat{y} = 15.9096 - 5.4894x - 1.625x^2 + 1.1945x^3.$$

The reader is invited to check that this equation yields the same $\hat{y}_1$ and $\hat{y}_2$ as calculated above. Note that instead of the raw scores x, the difference values x from Table 6.9 must be inserted to obtain the estimates for y. The difference values in Table 6.9 result from subtracting the mean $\bar{x} = 3.5$ from each original x-value. Also, it is important to note that the interpretation of polynomial coefficients as means, linear, cubic, or higher degree trend is possible only for the coefficients a_i given in (6.27). The coefficients given in the last equation of the present example do not allow this interpretation. Figure 6.1 gives the observed values for y and the estimates from the second and the third degree polynomial.

▲

The following example of CFA of polynomial coefficients is taken from von Eye and Nesselroade (in press). It analyzes data from a longitudinal study in which $n = 42$ college students were observed four times for state anxiety (cf. Nesselroade, Pruchno, and Jacobs 1986). On each occasion, the students completed the two parallel forms A and B of a state anxiety questionnaire. For the present purposes we approximate the four measures with second degree polynomials. Thus, for each student the parameters of the following quadratic form was estimated

$$\hat{y} = \bar{y} + b_1 t + b_2 t^2,$$

with $t = \{1, 2, 3, 4\}$ being the equidistant points in time. For instance, student no. 27 has values $\bar{y} = 37.8$, $b_1 = 1.0$, and $b_2 = -0.8$ for Form A (see von Eye and Nesselroade, in press). These values indicate that the mean of this student's four anxiety scores in Form A is 37.8 and is slightly above the group mean. His linear trend is 1.0, indicating that the overall trend is toward increasing scores. His quadratic trend was -0.8, indicating that toward the end of the observation period the student's score went down.

For the present purposes we use only the mean and the linear trend of the time series. (von Eye and Nesselroade (in press) used the linear and the quadratic trend coefficients.) The means of both scales were dichotomized at their respective medians. The linear trend coefficients were dichotomized at zero. This can be considered a natural cut-off because positive coefficients indicate increasing state anxiety, and negative coefficients indicate decreasing state anxiety. Thus, the four scales A0, A1, B0, and B1 resulted. A0 and B0 are the scales for the dichotomized mean scores and A1 and B1 are the scales for the dichotomized trends. The frequencies of the resulting cross-classification were analyzed with first order CFA, that is, under the assumption of total independence of all four scales. The binomial test was used for significance testing. Alpha was adjusted using the Bonferroni method to $\alpha^* = 0.05/16 = 0.003125$. Table 6.10 summarizes the results of the analysis.

The data in Table 6.10 were analyzed to determine if the two forms are parallel across the four observations. In the present context, we consider the tests parallel if subjects display the same configuration of mean and linear trend in both tests. First order CFA reveals two types, both of which support the

Table 6.10. *First order CFA of dichotomized mean and linear trend scores of two parallel state anxiety tests (n = 42).*

Configurations				Frequencies		$B(o)$	T/A
A0	A1	B0	B1				
+	+	+	+	10	3.10	0.0015	T
+	+	+	−	0	2.11	0.2306	
+	+	−	+	1	2.56	0.5317	
+	+	−	−	0	1.74	0.3384	
+	−	+	+	5	3.75	0.6394	
+	−	+	−	4	2.55	0.4995	
+	−	−	+	0	3.10	0.0802	
+	−	−	−	1	2.11	0.7417	
−	+	+	+	2	3.10	0.7855	
−	+	+	−	1	2.11	0.7417	
−	+	−	+	5	2.56	0.2207	
−	+	−	−	0	1.74	0.3384	
−	−	+	+	0	3.75	0.0394	
−	−	+	−	1	2.55	0.5355	
−	−	−	+	2	3.10	0.7855	
−	−	−	−	10	2.11	0.00006	T

1... = 21, 2... = 21
.1.. = 19, .2.. = 23
..1. = 23, ..2. = 19
...1 = 25, ...2 = 17

notion of the two test forms being parallel. The first type has pattern + + + +, indicating that far more subjects than expected under the assumption of total independence displayed in both state anxiety test forms scores above the group median with a tendency toward increasing scores. The second type contains subjects with just the opposite pattern.

These two types strongly support the notion of two parallel test forms. The two other configurations supporting this interpretation have pattern + − + − and − + − +. Both of these show only a nonsignificant tendency in the right direction, that is, were observed more often than expected.

All configurations but one $(+ - + +)$, that contradict the notion of two parallel test forms, tend to occur less often than expected. Two of those configurations $+ - - +$ and $- - + +$, almost form antitypes. These patterns did not occur at all. Of the other two contradictory patterns, $+ + - -$ and $- + + -$, $- + + -$ was observed only once. However, none of these configurations deviates from its expected values dramatically enough to form antitypes.

Overall, these results support the notion that the two test forms are parallel. Those configurations which indicate same responses of subjects to both forms either form types or tend to occur more often than expected. Configurations contradictory to the notion of parallelism tend to occur less often than expected. These results complement those reported by von Eye and Nesselroade (in press) where a similar pattern of responses was found using the first and second degree polynomial coefficients.

6.4.3 CFA of orthogonal polynomial coefficients for nonequidistant time points

In many social science research studies observation points are not equidistant. Suppose students are observed at the beginning and the end of the school year for five years. Then, the observation points within each school year are about nine months apart and those between school years are about three months apart. The algorithms described in the following section allow one to take the size of the differences between these intervals into account. The estimated polynomial coefficients are also orthogonal. Therefore, the conditions given in Section 6.2.3 are fulfilled, and the coefficients are interpretable in the same fashion as for orthogonal polynomials for equally spaced observation points (cf. Krauth and Lienert 1975, 1978; Krauth 1980b; von Eye and Hussy 1980).

▼

Suppose a variable was measured several times at non-equidistant occasions. Then, the coefficients a_i of the orthogonal polynomials can be calculated by

$$a_i = \frac{\sum_j \beta_j y_j}{\sum_j \beta_j^2}, \quad \text{for } i = 1, \ldots, t \tag{6.33}$$

(cf. (6.27)). The polynomials can be calculated using the following recursive formula

$$\beta_{i+1} = (2x + \alpha_i)\beta_i + \gamma_{i-1}\beta_{i-1}, \tag{6.34}$$

where x denotes the values of the observation points. The starting values for the β_i are $\beta_{-1} = 0$ and $\beta_0 = 0.5$. The values for α_i and γ_{i-1} are calculated using

$$\alpha_i = \frac{-2 \sum_{j=1}^t x_j \beta_{ij}^2}{\sum_{j=1}^t \beta_{ij}^2} \tag{6.35}$$

and

$$\gamma_{i-1} = \frac{-\sum_{j=1}^t \beta_{ij}^2}{\sum_{j=1}^t \beta_{i-1,j}^2}. \tag{6.36}$$

Application of these equations is illustrated using an example from a learning experiment (cf. von Eye and Hussy 1980). In an experiment on retroactive inhibition, the effects of the duration of a pause before an interfering activity was studied. The duration of the pause was $x = \{1, 5, 10, 20, 40\}$ min. The respective recall rates were $y = \{6.28, 8.50, 8.67, 10.06, 12.94\}$.

The coefficient a_0 is easily calculated as $a_0 = \bar{y} = 9.29$. Inserting into (6.34)–(6.36), yields $a_1 = 0.15$ and $a_2 = 0.00076$, and the second degree polynomial $\hat{y} = 9.29 + 0.15\beta_1 + 0.00076\beta_2$. (Note that a_1 is identical to the usual linear regression coefficient.) For interpolation purposes, the β_i can be calculated and values for y for any value of x between 1 and 40 can be estimated. Inserting the polynomials for the β_i yields, after some elementary algebraic transformations, the interpolation polynomial $\hat{y} = 6.69 + 0.21x - 0.0015x^2$. For instance, the recall rate after a pause of 25 min between the end of a learning trial and interfering activity is $y = 6.69 + (0.21 \times 25) - 0.0015(25 \times 25) = 11.00$.   ▲

The following example, taken from von Eye and Lienert (1987) (cf. Krauth 1980b), analyzes a biomedical data set. A sample of $n = 20$ obese patients was compared to a sample of $n = 13$ control patients with respect to $t = 8$ plasma measurements in inorganic phosphate. The obese were orally administered a standard dose of glucose. The plasma samples were taken after the following time intervals: immediately after glucose application (0 min), 30 min, 1 h, 90 min, 2 h, 3 h, 4 h, and 5 h. Each subject's response curve was approximated using second degree orthogonal polynomials for nonequidistant observations (the raw data are given in Zerbe 1979).

The present analysis compares the two samples with respect to the first three polynomial coefficients, a_0, a_1, and a_2. Two sample CFA was conducted. X^2-tests are used under Bonferroni adjustment. Each of the three polynomial coefficients was dichotomized. The first coefficient, a_0, was dichotomized at the median, and the other two coefficients were dichotomized at $a_1 = a_2 = 0$. Together with the two groups of patients, the dichotomized coefficients form a $(2 \times 2 \times 2) \times 2$ contingency table. Two-sample CFA performs one test per row of this table or eight tests. Thus, $\alpha^* = 0.05/8 = 0.00625$. Table 6.11 gives the results of two-sample CFA; $+$ signs indicate coefficients above the cut-off, and $-$ signs indicate coefficients below the cut-off.

Even though the overall X^2 for the cross-tabulation is significant ($X^2 = 14.9896$, $df = 7$, $p = 0.0361$), no tests against the null hypothesis of no local differences between the two groups were significant. However, configurations $+ - -$ and $- + +$ seem to show that pattern $+ - -$ occurs only in the obese group while $- + +$ occurs only in the control group. To test this, biprediction CFA can be applied. Biprediction CFA requires condensation of the cross-tabulation such that the two complementary configurations form two rows and all other configurations together form a third one (see Section 5.5.2). Table 6.12 gives this cross-tabulation for the present data set.

Table 6.11. *Two-sample CFA of polynomial coefficients of plasma measures.*

Configurations		Frequencies			X^2 – components			p
		o	e					
+	+	1	1.576	2.424	0.210	0.137	0.347	0.5558
+	−	2	1.182	1.818	0.566	0.368	0.934	0.3337
+	+	1	1.576	2.424	0.210	0.137	0.347	0.5558
+	−	0	2.364	3.636	2.364	1.536	3.900	0.0483
−	+	4	1.576	2.424	3.730	2.424	6.154	0.0131
−	−	4	2.364	3.636	1.133	0.736	1.869	0.1716
−	+	1	0.394	0.606	0.394	0.256	0.650	0.4201
		13	20					

Table 6.12. *Biprediction CFA for the comparison of the complementary configurations* $+ - -$ *and* $- + +$ *in the two samples of obese and normals*

Configuration	Obese	Normals	Sums
$+ - -$	0	6	6
$- + +$	4	0	4
Others	9	14	23
Sums	13	20	33

Application of equation (5.11) yielded a $X^2 = 10.05$ which has for $df = 1$, a tail probability of 0.0015. This value is smaller than the critical $\alpha^* = 0.0125$ required for four simultaneous biprediction CFA tests. Thus, we may conclude that even though simple configurations do not allow one to discriminate between the two samples, pattern $+ - -$ is typical for obese and pattern $- + +$ is typical for subjects in the control sample. This result suggests that when compared with normals, obese patients display above median levels of phosphate, negative trends, and inversely U-shaped slopes of acceleration. The control sample, on the other hand, displays below median phosphate levels, positive trends, and U-shaped slopes of acceleration during the first five hours after glucose challenge.

6.5 CFA of time series of different length

In empirical research, time series often differ in length. For example, subjects participating in a problem solving experiment may need different numbers of attempts before arriving at the solution. Patients in psychotherapy may become better at different rates and, therefore, conclude therapy after different numbers of sessions. This section presents approaches to deal with time series of different length, not only with respect to the number of observation points but also with respect to slope and trend. Special emphasis is placed on including even those cases that show only a very small number of measures.

There are several approaches to ensure that a maximum number of cases can be included in an analysis. A first approach confines itself to estimating parameters of even very short time series. For instance, the mean and regression coefficient for a time series can be estimated even if there are only two observations. A second approach combines parameter information with information on the length of time series. Both of these methods are very simple and can be applied to practically any time series. However, they may do justice only to very simple patterns of repeated observations and may not be sensible for some substantive questions. Therefore, the present section describes how these two approaches can be combined (Lienert and von Eye 1986).

The method is introduced using data from a learning experiment. A total of $n = 89$ subjects ($n = 52$ males and $n = 37$ females) participated in an experiment in which they were presented with a paired-association learning task. Twelve pairs of nouns were presented using a memory drum. After each of eight trials, only the stimulus words were presented and subjects were asked to provide the response word. Eight correctly recalled words were required as a learning criterion (see criterion 3, below). Thus, it was relatively easy to reach the criterion before the maximum alotted number of eight trials. To identify gender-related types of learning, these curves were evaluated with respect to the following three criteria:

(1) *Monotonic trend criterion (M)*. This criterion refers to the linear trend in the data. For the present data, a monotonic increase, denoted by $M+$, was assigned if, over the eight trials, the inequality $y_{i+1} \geqslant y_i$ held true (weak monotonicity, for $i = 1, \ldots, t - 1$). If this inequality was violated for at least one pair of adjacent measures, the value $M-$, that is, lack of monotonicity, was assigned. For subjects with less than eight trials all available recall scores were considered. This criterion requires a minimum of two responses.

(2) *Early success criterion (K)*. The learning criterion of the noun pairs was reached if a subject recalled a minimum of eight nouns correctly before the maximum number of trials was reached. Learning curves for subjects who reached this

criterion were labeled with $K+$, and $K-$ otherwise. This criterion distinguishes between subjects who needed eight trials and those who needed fewer trials. More refined scales could have been considered, the most refined one counting the number of trials needed by a subject. This criterion requires a minimum of one response.

(3) *Mistake-avoidance-criterion (S).* In addition to the number of correctly recalled nouns, the number of errors made in terms of nouns associated to the wrong stimulus word was counted. This measure was interpreted as an indicator of how certain subjects reacted with respect to their associations. Subjects were classified based on their position with respect to the overall median. Thus, subjects whose average number of wrong associations was below the median were assigned a $S+$, and a $S-$ otherwise. The criterion requires a minimum of one response.

The first of these three criteria refers to the slope of the curve. The second and third criteria refer to substantive phenomena. This example shows that slope and substantive parameters can be combined to form a multivariate vector describing a subject's learning characteristics. Obviously, the strategy of combining substantive and slope characteristics is not restricted to incomplete curves. One can combine these interests, for instance, when investigating learners with respect to personality characteristics or evaluating differential treatment effects depending on patterns of symptoms.

Table 6.13 gives the present data. Crossing the three variables M, K, and S led to a $2 \times 2 \times 2$ contingency table. To compare male with female subjects, two-sample CFA was conducted. Instead of performing a complete two-sample CFA, we investigate only whether the configuration of overall poor performers, $- - -$, discriminates between males and females. Application of (5.12) yields a $X^2 = 5.0291$. For $df = 1$ this value has a tail probability of $p = 0.0249$. Since for one test, alpha need not be adjusted we may conclude that configuration $- - -$ constitutes a discrimination type. This type suggests that males, significantly more than females, do not show increase in recall rates, do not reach the early success criterion, and make more than average association errors.

Table 6.13. *Two-sample CFA of incomplete learning curves* ($n = 85$).

MKS	Males	Females	Sum
+ + +	12	12	24
+ + −	2	3	5
+ − +	3	2	5
+ − −	6	6	12
− + +	5	6	11
− + −	3	2	5
− − +	2	2	4
− − −	12	4	19
	48	37	85

6.6 CFA in the analysis of treatment effects

Previous chapters in this book covered treatment effects under several perspectives. For instance, Table 5.12 compared the effects of two nicotine doses and a placebo on finger pulse volume. Table 5.22 showed data from blood plasma samples drawn under varying stress conditions. The present section introduces CFA methods for a more detailed analysis of treatment effects (Lienert and Straube 1980; Krauth and Lienert 1980). More specifically, the following four questions will be considered:

(1) Does a treatment reduce the number of undesirable behavior patterns?
(2) Will the number of individuals showing a particular pattern of undesirable behaviors be reduced by the therapy?
(3) Will the number of individuals displaying a particular pattern of undesirable behaviors change?
(4) Does a treatment produce a shift from one particular configuration to another?

A very simple strategy can be applied to answer the first question. Count first those individuals, e.g., patients, who display fewer symptoms after the treatment than before, then count those who display more symptoms. Let the number of patients who got better be denoted as b, and the number of patients who get worse, w. Then, these two figures can be compared with the *diagonal half sign test*. It uses the – under the null hypothesis – standard normally distributed test statistic

$$z = \frac{(b - w)}{(b + w)^{1/2}} . \qquad (6.37)$$

Alternatively, the binomial test given in (2.8) can be used with $p = w/n$. If one assumes changes for the better and changes for the worse are equally likely, $p = 1/2$. To illustrate this test statistic, a psychiatric data set is used (Lienert and Straube 1980). A sample of $n = 75$ acute schizophrenics was treated with neuroleptic drugs for two weeks. Before and after the treatment they were observed for seventeen symptoms with the brief psychiatric rating scale (BPRS) (Overall and Gorham 1962). From these seventeen symptoms, the three dichotomous scales W = emotional withdrawal, T = thought disturbances, and H = hallucinations were constructed for analysis with CFA. For all scales + denotes the presence and − the absence of symptoms.

To investigate if neuroleptic drugs reduce the number of symptoms, Table 6.14 was set up. This table contains the number of symptoms as a proxy for severity of schizophrenia, with symptoms observed once before and once after the treatment. (For the raw frequencies see Lienert and Straube 1980).

To apply (6.37), b is determined as the sum of those cell frequencies that indicate a reduction in the number of symptoms. Relevant cell frequencies in this case are in cells 32, 31, and 30 in the first row of the cross-tabulation, cells 21 and 20 in the second row, and cell 10 in the third row. Altogether, a total of $b = 10 + \cdots + 4 = 39$ patients displayed fewer symptoms after treatment with neuropleptic drugs. Similarly, cells 23, 12, 13, 01, 02, and 03 contain patients whose status worsened, and thus $w = 14$. Inserting these values into (6.37) yields $z = (39 - 14)/(39 + 14)^{1/2} = 3.4340$, for which $p =$

Table 6.14. *Analysis of change in number of symptoms in pre-post treatment designs.*

No. of symptoms before treatment	Configurations	No. of symptoms after treatment				Sums
		3	2	1	0	
		+++	++− +−+ −++	+−− −+− −−+	−−−	
3	+++	1	10	4	0	15
2	++− +−+ −++	6	11	17	4	38
1	+−− −+− −−+	1	4	7	4	16
0	−−−	0	1	2	3	6
	Sums	8	26	30	11	75

0.0003. From this we may conclude that application of neuroleptic drugs reduces the number of symptoms in schizophrenic patients.

To investigate if the relative frequency of single symptoms change with time, two approaches may be adopted. The first approach generates a fourfold table for each symptom, with the numbers of symptoms present versus absent before and after treatment cross-tabulated. For instance, for symptom W one obtains cell frequencies $+ + = 46$, $+ - = 11$, $- + = 8$, and $- - = 10$, where $+$ denotes the presence and $-$ the absence of emotional withdrawal.

This 2×2 table can be analyzed with McNemar's X^2-test. The test statistic is

$$X^2 = \frac{(b - c)^2}{b + c} \tag{6.38}$$

for $df = 1$ (cf. (6.37)). With continuity correction one obtains

$$X^2 = \frac{(|b - c| - 0.5)^2}{b + c}. \tag{6.39}$$

Application of these equations to the present data yields $X^2 = 0.47$ and $X^2 = 0.33$, respectively. Neither value comes even close to the critical $X^2 = 3.84$ ($\alpha = 0.05$), indicating that the number of patients freed from symptom W is not significantly different from the number of patients attaining that symptom during the two week study period. Thus, we may conclude that emotional withdrawal is not a symptom that can successfully be treated with neuroleptic drugs.

On the other hand, the neuroleptic drug treatment is clearly successful for hallucinations. The 2×2 table for H, formed from Table 6.14, has frequencies $+ + = 8$, $+ - = 21$, $- + = 9$, and $- - = 32$. Application of (6.38) yields $X^2 = 4.80$. The tail probability for this value is 0.0285 ($df = 1$), less than the usual $\alpha = 0.05$. We may conclude that application of neuropleptic drugs leads to a significant reduction in the number of observed hallucinations.

The second approach used to examine the stability of a relative frequency of a given symptom complements the first approach. This second approach consists of estimating a stability coefficient for each symptom. For the present purposes the phi coefficient is suggested. Phi is

$$\Phi = (ad - bc)/((a + b)(c + d)(a + c)(b + d))^{1/2}$$

(cf. (1.3)). Under the null hypothesis Φ is normally distributed and can be tested via

$$z = \Phi n^{1/2}$$

(cf. (5.13)). Application of these equations to the 2×2 table for W yields $z = 2.9867$. Application to the table for H yields $z = 0.9955$. The tail probability for the first z-value is $p = 0.0014$, indicating that the number of hallucinations is not very stable over the two occasions. Thus, we may conclude, again, that emotional withdrawal cannot be successfully treated with neuroleptic drugs, while hallucinations can.

The third question discussed in this section is more pertinent to the configural approach. This is the question as to whether particular configurations of symptoms respond to a given treatment. Suppose a researcher is interested in the effects of a treatment on a particular combination of symptoms for which the prognosis is most unfavorable. In a two observation point design, we can compare those patients who responded to the treatment with those who did not. Let b be the number of patients who display the relevant symptoms at both observation points, not responding to the treatment. Let $m1$ denote the observed frequency of the symptom pattern before the treatment and $m2$ the frequency after the treatment. Then, a test for homogeneity of $m1$ and $m2$ with respect to b is

$$z = (m3 - m4)/(m3 + m4)^{1/2}, \qquad (6.40)$$

where $m3 = m1 - b$, and $m4 = m2 - b$ (Lehmacher 1981; Lienert and Straube 1980). Under the null hypothesis, the test statistic z is normally distributed.

Suppose configuration $+ + +$, containing patients who suffer from all three symptoms of schizophrenia, was observed with frequencies $m1 = 15$ before, and $m2 = 8$ after treatment. Suppose also configuration $+ + +/+ + +$, containing those patients who did not respond to treatment with neuroleptic drugs, was observed only once. Then, we obtain $z=(15-1-8+1)/(15-1+8-1)^{1/2}=1.5275$. The one-sided tail probability for this value is $p = 0.0633$. Thus, we may conclude that treatment with neuroleptic drugs does not significantly reduce the number of occurrences of symptom pattern $+++$.

Notice that this test was performed one-tailed. This is because we expected the treatment to reduce the number of cases with all three symptoms. In exploratory studies or when effects of combined treatments are investigated, the direction of a particular treatment combination may not be known a priori. In such instances the two-tailed test may be preferred over the one-tailed version.

The fourth question discussed in this section concerns change patterns. Consider, for instance, a researcher who is interested in discovering which symptom pattern is most likely to follow a given configuration of symptoms after treatment. To answer this question prediction analysis (Hildebrand et al. 1977) or analysis of conditional probabilities (Sacket 1977) are suitable. In the present context, however, prediction CFA will be used (see Section 5.4). Suppose a researcher is interested in the hypothesis that configuration $+-+$ is most likely to follow from configuration $+++$. Then, a 2×2 table can be set up as schematized in Table 6.15.

As discussed in Table 5.17, a table of the form given in (6.15) can be analyzed using fourfold test of homogeneity. Such tests include Fisher's exact test (cf. (5.22) and (5.23)), the X^2 test as given in (5.24), z-tests as given in (5.26), log-ratio tests, or association coefficients.

In the present data example, the following 2×2 table was observed for the transition from symptom pattern $+++$ to pattern $++-$ (Lienert and Straube 1980): $a = 9$, $b = 6$, $c = 11$, $d = 48$. Inserting these values into (5.24) yields $X^2 = 10.6534$, for which the tail probability is $p = 0.0011$. This result supports the notion that neuroleptic drugs set schizophrenics who suffer from emotional withdrawal, thought disturbances, and hallucinations free from hallucinations.

Table 6.15. *Scheme of a fourfold table for the analysis of symptom shifts in pre-post treatment designs.*

		Pretreatment		
		$+-+$	All others combined	Marginals
Pretreatment	$+++$	a	b	f_{+++}
	All others combined	c	d	$n - f_{+++}$
		f_{+-+}	$n - f_{+-+}$	n

The tests presented in this section allow one to interpret loss or shifts of symptoms in a conclusive fashion only if spontaneous recovery can be excluded. Usually, a nonnegligible number of patients show spontaneous recovery from symptoms, this change not due to drug or therapeutic treatment. Therefore, to avoid overestimations of the efficiency of a given treatment, control group designs are strongly recommended. The next section introduces methods of CFA for the analysis of treatment effects in control group designs.

6.7 CFA of treatment effects in control group designs

Control groups are an integral part of the research on treatment effects. They are necessary to avoid wrong conclusions about the treatment effects. If one cannot a priori exclude the possibility of spontaneous symptom shifts or spontaneous recoveries, groups of subjects who received a certain treatment must be compared with either a control group or with another experimental group of subjects receiving another treatment.

Suppose a researcher compares the data in the last example in the last section with data from a control group. Then, two 2×2 tables of the form given in (6.15) must be compared with

Table 6.16. *Scheme of a fourfold table for the comparison of experimental and control groups with respect to symptom shifts in pre-post treatment designs.*

	Experimental group	Control group	Marginals
$+++/+-+$	a	a'	$f_{+++/+-+}$
All others combined	$b + c + d$	$b' + c' + d'$	$n + n' - f_{+++/+-+}$
	n	n'	$n + n'$

each other. For this comparison, a cross-tabulation of the form given in Table 6.16 can be formed.

Table 6.16 compares the shift of the control and experimental groups from symptom pattern $+++$ to pattern $+-+$, expressed as $+++/+-+$. If all subjects in the experimental group make this shift and none in the control group do, cells $b + c + d$ and a' are empty. To test whether relatively more subjects in the experimental group than in the control group made this shift, the null hypothesis that there is no association between the frequency distribution of the pattern shifts and group membership is set forth. Again, the tests discussed in Section 5.6.1 can be used.

Suppose a control group was included in the experiment on the effects of neuroleptic drugs on symptoms of schizophrenia. Suppose two of fifty-four patients who were not treated with neuroleptic drugs showed the symptom shift from pattern $+++$ to pattern $++-$. Then, a fourfold table results with cell frequencies $a = 9$, $b + c + d = 66$, $a' = 2$, and $b' + c' + d' = 52$. Application of (5.24) yields a $X^2 = 2.7361$. The tail probability for this value is $p = 0.0981$ which is greater than the usual $\alpha = 0.05$. This result indicates that in the above interpretation, that the drug caused a significant reduction in hallucinations for those patients who suffered from all three schizophrenia symptoms must be revised. Given that the spontaneous rate of recovery is about 4%, the observed reduction rate is no longer significant.

The present section discussed the statistical analysis of shifts from one pattern to another while comparing two groups of individuals. K-sample comparisons of all shifts or, in more general terms, of all change patterns, are possible with k-sample CFA. Lienert and Rudolf (1983) give an example of change in three variables. The authors analyzed the effects of client centered psychotherapy by comparing a group of patients who underwent therapy with a control group who did not. The two groups were compared with respect to their neuroticism, extraversion, and tendency to dissimulate. Results showed that an increase in extraversion, neuroticism, and dissimulation is found more often in the control group than in the treatment group.

6.8 CFA of patterns of correlation or of distance sequences

Longitudinal CFA of patterns of change, polynomial coefficients, or shifts in configurations requires relatively large samples if the number of variables is large. Let e denote the minimum cell frequency required for a CFA. Suppose, a researcher observes d variables t times, and the ith variable has c_i categories $(i = 1, \ldots, d)$. Then, the minimum sample size for a one wave investigation, analyzed with CFA, is

$$n = e \prod_{i=1}^{d} c_i. \tag{6.41}$$

To investigate, for instance, shifts in categories over t points in time, the required sample size increases to n^t. Thus, it is obvious that application of CFA methods to longitudinal designs confines one to relatively small sets of variables. The number of observation points is less of a problem if polynomials can be approximated. Polynomials typically reduce a long univariate time series to a small number of parameters. The following paragraphs describe two approaches to analyze multivariate time series: CFA of patterns of correlation; and CFA of patterns of distance sequences (von Eye 1984).

Suppose a sample of n subjects is observed t times on d variables. Then, the raw data box has dimensions $n \times d \times t$. The front slice of this matrix contains the data observed at the first observation. The second slice contains the data from the second observation, and the last slice, the data from the last observation. The top layer of this matrix contains the t vectors of data for the first subject. The second layer contains the t vectors for the second subject, and so on.

CFA of patterns of correlation uses the following strategy to analyze these data. Rather than evaluating changes variable-wise, the unit of analysis is shifted to the entire data vector of a person at each point in time. Each vector is compared with its adjacent vectors. More concretely, the first vector of the ith person is correlated with the second vector, the second with the third, and the t-1st with the tth. Altogether, this method transforms the $n \times d \times t$ box of raw data into the two-dimensional $n \times t$ matrix of correlations. Figure 6.2 depicts this process of data reduction.

The next steps parallel the process of longitudinal CFA. The correlations are categorized using, for instance (6.1), (6.4), or the method of first differences, and a matrix of the cross-classified change variables is formed in order to search for types and antitypes.

The following example analyzes data from an investigation on fatigue and mood changes caused by memory experiments. Immediately before and after a memory experiment in which participants read and recalled narratives, a questionnaire was administered to the $n = 148$ subjects measuring anxiety, arousal, and fatigue. The entire experimental procedure was repeated once. Thus, the fatigue and mood variables were observed a total of four times.

The first step in CFA of correlation sequences involves correlating adjacent data vectors. This step transforms the 3×4 data matrix for each person into a vector comprised of the three correlations between the first and the second, the second and the third, and the third and the fourth observation, respectively.

The distribution of the correlation coefficients was bimodal. One mode was located at $r = -0.80$, and the other at $r = 0.99$.

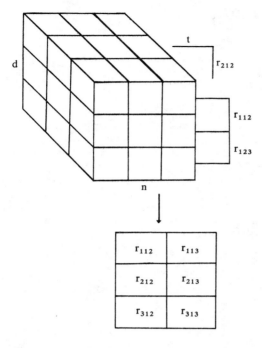

Fig. 6.2. Transformation of a raw data-matrix into a matrix of correlations of time adjacent data vectors.

The distribution is strongly skewed and shows many more positive than negative correlations. Therefore, rather than the median of $r = 0.90$, the value $r = 0.50$ was chosen as a cut-off. This value characterizes the lowest point in the "valley" between the two peaks.

Table 6.17 gives the cross-tabulation of the three dichotomized correlation coefficients. First order CFA of this table was done using Lehmacher's test under Küchenhoff's continuity correction and Holm's adjustment. The starting value for alpha was $\alpha^* = 0.05/8 = 0.00625$.

Table 6.17 shows that CFA detected one type and one antitype. The type has pattern 111. It contains subjects whose

Table 6.17. *First order CFA of correlation patterns of fatigue and mood changes (n = 148).*

Configuration	Frequencies		Significance tests		p		T/A
	o	e	$|z|$	p	Rank	Critical	
111	65	56.406	2.613	0.0045	1	0.006	T
112	12	13.161	0.272	0.3927	6	0.017	
121	31	38.459	2.335	0.0098	3	0.008	
122	9	8.974	0.208	0.4176	7	0.025	
211	8	14.945	2.548	0.0054	2	0.007	A
212	3	3.487	0.008	0.4969	8	0.05	
221	16	10.190	2.228	0.0129	4	0.01	
222	4	2.378	0.797	0.2130	5	0.0125	

1.. = 117, 2.. = 31
.1. = 88, .2. = 60
..1 = 120, ..2 = 28

repeated measures are always correlated above the cut-off. These constantly very high correlations indicate that the pattern of anxiety, arousal, and fatigue values is not affected by the memory experiments between the first and the second, and between the third and the fourth observation. Clearly more subjects than expected display this correlation pattern.

The antitype has pattern 211. The fatigue-mood pattern of these subjects is characterized by a low or negative correlation between the observations before and after the first experiment and a high correlation before and after the second experiment.

In many instances researchers wish to complement the correlations between adjacent vectors of measures with information on shifts in locations. Correlations are not sensitive to mean differences and therefore, high correlations can be associated with both large and small spatial distances. In the present data example, it was investigated whether there are types of shifts in location, that is, trends. To determine shifts in location Euclidean distances, s, between adjacent observations were calculated using

$$s = \left(\sum_i (y_{i+1} - y_i)^2 \right)^{1/2}, \quad \text{for } i = 1, \ldots, t - 1. \quad (6.42)$$

The resulting distance values were assigned a 1, if, on average, the observed values at point in time $i + 1$ were greater than at point in time i and a 2 otherwise. Fatigue was inversely scored, so that high scores indicate low fatigue. The dichtomization used the zero point as cut-off. Table 6.18 gives the results calculated using the same methods as for Table 6.17.

CFA of patterns of distance sequences revealed two types and two antitypes. Reading from the top to the bottom of the table, the first antitype includes subjects whose scores in all fatigue and mood variables increased over all four observations, indicating a decrease in self-reported fatigue and an increase in anxiety and arousal. These values increased even between the two experiments. Therefore, this trend can be considered independent of the experiments. CFA shows this pattern is highly unlikely.

Table 6.18. *First order CFA of distance patterns of fatigue and mood changes (n = 148).*

Configuration	Frequencies		Significance tests		p		T/A
	o	e	$|z|$	p	Rank	Critical	
111	17	26.248	2.674	0.0037	4	0.01	A
112	18	17.400	0.003	0.4867	7	0.025	T
121	38	24.867	3.905	0.00005	2	0.007	
122	12	16.484	1.357	0.0874	5	0.013	
211	16	19.454	0.965	0.1673	6	0.017	
212	25	12.897	4.228	0.00001	1	0.006	T
221	18	18.431	0.023	0.4908	8	0.05	
222	4	12.218	2.847	0.0021	3	0.008	A

1.. = 85,   2.. = 63
.1. = 76,   .2. = 72
..1 = 89,   ..2 = 59

Pattern 121 occurred more often than expected. This type includes subjects whose mood and fatigue scores increased during the experiments and decreased between them. Also more often than expected by chance was the complementary pattern, 212. This describes subjects whose overall mood and fatigue scores decreased during the experiments and increased between them.

The second antitype is also complementary to the first antitype. It contains subjects whose scores decreased between each observation. Hence, we can conclude, again, that a monotonic trend, not affected by the experiments, is most unlikely.

CFA of patterns of correlation or of distance sequences can be generalized in several ways. First, similarity measures other than the Pearson correlation coefficient can be used. Examples of such coefficients include phi coefficients for categorical variables and biserial coefficients for the similarity between categorical and continuous variables. Secondly, measures of distance and correlation can be combined. This last approach is most meaningful if measures are selected such that they are independent of each other, as are Pearson's r and the Euclidean distance.

It should be emphasized that the Euclidean distance is not invariant against scale differences in mean and variance. Suppose a researcher compares distances measured in both millimeters and miles. Then, the use of the Euclidean distance as given in (6.42) will lead to a heavy overemphasis of the millimeter scale simply because of its larger absolute values. Therefore, suitable scale transformations, such as standardization, are strongly recommended if scales are not commensurable.

Part IV:
Strategies of CFA and
computational issues

7

Exploratory and confirmatory search for types and antitypes

The following sections discuss exploratory and confirmatory strategies for CFA application. First exploratory then confirmatory approaches are introduced.

7.1 Exploratory and hybrid CFA

The exploratory search for types and antitypes has two main characteristics:

(1) The configurations for which one expects types or antitypes are not specified a priori. Rather, simultaneous CFA tests are applied to all cells. The obvious disadvantage of this strategy lies in the large number of tests performed. For large tables the adjustment of the critical level of alpha can lead to prohibitively small critical alphas and thus, result in the identification of only a very small number of types and antitypes.

(2) Because no explicit configuration predictions are set forth, emerging types and antitypes can be interpreted only tentatively. Interpretation of types and antitypes emerging from exploratory CFA typically relies on plausibility arguments rather than confirming theory generated hypotheses.

The second of these two characteristics can only be changed by introducing confirmatory characteristics in one's data analysis (cf. Abt 1987). The first characteristic led to three approaches to define more efficient test strategies. The first approach is to derive more powerful tests for the identification of types and antitypes (e.g., Lehmacher 1981; Lindner 1984), or to use more powerful tests based on residual analysis of log-linear models within a CFA framework (Lehmacher 1980b). The second approach involves the application of more efficient strategies of alpha-adjustment. Chapter 2 described the results of some of these attempts. The third approach is a hybrid of exploratory and confirmatory strategies (Lienert and Rey 1982; Lautsch, Lienert, and von Eye 1988).

Basically, the hybrid approach consists of two steps. First, CFA is applied heuristically, that is, without adjusting the alpha level to the number of tests, to a random half of the total sample. This application typically leads to the detection of candidate types and antitypes. Second, simultaneous tests are applied only to those candidate configurations in the second random half of the data or in another independent sample.

Lienert and Rey (1982) applied this method to increase the efficiency of CFA testing. However, the major disadvantage of this approach is that the final results may be severely biased by sample fluctuations. To correct for this bias, Lautsch et al. (1988) applied bootstrap methods to the first random half of a sample and selected for more rigorous testing those type and antitype patterns that were observed most often. This strategy both increases the efficiency of testing and reduces the bias due to fluctuations caused by the sample split. However, it cannot completely exclude such bias. The following example, taken from Lautsch et al. (1988), illustrates both the use of the hybrid CFA strategy and the risk of failing to cross-validate bootstrap results.

The example analyzes data from a sample of $n = 704$ preschoolers (Enke 1980) who displayed neurotic behaviors. The following variables were included in the analysis: behavior disorders (A, with levels $A1$ = no disorders, $A2$ = language disorders, $A3$ = both language and behavior disorders), mother's occupation (B, with levels $B1$ = unskilled worker, $B2$ = employee with little training, $B3$ = job requiring higher education), number of siblings (C, with levels $C1$ = less than 3 siblings and $C2$ = more than two siblings), and sex of child (D, with levels $D1$ = male and $D2$ = female). To do the bootstrap runs, the total sample was first split in two random halves.

Table 7.1 gives the frequencies for the entire sample and for the two random halves. The table is set up in a two-dimensional format to show that for the following analyses, behavior disorders will be considered the criterion variable, and all other variables predictors.

The first step of Lautsch et al.'s strategy consists of performing a bootstrap simulation on the first random half of the sample. These simulations consider the first random half the pool from which, for a given n, bootstrap samples are randomly drawn (with replacement). Each of the random samples has the same size. Each of the random samples is heuristically, without alpha adjustment, analyzed with CFA. The present example used prediction CFA (see Section 5.4). As a result of these bootstrap runs a pattern of types and antitypes is obtained for each random sample. The pattern that occurs most often usually is selected for more rigorous CFA testing in the second half of the total sample.

The present example uses the program SICFA (Lautsch and von Weber, in press). Altogether, 250 simulations were performed. The Pearson's X-square component test was applied. Table 7.2 lists the 20 patterns that occurred most frequently in the 250 runs. The left most column in the table contains the three levels of the criterion behavior disorders. The second column lists the 12 levels of the combined predictors. The following columns each represent one pattern of types and antitypes. A "1" indicates that the predictor-criterion configuration of the respective row was identified as a type, a "-1" indicates an antitype. The bottom of each column lists the frequency for each pattern.

Table 7.2 shows that the pattern with antitype 32 and the three types 33, 312, and 37 each occurred twelve times. The next most frequent pattern occurred seven times and shared with the first pattern the last two types. The three hypothetical types signify that language and behavior disorders ($A3$) can be predicted to occur more often than expected in male children ($C1$) with more than two siblings ($C2$) and with mothers working in unskilled jobs or with little training. For girls, language and behavior problems occur more often than expected by chance if the child has more than two siblings and

Table 7.1. Frequency distributions of behavior disorders of children for two random halfs and total sample.

V	BCD	A1			A2			A3		
		Total	Half	Half	Total	Half	Half	Total	Half	Half
1	111	72	39	33	32	19	13	23	14	9
2	112	90	43	47	22	14	8	8	2	6
3	121	13	7	6	8	2	6	7	5	2
4	122	20	11	9	6	3	3	9	3	6
5	211	95	56	39	41	22	19	24	15	9
6	212	89	56	39	25	14	11	9	4	5
7	221	8	6	2	6	2	4	7	5	2
8	222	11	5	6	7	2	5	1	0	1
9	311	24	15	9	14	4	10	4	2	2
10	312	17	9	8	4	1	3	0	0	0
11	321	2	1	1	1	0	1	0	0	0
12	322	3	1	2	0	0	0	2	2	0

Table 7.2. *Results of 250 bootstrap simulations using the first random half of the total sample from Table 7.1.*

A	V	Pattern[a]												
1	1	0	0	0	0	0	0	0	0	0	0	0	0	0
1	2	0	0	0	0	0	0	0	0	0	0	0	0	0
1	3	0	0	0	0	0	0	0	0	0	0	0	0	0
1	4	0	0	0	0	0	0	0	0	0	0	0	0	0
1	5	0	0	0	0	0	0	0	0	0	0	0	0	0
1	6	0	0	0	0	0	0	0	0	0	0	0	0	0
1	7	0	0	0	0	0	0	0	0	0	0	0	0	0
1	8	0	0	0	0	0	0	0	0	0	0	0	0	0
1	9	0	0	0	0	0	0	0	0	0	0	0	0	0
1	10	0	0	0	0	0	0	0	0	0	0	0	0	0
1	11	0	0	0	0	0	0	0	0	0	0	0	0	0
1	12	0	0	0	0	0	0	0	0	0	0	0	0	0
2	1	0	0	0	0	0	0	0	0	0	0	0	0	0
2	2	0	0	0	0	0	0	0	0	0	0	0	0	0
2	3	0	0	0	0	0	0	0	0	0	0	0	0	0
2	4	0	0	0	0	0	0	0	0	0	0	0	0	0
2	5	0	0	0	0	0	0	0	0	0	0	0	0	0
2	6	0	0	0	0	0	0	0	0	0	0	0	0	0
2	7	0	0	0	0	0	0	0	0	0	0	0	0	0
2	8	0	0	0	0	0	0	0	0	0	0	0	0	-1
2	9	0	0	0	0	0	0	0	0	0	0	0	0	0
2	10	0	0	0	0	0	0	0	0	0	0	0	0	0

Table 7.2 (cont.)

211

Table 7.2. (cont.)

A	V	Pattern[a]																		
2	11	0	0	0	0	0	0	0	0	0	0	0	0	0	0	0	0	0	0	0
2	12	0	0	0	0	0	0	0	0	0	0	0	0	0	0	0	0	0	0	0
3	1	0	1	0	0	1	0	0	0	0	0	0	0	0	0	0	0	-1	0	0
3	2	-1	-1	-1	0	-1	-1	-1	-1	-1	-1	-1	-1	0	-1	-1	0	-1	-1	0
3	3	1	1	0	0	1	1	1	0	1	1	1	1	0	1	-1	-1	0	0	0
3	4	0	0	0	0	0	0	0	0	0	1	0	0	0	0	0	0	0	0	0
3	5	0	0	0	0	0	0	1	0	0	0	0	0	0	0	0	0	0	0	0
3	6	0	0	0	0	-1	-1	0	0	-1	0	0	-1	-1	-1	0	-1	0	0	-1
3	7	1	0	0	1	1	1	1	1	1	1	1	1	1	1	0	1	0	0	-1
3	8	0	0	0	0	0	0	0	0	0	0	0	0	0	0	0	0	0	0	0
3	9	0	0	0	0	0	0	0	0	0	0	0	0	0	0	0	0	0	0	0
3	10	0	0	0	0	0	0	0	0	0	0	0	0	0	0	0	0	0	0	0
3	11	0	0	0	0	0	0	0	0	0	0	0	0	1	0	-1	0	0	0	0
3	12	1	0	1	1	1	0	1	1	1	0	1	1	1	1	1	1	0	0	1

Frequencies of type/antitype patterns

		12	4	1	47	4	2	2	1	1	1	2	11	1	21	1	4	4	2	1

[a] 1 = type in heuristic bootstrap simulation; −1 = antitype.

212

Table 7.3. *Expected frequencies e1, e2 and test statistic z for cross-validation in second half.*

Prediction type/ antitype A/BCD	f	$e1$	$e2$	s	z	Rank	Critical z
3/112	6	7.8	7.48	2.30	0.56	1	2.58
3/121	2	1.8	1.62	1.22	0.25	4	1.56
3/221	2	1.0	0.87	0.93	0.54	2	2.12
3/322	0	0.3	0.13	0.50	0.40	3	1.96

if their mothers work in positions that require higher education. The antitype suggests that language and behavior disorders occur less often than expected if the children have no more than two siblings and are daughters of mothers who are unskilled workers.

The second step of the hybrid test strategy applies CFA testing with alpha adjustment exclusively to the most frequently observed pattern of types and antitypes. The major advantage of this strategy is that alpha must be adjusted to take into account only the number of types and antitypes of this pattern. Benefits of this strategy include a large gain in efficiency. Costs of this strategy include the reduced sample size, which reduces the power of the statistical tests. However, if the total sample size is large, the benefits typically exceed the costs.

However, the present example shows that even bootstrap methods do not ensure unbiased results. Here we see that results from the first random half are biased and cannot be cross-validated in the second half. Table 7.3 shows that although the Holm-adjustment and the powerful Lehmacher test were applied to only four configurations, none of the types and antitypes was replicated.

7.2 Confirmatory CFA

In contrast to exploratory research, confirmatory research has the following characteristics (see Bock 1980): (1) questions are asked precisely; (2) the populations are well defined and the selection of subjects, measures, occasions etc. (Nesselroade 1983, in press) are ecologically valid; (3) the proper probability models are selected; (4) hypotheses are precisely stated; (5) alpha and beta are determined a priori; (6) the design for data collection is valid with respect to the hypotheses; (7) sampling does not contain major errors; and (8) statistical decisions are possible.

With respect to the application of CFA we discuss and exemplify chiefly the fourth of these characteristics. If a researcher states a confirmatory hypothesis in CFA he/she determines (1) the configurations expected to have frequencies significantly different from the expected ones, and (2) for each of these configurations, the direction of the expected discrepancy. As a result, confirmatory test procedures differ from exploratory ones in two major respects. First, the number of tests will be considerably smaller than in exploratory research, because researchers generally do not state a type/antitype hypothesis for each cell of a contingency table. Second, the tests will be one-sided rather than two-sided.

The following example shows that significance testing, in most instances, is much more efficient in confirmatory than in exploratory CFA. However, it will show also that lack of background knowledge can lead to prematurely stated hypotheses and thus, to wrong conclusions. The example uses the data from Table 2.2. The data are from a sample of $n = 65$ students who took LSD 50. They were observed for narrowed consciousness (B), thought disturbances (D), and affective disturbances (A). Each symptom was scaled as either present ($+$) or absent ($-$). Suppose a researcher is interested in whether Leuner's (1962) syndrome ($+ + +$) is present in the data. Under this assumption he/she can formulate the following one-sided hypothesis: $o(+ + +) > e(+ + +)$. The corresponding null hypothesis is $o(+ + +) = e(+ + +)$. The null hypothesis also assumes total independence among the three symptoms.

Because there is only one significance test, there is no need to protect alpha. Therefore, the a priori determined $\alpha = 0.05$ applies to this significance test. As one can see from Table 2.2,

$o(+ + +) = 20$ and $e(+ + +) = 12.506$. This difference is significant under all eight significance tests. Thus, we may conclude the confirmatory CFA test provided evidence in favor of the Leuner syndrome hypothesis.

However, as is obvious from Table 2.2, all observed frequencies in this data matrix deviate from their expectancies by about the same amount. Therefore, it is recommended that confirmatory application of CFA always go hand in hand with a second, exploratory run that prevents the researcher from overlooking important types or antitypes. In more general terms, the threat in exploratory research that sampling fluctuations dictate results has its pendant in confirmatory research. Hypotheses formulated prematurely or from deficient background knowledge can lead to the cementation of incomplete pictures of the existing relationships.

8

CFA and log-linear models

This section describes the relationship between log-linear modeling and CFA. Log-linear modeling is a widely used method for the analysis of contingency tables (cf. Haberman 1973; Bishop et al. 1975; Fienberg 1980; Agresti 1984). Log-linear modeling can be used, for instance, for the following tasks (cf. Goodman 1981):

(1) to analyze the joint distribution of variables;
(2) to investigate the dependence of dependent variables on independent variables; and
(3) to investigate the patterns of association between variables.

Typically, log-linear models parameterize cell frequencies, or, more precisely, the logarithms of cell frequencies, in terms of main effects and interactions. The status of variable categories as ordinal can be considered. Many applications of log-linear modeling attempt to set certain parameters equal to zero and check if the relationships present in the observed frequency distribution can be accounted for by a reduced set of main effects and interactions. Suppose a researcher investigates the four variables A, B, C, and D. Then, the saturated log-linear model, which considers all possible main effects and interactions, is

$$
\begin{aligned}
\log(y) = u_0 &+ u_A + u_B + u_C + u_D \\
&+ u_{AB} + u_{AC} + u_{AD} + u_{BC} + u_{BD} + u_{CD} \\
&+ u_{ABC} + u_{ABD} + u_{ACD} + u_{BCD} \\
&+ u_{ABCD}.
\end{aligned}
\tag{8.1}
$$

This model explains the observed frequency distribution perfectly; the expected frequencies are identical to the observed ones. However, the model exhausts all degrees of freedom and is, therefore, no more parsimonious than the observed frequencies themselves. More parsimonious models result from setting some of the u-terms in equation (8.1) to zero. For instance, as explained in Section 4.2 (see equation (4.16)), the model of total independence assumes the observed frequency distribution can be reproduced by considering only main effects, in this case, only the first five terms of (8.1).

For models including fewer terms than the saturated model, Pearson or likelihood-ratio chi-square tests are applied to test whether the discrepancies between the observed and the expected frequency distributions are significant. Pearson's chi-square statistic is

$$X^2 = \sum (o - e)^2/e \tag{8.2}$$

where the summation is over all cells of the cross-tabulation. The likelihood ratio chi-square test statistic is

$$G^2 = 2 \sum o \log(o/e). \tag{8.3}$$

Here, the summation is also over all cells in the table. However, because $\log(0)$ is not defined, cells for which $o = 0$ usually are omitted and the degrees of freedom are reduced by the number of omitted cells. Both X^2 and G^2 are good chi-square approximations.

Chi-square tests allow one to make decisions as to what pattern of associations among the variables best explains the observed frequency distribution. They are summary statistics that make global statements about the entire contingency table. However, for substantive reasons, one can be interested in those cells for which the observed frequencies greatly deviate from the expected ones. Two approaches have been developed for such situations. The first is residual analysis (Haberman 1973, 1974a). Haberman showed that for the square root of the components of (8.2), that is, the standardized residuals, the relation

$$(o - e)/e^{1/2} \cong N(0, \sigma) \tag{8.4}$$

holds, with $\sigma^2 < 1$, where σ^2 is the cellwise variance. In other words, the chi-square components are normally distributed. This relation holds for any model. Exact variances can be given.

The main purpose of residual analysis is to determine where and why a given model does not fit. Thus, the goal is still the identification of a model which provides good fit (Agresti 1984). The individual cell is not of interest per se, but rather as a source of information for improved model formulation.

If one is interested in specific cells in a cross-tabulation, a second approach is CFA. This method differs from residual analysis in three major respects. First, the researcher applies CFA not to make global statements about relationships among variables, but rather to make statements concerning single cells or patterns of cells that deviate from a local hypothesis concerning variable relationships. Thus, CFA is a method for differential research.

The second major difference between CFA and residual analysis concerns the selection of models. Whereas residual analysis can be meaningfully applied to any model more parsimonious than the saturated model, CFA refers to a subset of models. Examples include first order CFA, in which types and antitypes emerge only if, counter to the independence model, there are interactions among the variables. Another example is interaction structure analysis (ISA), in which types and antitypes emerge only if, counter to the model of independence between predictors and criteria, relationships between these two groups of variables do exist. In other words, CFA considers only a subset of models entertained by log-linear analysis.

The third respect in which CFA and log-linear models differ concerns the application of statistical tests. Log-linear modeling applies significance tests to retain global null hypotheses. The researcher searches for a model that is substantively meaningful and produces observed and expected frequencies not statistically different from each other. In contrast, CFA applies significance tests to reject local null hypotheses. Types and antitypes result from the conclusion that model assumptions do not locally hold.

To conclude, the relation of log-linear modeling, in particular model fitting and residual analysis, to CFA has three characteristics. First, log-linear modeling and CFA use the same procedures for the estimation of expected frequencies. Second, CFA is typically applied in differential research. Rather than stating results in terms of a cross-tabulation as a whole, CFA selects individual cells. Third, rather than fitting models, CFA attempts to reject local null hypotheses.

There are two ways in which CFA and log-linear models can complement each other. First, CFA may be used in an attempt to support log-linear modeling. Suppose a researcher has theoretical reasons for suspecting a particular model should explain the data. However, log-linear modeling fails to give the researcher an acceptable fit. CFA can then be used to identify cells with observed frequencies significantly deviating from the expected ones. These cells, configurations, can be interpreted in CFA fashion as those events which contradict a theory by occurring either more often or less often than expected. In addition, the results of CFA can be used in the process of continued model fitting. If the number of types and antitypes is not large, a result that would make a theory hard to defend, one can blank these cells out, declaring them structural zeros, and see if the model assumed to explain the whole table explains at least the remainder of it.

The following example uses the data from Table 5.25 which contains the frequencies of the eight combinations of three dichotomously scaled verbal tasks used to diagnose aphasia. The tasks are naming of objects (O), forming alliterations (A), and number of errors made in the first two tasks (E). CFA of directed relations had revealed the two antitypes (111) and (122) and one type (112). Suppose the researcher still assumes that the number of alliterations allows one to predict performance in the other two tasks, but that he/she allows local deviations from this assumption. Then, one can use CFA to guide the following steps in log-linear analysis. The researcher can, for instance, assume that configuration 122, an antitype, is a structural zero, and that the basic hypothesis regarding the predictability of O and E from A holds true when this one configuration is blanked out.

Table 8.1. *Analysis of three variables measuring aphasia under two log-linear models.*

OAE	o	e1	z = X	p(z)	e2	z = X
111	6	15.11	2.34	0.0096	7.64	−0.59
112	43	18.47	5.71	6×10^{-9}	42.97	0.01
121	30	20.89	1.99	0.0233	28.30	0.31
122	1	25.53	−4.85	6×10^{-7}	—	—
211	7	17.63	−2.53	0.0057	8.91	−0.64
212	12	16.79	−1.17	0.1210	8.49	1.21
221	35	24.37	2.15	0.0158	33.10	0.33
222	28	23.21	0.99	0.1611	31.53	−0.63

Results for log-linear models[a]
Model 1 $df = 3$ $X^2 = 91.69$ $p(X^2) = 8 \times 10^{-11}$
Model 2 $df = 2$ $X^2 = 2.72$ $p(X^2) = 0.2567$

[a]For explanation, see text.

Table 8.1 shows the result of this analysis. The expected frequencies in this table were calculated under the assumption that variable A is independent of variables O and E. Variables O and E, however, may interact. (Note that this is the model of prediction CFA (PCFA) which allows the criteria to interact. In contrast, DCFA allows only the predictors to have any effects.) Table 8.1 gives the expected frequencies for two models. The first is the model which considers all cells. The second blanks cell 122 out.

One of the results shown in Table 8.1 is that DCFA and PCFA suggest different conclusions. Both approaches identify configurations 112 as a type and 122 as an antitype. However, PCFA does not identify 111 as an antitype. Instead, it identifies configuration 211 as the second antitype. More importantly, the models fit under the two approaches differ. Model 1, which assumed independence between variable A and the group of variables O and E, provided a poor fit. The likelihood ratio X^2 was too large to allow one to keep the assumptions of PCFA. In dramatic contrast, note the results obtained after blanking out cell 122. The likelihood ratio X^2 is only 2.72, smaller than the critical value of 5.99 ($df = 2$).

The researcher can conclude from these results that the assumption of independence between A and the group of O and E holds throughout the table with one exception. Configuration 122 must be excluded from the model, and therefore, requires separate interpretation.

The second approach that demonstrates the complimentarity of log-linear modeling and CFA combines the goals of both by performing a CFA first and then using log-linear modeling to investigate the pattern of associations underlying the obtained types and antitypes. Examples of this approach were given throughout the book. A specific example is found in the analysis of Table 4.2 (see Section 4.2). This table contains the data from students taking examinations in three social sciences courses. CFA revealed three types and one antitype. After interpreting these configurations, a log-linear analysis was performed. The analysis showed that the joint frequency distribution of the grades in the three examinations can be explained by all pairwise associations.

From these results one can conclude that log-linear modeling and CFA complement each other. The analysis of type and antitype patterns as well as patterns of interactions among variables are complementary goals.

9
Computational issues

The present chapter introduces programs and shows how to apply some of the larger statistical software packages to obtain CFA results. Three levels of application will be covered: (1) pocket calculators; (2) microcomputers (PCs); and (3) main frame computers.

9.1 Programs for pocket calculators

Relatively small data problems can be handled using programmable pocket calculators. A program for first order CFA of dichotomous variables is available for calculators of the type HP 41 C, HP 41 CV, and HP 41 CX (von Eye 1982; the program is printed in this reference; mag-card versions are also available.) The program can be applied if the following periphery is available in addition to the calculator:

(1) Quad-memory (required for HP 41 C only);
(2) mag-card reader or digital cassette drive to read program;
(3) printer.

This program allows one to analyze up to seven variables. All variables must be dichotomous. The program calculates the marginals and the expected frequencies from the raw frequencies, gives both the Pearson chi-square components and Lehmacher's z, and calculates the tail probabilities for z using an algorithm from Abramowitz and Stegun (1970).

A second program for the same type pocket calculators computes second order CFA for three variables using the approximation given in Appendix B. Application of this program requires the same periphery as above. The program calculates marginals, expected frequencies, Pearson chi-square components, and the tail probabilities for the chi-square values using an approximation given in Abramowitz and Stegun (1970).

9.2 Programs for microcomputers

The following programs are introduced:

(1) BASIC programs for zero and first order CFA (von Eye 1987);
(2) FORTRAN77 program for first order CFA which estimates expected frequencies using an ordinary least squares solution (von Eye, 1988); and
(3) SYSTAT, TABLES module (SYSTAT 1986).

The BASIC programs for CFA are available in several versions and share the following characteristics. They can all handle up to ten variables with up to 100 categories each. Limitations within this range reflect limitations of the memory of the microcomputer. The programs are all written in interpreted Microsoft BASIC. They are all interactive but allow one to read raw frequencies from a file. Results are printed rather than written on file. The programs differ in the significance tests they provide. A copy of one program comes with this book. The program has been tested on a HP 110 and on a HP 110 plus under DOS 2.1 and runs on IBM and compatible PCs (16 bit processors). The program requires about 13 K bytes resident memory without the data; it has been used for most of the examples of this book but has also been successfully used on larger data sets, for instance on one data set including over 55,000 cases (Chipuer and von Eye 1989).

A sample print-out of the version of the program that uses the standard normal z as an approximation of the binomial test appears in Table 9.1. The print-out shows the analysis of the data from Table 1.4.

Table 9.1. *BASIC-Program CFA.*

Program Author: Alexander von Eye, 1985
Limitations: min 2. max 10 variables
and 100 categories per variable

Number of variables = 3
Sample size n = 362
Alpha* = 0.00625 (two-sided)

Marginal sums of variable 1
161   201

Marginal sums of variable 2
159   203

Marginal sums of variable 3
193   169

Table of results

Configuration			fo	fe	z	p(fo)
1	1	1	38	37.70189	5.129475E-02	.9590902824966968
1	1	2	52	33.01358	3.466268	5.2782993088l987D-04
1	2	1	23	48.13513	−3.890747	9.9975495395963262D-05
1	2	2	48	42.14941	.9587048	.3377074734711635
2	1	1	39	47.06883	−1.260927	.2073351328078506
2	1	2	30	41.21571	−1.85585	6.3474757157010l24D-02
2	2	1	93	60.09416	4.6481	3.3537412857802720D-06
2	2	2	39	52.62131	−2.031174	4.2237193208063620D-02

Table 9.2. *Least squares configural frequency analysis.*

Author of program: Alexander von Eye (1986)

Table of results

Configuration	fo	fe	z = sqrt(chi2)	p(z)
111	38.	37.750000	.042993	.96570711
112	52.	31.750000	3.762583	.00016822
121	23.	48.750000	3.964594	.00007355
122	48.	42.750000	.855027	.39253581
211	39.	47.750000	1.359058	.17412831
212	30.	41.750000	1.933389	.05318810
221	93.	58.750000	4.882143	.00000105
222	39.	52.750000	2.048287	.04053171

n = 362
alpha*(0.05) = .0062500   alpha*(0.01) = .0012500

The FORTRAN77 program for CFA can handle contingency tables with up to 600 cells. The number of categories per variable must be less than seven, and the number of variables must be less than ten. The program was compiled using the Microsoft FORTRAN77 compiler on a HP 110 plus. Data input is interactive. The program writes results to a disk file. The program runs on IBM and compatible microcomputers (16 bit processors) and requires about 85 K bytes resident memory, including the data matrices. A sample print-out is provided in Table 9.2. Here, the program analyzed the data from Tables 1.4 and 9.1.

SYSTAT is a multipurpose statistical software package available for micro, mini, and main frame computers. The following examples use SYSTAT 3.0 (1986). The package contains modules for virtually all standard applications of statistics in the social sciences. CFA can be simulated using the TABLES module, which generates cross-tabulations and estimates log-linear models to test assumptions regarding the joint frequency distribution of two or more variables. The

Table 9.3.

		U1	U2	U3	F
CASE	1	1.000	1.000	1.000	38.000
CASE	2	1.000	1.000	2.000	52.000
CASE	3	1.000	2.000	1.000	23.000
CASE	4	1.000	2.000	2.000	40.000
CASE	5	2.000	1.000	1.000	39.000
CASE	6	2.000	1.000	2.000	30.000
CASE	7	2.000	2.000	1.000	93.000
CASE	8	2.000	2.000	2.000	39.000

SYSTAT PROCESSING FINISHED
INPUT STATEMENTS FOR THIS JOB:

```
OU@
USE TAB14
LIST
RUN
```

module performs all computations in double precision. The data are stored in RAM memory. Therefore, there is an upper limit on the number of cells that can be handled. The manual says around 500 cells is the maximum number for a 64 K computer. On a larger computer, around 2,500 cells are possible with the earlier version SYSTAT 2.1. A large version of SYSTAT 3.0 has limits only because some DOS versions do not allow one to break the 640 K barrier. On a 640 K computer this version is able to process about 5,000 cells.

To simulate a CFA one either uses raw data written on a system file and forms a cross-tabulation with the TABLES module, or generates a system file that contains the matrix and the frequencies with the DATA module. System files can be read directly by the TABLES module. The present example used the data from Table 1.4, again, and transformed them into a system file. Table 9.3 gives a sample print out of this file. At the bottom of the table there is a list of the statements used to print the file.

The TABLES module can be used to estimate expected frequencies for CFA and to calculate standardized residuals, that is, the square root of Pearson chi-square components for the cellwise tests. The program gives for the expected frequencies (the program calls them fitted values) and the residuals, only two decimal places. Even with the FORMAT statement, the user cannot specify the desired number of decimal places. Thus, CFA tests cannot be estimated as precisely as necessary. Table 9.4 gives a sample print out. A main effect log-linear model corresponding to first order CFA, was estimated for the data from Table 1.4. The upper panel of the table contains the cell frequencies, the middle panel the expected frequencies, and the lower panel the residuals. At the bottom there is a list of the statements needed to perform the calculations.

The TABLES module in SYSTAT contains the most flexible of programs discussed in this section. It handles any standard hierarchical log-linear model, and allows one to consider structural zeros. The FORTRAN77 program computes only first order CFA, and the BASIC programs compute only zero and first order CFAs. However, SYSTAT allows only approximations of the CFA tests and provides only one test statistic. Other microcomputer programs for log-linear models include Rindskopf's (1987) BASIC and PASCAL programs. Mini and main frame versions of SYSTAT are also available.

9.3 Programs for main frame computers

There are several statistical software packages available that allow one to simulate or directly perform CFA, mostly first order CFA. Examples include Bergman and El-Khouri's (1987) FORTRAN77 program for the exact analysis of single cells in two-dimensional cross-tabulations and Roeder's (1977) (cf. Roeder 1974, 1976) FORTRAN program for first order CFA of tables with up to 1,024 cells. The present section focuses on the application of major statistical software packages for CFA. In particular, this section presents sample

Table 9.4.

TABLE OF   V2   (ROWS) BY   V3   (COLUMNS)
    FOR THE FOLLOWING VALUES:
           V1   =   1

FREQUENCIES

	1	2	TOTAL
1	38	52	90
2	23	40	63
TOTAL	61	92	153

TABLE OF   V2   (ROWS) BY   V3   (COLUMNS)
    FOR THE FOLLOWING VALUES:
           V1   =   2

FREQUENCIES

	1	2	TOTAL
1	39	30	69
2	93	39	132
TOTAL	132	69	201

MODEL WAS FIT AFTER 2 ITERATIONS.
TABLE OF   V2   (ROWS) BY   V3   (COLUMNS)
    FOR THE FOLLOWING VALUES:
           V1   =   1

FITTED VALUES

	1	2
1	37.47	31.25
2	45.95	38.33

228

Table 9.4 (*cont.*)

TABLE OF   V2   (ROWS) BY   V3   (COLUMNS)
FOR THE FOLLOWING VALUES:
                V1   =   2

FITTED VALUES

	1	2
1	49.22	41.06
2	60.36	50.36

TABLE OF   V2   (ROWS) BY   V3   (COLUMNS)
FOR THE FOLLOWING VALUES:
                V1   =   1

STANDARDIZED RESIDUALS: (OBSERVED-FITTED)/SQRT(FITTED)

	1	2
1	.09	3.71
2	−3.39	.27

TABLE OF   V2   (ROWS) BY   V3   (COLUMNS)
FOR THE FOLLOWING VALUES:
                V1   =   2

STANDARDIZED RESIDUALS: (OBSERVED-FITTED)/SQRT(FITTED)

	1	2
1	−1.46	−1.73
2	4.20	−1.60

229

Table 9.4 (*cont.*)

TEST OF FIT OF MODEL

DEGREES OF FREEDOM = 4
PEARSON CHI-SQUARE =   50.62   PROBABILITY = .000
LIKELIHOOD RATIO CHI-SQUARE =   49.07   PROBABILITY = .000

SYSTAT PROCESSING FINISHED

INPUT STATEMENTS FOR THIS JOB:


```
OU@
USE TAB14
WEIGHT=F
TABULATE V1*V2*V3
MODEL V1+V2+V3/FITTED,RESIDUALS
```

results from the SPSSX (Nie, Hull, Jenkins, Steinbrenner, and
Bent 1975) and the BMDP (Dixon 1983). Both are multipurpose program packages that allow a wide variety of statistical
analyses and are implemented on most university main frame
computers.

The BMDP package includes the module 4F, which allows
one to form cross-tabulations and to estimate hierarchical log-
linear models. To simulate a first order CFA one computes a
main effects model. Print outs include, for instance, expected
frequencies, the standardized residuals, or chi-square components. The program prints the observed and the requested
calculated values in tabular form. The calculated values are
given with only one decimal place and provide, therefore, only
crude approximations for CFA tests. Table 9.5 gives a sample
print out from a BMDP 4F run that used the same data as in
Table 9.4. The upper panel of the table contains the com-
mands, and the lower panel contains observed frequencies,
expected values, standardized deviates, differences between
observed and expected frequencies, and chi-square components. The information on the goodness of fit is omitted.
Program version 1987 for IBM/OS was used.

Table 9.5. *Sample print-out of a BMDP 4F run.*

Program instructions

```
/ PROBLEM   TITLE IS 'MAIN EFFECT MODEL WITH EXPECTED AND STAND'.
/ INPUT     VARIABLES ARE 4.
           FORMAT IS '(3(1F1. 0, 1X), 1F2. 0)'.
/ VARIABLE  NAMES ARE A, B, C, FREQ.
/ TABLE     INDICES ARE A, B, C.
           COUNT IS FREQ.
/ FIT       MODEL IS A, B, C.
/ PRINT     EXPECTED. STANDARDIZED. DIFFERENCE. CHISQUARE.
/ END
```

PAGE   5   BMDP4F MAIN EFFECT MODEL WITH EXPECTED AND STAND

```
********************************
 *  TABLE PARAGRAPH  1  *
********************************
```

***** OBSERVED FREQUENCY TABLE 1

```
VARIABLE    4    FREQ    USED AS COUNT VARIABLE.
                     *********
```

231

Table 9.5 (*cont*).

C	B	A 1	2	TOTAL
1	1	38	39	77
	2	23	93	116
	TOTAL	61	132	193
2	1	52	30	82
	2	40	39	79
	TOTAL	92	69	161

TOTAL OF THE OBSERVED FREQUENCY TABLE IS   354
ALL CASES HAD COMPLETE DATA FOR THIS TABLE.

PAGE   6   BMDP4F MAIN EFFECT MODEL WITH EXPECTED AND STAND

232

```
****************
*  MODEL  1  *
****************

MODEL
-----
A, B, C.

*****  EXPECTED VALUES USING ABOVE MODEL
```

C	B	A		TOTAL
		1	2	
1	1	37.5	49.2	86.7
	2	45.9	60.4	106.3
	TOTAL	83.4	109.6	193.0
2	1	31.3	41.1	72.3
	2	38.3	50.4	88.7
	TOTAL	69.6	91.4	161.0

233

Table 9.5 (*cont.*)

***** STANDARDIZED DEVIATES = (OBS − EXP)/SQRT(EXP) FOR ABOVE MODEL

C	B	A	
		1	2
1	1	0.1	−1.5
	2	−3.4	4.2
2	1	3.7	−1.7
	2	0.3	−1.6

**** DIFFERENCES BETWEEN OBSERVED AND EXPECTED USING ABOVE MODEL

C	B	A	
		1	2
1	1	0.5	−10.2
	2	−22.9	32.6

2	1		20.7	−11.1
	2		1.7	−11.4

***** COMPONENTS OF CHI-SQUARE = (OBS − EXP)**2/EXPECTED FOR MODEL ABOVE

C	B	A	
		1	2
1	1	0.0	2.1
	2	11.5	17.6
2	1	13.8	3.0
	2	0.1	2.6

235

The SPSSX package includes several modules for log-linear analyses. The following example uses the LOGLINEAR module which allows one to calculate a wide variety of log-linear models. The program calculates nonhierarchical log-linear models. As a consequence, higher order interactions do not include lower order terms. Rather, the user must explicitly include them. The following example uses the same data as in Tables 1.4 and 9.5. Table 9.6 gives a sample print out. It includes the listing of program instructions, and a table with the observed and the expected frequencies, residuals, and standardized residuals in tabular form. The program prints results with two decimal places. Note that the terminology used by SPSSX differs from that used by the BMDP. What the BMDP calls "differences between observed and expected" is called "residual" by the SPSSX. The adjusted residuals and information on the goodness of fit of the log-linear model, provided by the SPSSX, are omitted in Table 9.6.

Table 9.6. *Sample print-out of a SPSSX run.*

Program instructions

1	0	FILE HANDLE FIRST / NAMES = 'ALEX LOG A'
2	0	TITLE 'LOGLINEAR MAIN EFFECTS IN SPSSX'
3	0	DATA LIST FILE = FIRST FREE
4	0	/ A
5	0	B
6	0	C
7	0	FREQ
8	0	
9	0	WEIGHT BY FREQ
10	0	
11	0	LOGLINEAR A(1, 2) B(1, 2) C(1, 2)/
12	0	DESIGN A, B, C/

237

238

Table 9.6 (cont.)

CONVERGED AT ITERATION 4.   THE CONVERGE CRITERION =   .00011

OBSERVED, EXPECTED FREQUENCIES AND RESIDUALS

FACTOR	CODE	OBS. COUNT & PCT.	EXP. COUNT & PCT.	RESIDUAL	STD. RESID.
1					
1					
	1	38.00 (10.73)	37.47 (10.58)	.5338	.0872
	2	52.00 (14.69)	31.25 (8.83)	20.7458	3.7109
2					
	1	23.00 (6.50)	45.95 (12.98)	−22.9491	−3.3855
	2	40.00 (11.30)	38.33 (10.83)	1.6694	.2696
2					
1					
	1	39.00 (11.02)	49.22 (13.90)	−10.2203	−1.4568
	2	30.00 (8.47)	41.06 (11.60)	−11.0594	−1.7259
2					
	1	93.00 (26.27)	60.36 (17.05)	32.6355	4.2005
	2	39.00 (11.02)	50.36 (14.22)	−11.3559	−1.6003

Appendix A

Computational issues: the estimation of tail probabilities for the standard normal and the F distributions

The estimation of tail probabilities for the z statistic

In virtually all statistical textbooks tables are given that contain alpha levels for given values of z. Usually, values of z are tabulated ranging from $z = 0.0$ to $z = 3.09$. These z values correspond to one-tailed probabilities ranging from $p = 0.5$ to $p = 0.000048$. In CFA testing, however, decisions often involve more extreme alpha levels. (The reasons why extreme alpha levels occur in CFA are explained in Section 2.5.) Therefore, this Appendix gives an approximation of the standard normal and the F distributions that allow the researcher to estimate the tail probability for any value of z or F (see Abramowitz and Stegun 1970).

The one-sided tail probability of the standard normal distribution is given by

$$Q(z) = 1/(2\pi)^{1/2} \int_{x}^{r} e^{-1/2t^2} \, dt \qquad (A.1)$$

(t is explained below). To approximate this function, a fifth order polynomial

$$R = b_1 t + b_2 t^2 + b_3 t^3 + b_4 t^4 + b_5 t^5 + e(z) \qquad (A.2)$$

is used. The maximal difference between a value of this

239

polynomial and the exact $Q(z)$ is

$$e(z) < 7.5 \times 10^{-8}.$$

The variable t in (2.35) and (2.36) can be determined by

$$t = 1/(1 + r \times |z|) \tag{A.3}$$

with $r = 0.2316419$. The polynomial coefficients are

$b_1 = 0.31938153$, $b_2 = -0.356563782$, $b_3 = 1.781477937$,

$b_4 = -1.821255978$,   and $b_5 = 1.330274429$.

Using (A.2) and (A.3) one obtains as an estimator for the one-sided tail probability R, for which

$$Q(z) = \begin{cases} R & \text{if } z \geqslant 0, \\ 1 - R & \text{if } z < 0. \end{cases}$$

Whenever tail probabilities of the standard normal or the chi-square distributions are estimated in this text, equations (A.2) and (A.3) are used. Two-sided tail probabilities will result from multiplying R by 2.

The estimation of tail probabilities for the F statistic

As was mentioned in Section 2.1, the F distribution is tabulated for the most common alpha levels only. For more extreme alpha levels that may be the basis for decisions in CFA, values assumed by the function described in (2.26) may be determined using the following series

$$P(F) = t^{1/2 df 2} \left[1 + 1/2 df\, 2(1 - t) + \cdots \right.$$

$$\left. + \frac{df\, 2(df\, 2 + 2) \cdots (df\, 2 + df\, 1 - 4)}{2 \times 4 \times \cdots \times (df\, 1 - 2)} (1 - t)^{1/2(df\, 1 - 2)} \right]$$

$$\tag{A.4}$$

with $t = df\, 2/(df\, 2 + (df\, 1 \times F))$.

Equation (A.4) requires more computation than (2.36), in particular when there are many degrees of freedom. However, for unconventional alpha levels, tables are virtually unavailable. (It should be noted that (A.4) is applicable only if $df\,1$ is an even number. This constraint, however, does not affect the applicability of this equation in CFA, because both $df\,1$ and $df\,2$ are always even when the F test is applied in CFA.)

Appendix B

Estimation of expected frequencies in 2 × 2 × 2 tables under the assumption that main effects and first order interactions exist

(1) The following coefficients are defined for a cubic equation:

$C_3 = n.$

$C_2 = n_{100}n_{010} + n_{100}n_{001} + n_{010}n_{001}$
$\quad - n_{100}n_{011} - n_{010}n_{101} - n_{001}n_{110}$
$\quad - n(n_{110} + n_{101} + n_{011}).$

$C_1 = n(n_{110}n_{101} + n_{110}n_{011} + n_{101}n_{011}) + n_{100}n_{010}n_{001}$
$\quad - n_{100}n_{010}(n_{011} + n_{101}) - n_{100}n_{001}(n_{011} + n_{110})$
$\quad - n_{010}n_{001}(n_{101} + n_{110}) + n_{100}n_{011}^2 + n_{010}n_{101}^2$
$\quad + n_{001}n_{110}^2 + 2n_{110}n_{101}n_{011}.$

$C_0 = n_{110}n_{101}n_{011}(n_{001} + n_{010} + n_{100} - n_{110} - n_{101} - n_{011}n).$

(2) The normal form of the cubic equation is determined. One obtains

$$m^3 + rm^2 + sm + t = 0,$$

where

$$r = C_2/n, \quad s = C_1/n, \quad t = C_0/n.$$

(3) The reduced form of the cubic equation is determined by eliminating the quadratic term

$$y^3 + py + q = 0$$

242

where

$$y=m+(r/3), \quad p=s-(r^2/3), \quad q=(2r^3/27)-(sr/3)+t.$$

(4) To simplify the notation one sets

$$A = -0.5q, \quad B^3 = p^3/27, \quad C = A^2 + B^3$$

$$U = A + \sqrt{C}, \quad V = A - \sqrt{C}.$$

(5) Under the condition that $C > 0$, which is met here, the cubic equation has three solutions. The first solution is real, the other two complex. The real solution is

$$y = U^{1/3} + V^{1/3}.$$

(6) The second order CFA expected frequency for cell 111 is determined by

$$m = y - r/3.$$

The remaining expected frequencies are determined by subtracting from the marginals.

The cubic equation has three real solutions if $C = 0$. From these one selects the one for which $e < m < o$, where e denotes expected frequencies under first order CFA and o observed frequencies.

Appendix C

Critical alpha levels under Holm adjustment for up to 330 cells and a priori alphas 0.05 and 0.01

No. of tests	A priori α 0.05	A priori α 0.01	No. of tests	A priori α 0.05	A priori α 0.01
330	0.00015152	0.00003030	308	0.00016234	0.00003247
329	0.00015198	0.00003040	307	0.00016287	0.00003257
328	0.00015244	0.00003049	306	0.00016340	0.00003268
327	0.00015291	0.00003058	305	0.00016393	0.00003279
326	0.00015337	0.00003067	304	0.00016447	0.00003289
325	0.00015385	0.00003077	303	0.00016502	0.00003300
324	0.00015432	0.00003086	302	0.00016556	0.00003311
323	0.00015480	0.00003096	301	0.00016611	0.00003322
322	0.00015528	0.00003106	300	0.00016667	0.00003333
321	0.00015576	0.00003115	299	0.00016722	0.00003344
320	0.00015625	0.00003125	298	0.00016779	0.00003356
319	0.00015674	0.00003135	297	0.00016835	0.00003367
318	0.00015723	0.00003145	296	0.00016892	0.00003378
317	0.00015773	0.00003155	295	0.00016949	0.00003390
316	0.00015823	0.00003165	294	0.00017007	0.00003401
315	0.00015873	0.00003175	293	0.00017065	0.00003413
314	0.00015924	0.00003185	292	0.00017123	0.00003425
313	0.00015974	0.00003195	291	0.00017182	0.00003436
312	0.00016026	0.00003205	290	0.00017241	0.00003448
311	0.00016077	0.00003215	289	0.00017301	0.00003460
310	0.00016129	0.00003226	288	0.00017361	0.00003472
309	0.00016181	0.00003236	287	0.00017422	0.00003484

244

No. of tests	A priori α		No. of tests	A priori α	
	0.05	0.01		0.05	0.01
286	0.00017483	0.00003497	245	0.00020408	0.00004082
285	0.00017544	0.00003509	244	0.00020492	0.00004098
284	0.00017606	0.00003521	243	0.00020576	0.00004115
283	0.00017668	0.00003534	242	0.00020661	0.00004132
282	0.00017730	0.00003546	241	0.00020747	0.00004149
281	0.00017794	0.00003559	240	0.00020833	0.00004167
280	0.00017857	0.00003571	239	0.00020921	0.00004184
279	0.00017921	0.00003584	238	0.00021008	0.00004202
278	0.00017986	0.00003597	237	0.00021097	0.00004219
277	0.00018051	0.00003610	236	0.00021186	0.00004237
276	0.00018116	0.00003623	235	0.00021277	0.00004255
275	0.00018182	0.00003636	234	0.00021368	0.00004274
274	0.00018248	0.00003650	233	0.00021459	0.00004292
273	0.00018315	0.00003663	232	0.00021552	0.00004310
272	0.00018382	0.00003676	231	0.00021645	0.00004329
271	0.00018450	0.00003690	230	0.00021739	0.00004348
270	0.00018519	0.00003704	229	0.00021834	0.00004367
269	0.00018587	0.00003717	228	0.00021930	0.00004386
268	0.00018657	0.00003731	227	0.00022026	0.00004405
267	0.00018727	0.00003745	226	0.00022124	0.00004425
266	0.00018797	0.00003759	225	0.00022222	0.00004444
265	0.00018868	0.00003774	224	0.00022321	0.00004464
264	0.00018939	0.00003788	223	0.00022422	0.00004484
263	0.00019011	0.00003802	222	0.00022523	0.00004505
262	0.00019084	0.00003817	221	0.00022624	0.00004525
261	0.00019157	0.00003831	220	0.00022727	0.00004545
260	0.00019231	0.00003846	219	0.00022831	0.00004566
259	0.00019305	0.00003861	218	0.00022936	0.00004587
258	0.00019380	0.00003876	217	0.00023041	0.00004608
257	0.00019455	0.00003891	216	0.00023148	0.00004630
256	0.00019531	0.00003906	215	0.00023256	0.00004651
255	0.00019608	0.00003922	214	0.00023364	0.00004673
254	0.00019685	0.00003937	213	0.00023474	0.00004695
253	0.00019763	0.00003953	212	0.00023585	0.00004717
252	0.00019841	0.00003968	211	0.00023697	0.00004739
251	0.00019920	0.00003984	210	0.00023810	0.00004762
250	0.00020000	0.00004000	209	0.00023923	0.00004785
249	0.00020080	0.00004016	208	0.00024038	0.00004808
248	0.00020161	0.00004032	207	0.00024155	0.00004831
247	0.00020243	0.00004049	206	0.00024272	0.00004854
246	0.00020325	0.00004065	205	0.00024390	0.00004878

No. of tests	A priori α		No. of tests	A priori α	
	0.05	0.01		0.05	0.01
204	0.00024510	0.00004902	163	0.00030675	0.00006135
203	0.00024631	0.00004926	162	0.00030864	0.00006173
202	0.00024752	0.00004950	161	0.00031056	0.00006211
201	0.00024876	0.00004975	160	0.00031250	0.00006250
200	0.00025000	0.00005000	159	0.00031447	0.00006289
199	0.00025126	0.00005025	158	0.00031646	0.00006329
198	0.00025253	0.00005051	157	0.00031847	0.00006369
197	0.00025381	0.00005076	156	0.00032051	0.00006410
196	0.00025510	0.00005102	155	0.00032258	0.00006452
195	0.00025641	0.00005128	154	0.00032468	0.00006494
194	0.00025773	0.00005155	153	0.00032680	0.00006536
193	0.00025907	0.00005181	152	0.00032895	0.00006579
192	0.00026042	0.00005200	151	0.00033113	0.00006623
191	0.00026178	0.00005236	150	0.00033333	0.00006667
190	0.00026316	0.00005263	149	0.00033557	0.00006711
189	0.00026455	0.00005291	148	0.00033784	0.00006757
188	0.00026596	0.00005319	147	0.00034014	0.00006803
187	0.00026738	0.00005348	146	0.00034247	0.00006849
186	0.00026882	0.00005376	145	0.00034483	0.00006897
185	0.00027027	0.00005405	144	0.00034722	0.00006944
184	0.00027174	0.00005435	143	0.00034965	0.00006993
183	0.00027322	0.00005464	142	0.00035211	0.00007042
182	0.00027473	0.00005495	141	0.00035461	0.00007092
181	0.00027624	0.00005525	140	0.00035714	0.00007143
180	0.00027778	0.00005556	139	0.00035971	0.00007194
179	0.00027933	0.00005587	138	0.00036232	0.00007246
178	0.00028090	0.00005618	137	0.00036496	0.00007299
177	0.00028249	0.00005650	136	0.00036765	0.00007353
176	0.00028409	0.00005682	135	0.00037037	0.00007407
175	0.00028571	0.00005714	134	0.00037313	0.00007463
174	0.00028736	0.00005747	133	0.00037594	0.00007519
173	0.00028902	0.00005780	132	0.00037879	0.00007576
172	0.00029070	0.00005814	131	0.00038168	0.00007634
171	0.00029240	0.00005848	130	0.00038462	0.00007692
170	0.00029412	0.00005882	129	0.00038760	0.00007752
169	0.00029586	0.00005917	128	0.00039063	0.00007813
168	0.00029762	0.00005952	127	0.00039370	0.00007874
167	0.00029940	0.00005988	126	0.00039683	0.00007937
166	0.00030120	0.00006024	125	0.00040000	0.00008000
165	0.00030303	0.00006061	124	0.00040323	0.00008065
164	0.00030488	0.00006098	123	0.00040650	0.00008130

No. of tests	A priori α 0.05	0.01	No. of tests	A priori α 0.05	0.01
122	0.00040984	0.00008197	81	0.00061728	0.00012346
121	0.00041322	0.00008264	80	0.00062500	0.00012500
120	0.00041667	0.00008333	79	0.00063291	0.00012658
119	0.00042017	0.00008403	78	0.00064103	0.00012821
118	0.00042373	0.00008475	77	0.00064935	0.00012987
117	0.00042735	0.00008547	76	0.00065789	0.00013158
116	0.00043103	0.00008621	75	0.00066667	0.00013333
115	0.00043478	0.00008696	74	0.00067568	0.00013514
114	0.00043860	0.00008772	73	0.00068493	0.00013699
113	0.00044248	0.00008850	72	0.00069444	0.00013889
112	0.00044643	0.00008929	71	0.00070423	0.00014085
111	0.00045045	0.00009009	70	0.00071429	0.00014286
110	0.00045455	0.00009091	69	0.00072464	0.00014493
109	0.00045872	0.00009174	68	0.00073529	0.00014706
108	0.00046296	0.00009259	67	0.00074627	0.00014925
107	0.00046729	0.00009346	66	0.00075758	0.00015152
106	0.00047170	0.00009434	65	0.00076923	0.00015385
105	0.00047619	0.00009524	64	0.00078125	0.00015625
104	0.00048077	0.00009615	63	0.00079365	0.00015873
103	0.00048544	0.00009709	62	0.00080645	0.00016129
102	0.00049020	0.00009804	61	0.00081967	0.00016393
101	0.00049505	0.00009901	60	0.00083333	0.00016667
100	0.00050000	0.00010000	59	0.00084746	0.00016949
99	0.00050505	0.00010101	58	0.00086207	0.00017241
98	0.00051020	0.00010204	57	0.00087719	0.00017544
97	0.00051546	0.00010309	56	0.00089286	0.00017857
96	0.00052083	0.00010417	55	0.00090909	0.00018182
95	0.00052632	0.00010526	54	0.00092593	0.00018519
94	0.00053191	0.00010638	53	0.00094340	0.00018868
93	0.00053763	0.00010753	52	0.00096154	0.00019231
92	0.00054348	0.00010870	51	0.00098039	0.00019608
91	0.00054945	0.00010989	50	0.00100000	0.00020000
90	0.00055556	0.00011111	49	0.00102041	0.00020408
89	0.00056180	0.00011236	48	0.00104167	0.00020833
88	0.00056818	0.00011364	47	0.00106383	0.00021277
87	0.00057471	0.00011494	46	0.00108696	0.00021739
86	0.00058140	0.00011628	45	0.00111111	0.00022222
85	0.00058824	0.00011765	44	0.00113636	0.00022727
84	0.00059524	0.00011905	43	0.00116279	0.00023256
83	0.00060241	0.00012048	42	0.00119048	0.00023810
82	0.00060976	0.00012195	41	0.00121951	0.00024390

No. of tests	A priori α		No. of tests	A priori α	
	0.05	0.01		0.05	0.01
40	0.00125000	0.00025000	20	0.00250000	0.00050000
39	0.00128205	0.00025641	19	0.00263158	0.00052632
38	0.00131579	0.00026316	18	0.00277778	0.00055556
37	0.00135135	0.00027027	17	0.00294118	0.00058824
36	0.00138889	0.00027778	16	0.00312500	0.00062500
35	0.00142857	0.00028571	15	0.00333333	0.00066667
34	0.00147059	0.00029412	14	0.00357143	0.00071429
33	0.00151515	0.00030303	13	0.00384615	0.00076923
32	0.00156250	0.00031250	12	0.00416667	0.00083333
31	0.00161290	0.00032258	11	0.00454545	0.00090909
30	0.00166667	0.00033333	10	0.00500000	0.00100000
29	0.00172414	0.00034483	9	0.00555556	0.00111111
28	0.00178571	0.00035714	8	0.00625000	0.00125000
27	0.00185185	0.00037037	7	0.00714286	0.00142857
26	0.00192308	0.00038462	6	0.00833333	0.00166667
25	0.00200000	0.00040000	5	0.01000000	0.00200000
24	0.00208333	0.00041667	4	0.01250000	0.00250000
23	0.00217391	0.00043478	3	0.01666667	0.00333333
22	0.00227273	0.00045455	2	0.02500000	0.00500000
21	0.00238095	0.00047619	1	0.05000000	0.01000000

References

Abramowitz, M. and Stegun, I. A. (1970) *Handbook of Mathematical Functions*. Washington, DC: National Bureau of Standards.

Abt, K. (1987) Descriptive data analysis: a concept between confirmatory and exploratory data analysis. *Methods Inform. Med.* **26**, 77–88.

Agresti, A. (1984) *Analysis of Ordinal Categorical Variables*. New York: John Wiley.

Anderson, T. W. (1971) *The Statistical Analysis of Time Series*. New York: John Wiley.

Arminger, G. (1983) Multivariate Analyse von qualitativen abhängigen Variablen mit verallgemeinerten linearen Modellen. *Z. Soziol.* **12**, 49–64.

Bartoszyk, G. D. and Lienert, G. A. (1978) Konfigurationsanalytische Typisierung von Verlaufskurven. *Z. Exp. Angew. Psychol.* **XXV**, 1–9.

Bauer, P. and Hackl, P. (1985) The application of Hunter's inequality in simultaneous testing. *Biom. J.* **1**, 25–38.

Benton, A. L. (1974) *Der Benton-Test*. Bern: Huber.

Berchtold, H. (1972) Vertrauensgrenzen und Vergleich zweier Wahrscheinlichkeiten. *Z. Wahrscheinlichkeitstheor. Verw. geb.* **22**, 112–19.

Bergman, L. R. and El-Khouri, B. (1986) Some exact test of single cell frequencies in two-way contingency tables. In: D. Magnusson, T. Kunnapa, S. Dornic and B. Ekehammar (Eds.), *Reports from the Department of Psychology, University of Stockholm*, No. 645.

Bergman, L. R. and El-Khouri, B. (1987) Exacon: A FORTRAN77 program for the exact analysis of single cells in a contingency table. *Educ. Psychol. Meas.* **47**, 155–61.

Bergman, L. R. and Magnusson, D. (In press) A person approach to the study of the development of adjustment problems: an empirical example and some research strategical considerations. In: D. Magnusson and A. Ohman (Eds.), *Psychopathology: An Interactional Perspective*. New York: Academic Press.

249

Bergman, L. R. and von Eye, A. (1987) Normal approximations of exact tests in Configural Frequency Analysis. *Biom. J.* **29**, 849–55.

Bierschenk, B. and Lienert, G. A. (1977) Simple methods for clustering profiles and learning curves. *Didaktometry* **56**, 1–26.

Bishop, Y. M. M., Fienberg, S. E. and Holland, P. W. (1975) *Discrete Multivariate Analysis: Theory and Practice.* Cambridge, MA: MIT Press.

Bliss, C. I. (1970) *Statistics in Biology*, Vol. 2. New York: McGraw-Hill.

Blyth, C. R. and Still, H. A. (1983) Binomial confidence intervals. *J. Am. Statist. Assoc.* **78**, 108–16.

Bock, H. H. (1980) Explorative Datenanalyse. In: N. Victor, W. Lehmacher and W. van Eimeren (Eds.), *Explorative Datenanalyse*, pp. 6–37. Berlin: Springer.

Cattell, R. B., Coulter, M. A. and Tsujioka, B. (1966) The taxonometric recognition of types and functional emergents. In: R. B. Cattell (Ed.), *Handbook of Multivariate Experimental Psychology*, pp. 288–329. Chicago: Rand McNally.

Chapius, F. (1959) *Der Labyrinth-Test.* Bern: Huber.

Chernick, M. R. and Murthy, V. K. (1983) Chi-square percentiles: old and new approximations, with applications to sample size determination. *Am. J. Math. Manage. Sci.* **3**(2), 145–61.

Chipuer, H. and von Eye, A. (1989) Suicide trends in Canada and Germany: an application of configural frequency analysis. *Suicide Life-Threat. Behav.* **19**, 264–276.

Darroch, J. N. and Ratcliff, D. (1972) Generalized iterative scaling for log-linear models. *Ann. Math. Statist.* **43**, 1470–80.

Dawson, J. M. (1982) Stratification and the adjusted chi-square statistic: application to analysis of employment discrimination data. *Am. J. Math. Manage. Sci.* **2**(4), 289–318.

Deming, W. E. and Stephan, F. E. (1940) On a least squares adjustment of a sampled frequency table when the expected marginal totals are known. *Ann. Math. Statist.* **11**, 427–44.

Dixon, W. J. (Ed.) (1983) *BMDP Statistical Software* 1983. Berkeley: University of California Press.

Enke, H. (1980) Zur Erfassung von Zusammenhangsstrukturen in mehrdimensionalen kontingenztafeln. *Z. Gesamte Hyg.* **26**, 834–40.

Everitt, B. S. (1977) *The Analysis of Contingency Tables.* London: Chapman and Hall.

Feller, W. (1957) *Probability Theory and its Applications.* New York: Wiley.

Ferguson, G. A. (1965) *Nonparametric Trend Analysis.* Montreal: McGill University Press.

Fienberg, S. E. (1980) *The Analysis of Cross-classified Categorical Data*, 2nd edn. Cambridge, MA: MIT Press.

Fisher, R. A. and Yates, F. (1948) *Statistical Tables for Biological Agricultural, and Medical Research*. Edinburgh: Oliver and Boyd.

Fleischmann, U. M. and Lienert, G. A. (1982) Die Interaktionsstrukturanalyse als Mittel der Orthogonalitätsbeurteilung faktoriell einfach strukturierter Tests. *Psychol. Beiträge* **24**, 395–410.

Funke, W., Funke, J. and Lienert, G. A. (1984) Prädiktionskoeffizienten in der Konfigurationsfrequenzanalyse (Phi-Koeffizienten). *Psychol. Beiträge* **26**, 382–92.

Funke, J. and Hussy, W. (1979) Informationsverarbeitende Strukturen und Prozesse. Analysemöglichkeiten durch Problemlöseparadigmen. *Trierer Psychol. Ber.* **6**, Heft 8.

Gangestad, S. and Snyder, M. (1985) To carve nature at its joints: on the existence of discrete classes in personality. *Psychol. Rev.* **92**, 317–49.

Gilula, Z. and Krieger, A. M. (1983) The decomposability and monotonicity of Pearson's chi-square for collapsed contingency tables with applications. *J. Am. Statist. Assoc.* **78**, 176–80.

Gloning, K., Quatember, R. and Lienert, G. A. (1972) Konfigurationsfrequenzanalyse aphasie-spezifischer Testleistungen. *Z. Klin. Psychol. Psychother.* **20**, 115–22.

Gokhale, D. V. and Kullback, S. (1978) *The Information in Contingency Tables*. New York: Dekker.

Goodman, L. A. (1965) On simultaneous confidence intervals for multinomial proportions. *Technometrics* **7**, 247–54.

Goodman, L. A. (1978) *Analyzing Qualitative/Categorical Data*. Cambridge, MA: Abt Books.

Goodman, L. A. (1981) Three elementary views of log-linear models for the analysis of cross-classifications having ordered categories. *Sociol. Method.*, 191–239.

Görtelmeyer, R. (1988) *Typologie des Schlafverhaltens. Eine empirische Untersuchung an berufstätigen Personen*. Regensburg: Roderer.

Gottlieb, R., Lienert, G. A. and Ludwig, O. (1983) Standard normal deviates for unconventional alphas. *EDV Med. Biol.* **14**(3–4), 120–24.

Grobe, R. and Hofer, M. (1983) Kognitiv-motivationale Korrelate von Schulnoten: Typen motivierter Schüler. *Z. Entwicklungspsychol. Pädagog. Psychol.* **XV**, 292–316.

Haberman, S. J. (1973) The analysis of residuals in cross-classified tables. *Biometrics* **29**, 205–20.

Haberman, S. J. (1974a) *The Analysis of Frequency Data*. Chicago: The University of Chicago Press.

Haberman, S. J. (1974b) Log linear models for frequency tables with ordered classifications. *Biometrics* **30**, 589–600.

Haberman, S. J. (1978) *Analysis of Qualitative Data, Vol. 1. Introductory Topics.* New York: Academic Press.

Hager, W. (1987) Grundlagen einer Versuchsplanung zur Prüfung empirischer Hypothesen in der Psychologie. In: G. Lüer (Ed.), *Allgemeine Experimentelle Psychologie*, pp. 43–264. Stuttgart: Gustav Fischer.

Hald, A. (1965) *Statistical Theory with Engineering Applications* 6th edn. New York: John Wiley.

Harter, H. L. (1980) Early history of multiple comparison tests. In P. R. Krishnaiah (Ed.), *Handbook of Statistics: Analysis of Variance*, pp. 617–22. Amsterdam: North-Holland.

Hartigan, J. A. (1975) *Clustering Algorithms.* New York: John Wiley.

Havránek, T., Kohnen, R. and Lienert, G. A. (1986) Nonparametric evaluation of ANOVA designs by local, regional, and global contingency testing. *Biom. J.* **28**, 11–21.

Havránek, T. and Lienert, G. A. (1984) Local and regional vs. global contingency testing. *Biom. J.* **26**, 483–94.

Havránek, T. and Lienert, G. A. (1986) Remission control of pre-post treatment comparisons by two-sample symmetry testing. *Methods Inform. Med.* **25**, 116–22.

Hays, W. L. (1981) *Statistics for the Social Sciences*, 2nd edn. London: Holt, Rinehart & Winston.

Heilmann, W.-R. and Lienert, G. A. (1982) Predictive configural frequency analysis evaluated by simultaneous Berchtold-corrected fourfold X^2-tests. *Biom. J.* **24**, 723–28.

Heilmann, W.-R., Lienert, G. A. and Maly, V. (1979) Prediction models in configural frequency analysis. *Biom. J.* **21**, 79–86.

Heilmann, W.-R. and Schütt, W. (1985) Tables for binomial testing via F-distribution in configural frequency analysis. *EDV Med. Biol.* **16**(1), 1–7.

Hertzog, C. and Rovine, M. J. (1985) Repeated measures analysis of variance in developmental research: selected issues. *Child Dev.* **56**, 787–809.

Hicks, L. E. (1984) Conceptual and empirical analysis of some assumptions of an explicitly typological theory. *J. Pers. Soc. Psychol.* **46**, 1118–31.

Hildebrand, D. K., Laing, J. D. and Rosenthal, H. (1977) *Prediction Analysis of Cross-Classifications.* New York: John Wiley.

Hoernes, G. E. and Heilweil, M. F. (1964) *Introduction to Boolean Algebra and Logic Design.* New York: McGraw-Hill.

Holland, B. S. and Copenhaver, D. M. (1987) An improved sequentially rejective Bonferroni test procedure. *Biometrics* **43**, 417–23.

Holland, B. S. and Copenhaver, D. M. (1988) Improved Bonferroni-type multiple testing procedures. *Psychol. Bull.* **104**, 145–49.

Holm, S. (1979) A simple sequentially rejective multiple test procedure. *Scand. J. Statist.* **6**, 65–70.

Hommel, G., Lehmacher, W. and Perli, H.-G. (1985) Residuenanalyse des Unabhängigkeitsmodells zweier kategoriater Variablen. In: J. Jesdinsky and J. Trampisch (Eds.), *Prognose- und Entscheidungsfindung in der Medizin*, pp. 494–503. Berlin: Springer.

Hommers, W. (1987) Anti-Typen zur psychologischen Validität eines methodischen Konstrukts der Konfigurationsfrequenzanalyse. *Diagnostika* **33**, 301–18.

Hu, T.-C. (1988) A statistical method of approach to Stirlings formula. *Am. Statist.* **42**, 204–05.

Hütter, U., Müller, U. and Lienert, G. A. (1981) Die Konfigurationsfrequenzanalyse. XIII. Multiple, kanonische und multivariate Prädiktions-KFA und ihre Anwendung in der Medizinsoziologie. *Z. Klin. Psychol. Psychother.* **29**, 4–13.

Immich, H. and Sonnemann, E. (1974) Which statistical methods can be used in practice for the comparison of curves over few time-dependent measure points? *Biom. Praxim.* **14**, 43–52.

Jannarone, R. J. and Roberts, J. S. (1984) Reflecting interactions among personality items: Meehl's Paradox revisited. *J. Pers. Soc. Psychol.* **47**, 621–28.

Keuchel, I. and Lienert, G. A. (1985) DieKonfigurationsfrequenzanalyse. XXIIb. Typen ipsativer Skalenmuster. *Z. Klin. Psychol. Psychopathol. Psychother.* **33**, 232–38.

Kimball, A. W. (1954) Short-cut formulae for the exact partition of χ^2 in contingency tables. *Biometrics* **20**, 452–58.

Kirk, R. E. (1982) *Experimental Design*, 2nd edn. Belmont, CA: Wadsworth.

Koehler, K. J. and Larntz, K. (1980) An empirical investigation of goodness-of-fit statistics for sparse multinomials. *J. Am. Statist. Assoc.* **75**, 336–44.

Kohnen, R. and Rudolph, J. (1981) Die Konfigurationsfrequenzanalyse. XIVa. Remissionskontrollierte Symptommuster-Abfolgen im Therapie-Wartegruppen-Vergleich. *Z. Klin. Psychol. Psychother.* **29**, 119–26.

Kotze, P. J. V. and Hawkins, M. M. (1984) The identification of outliers in two-way contingency tables, using 2×2 subtables. *J. Appl. Statist.* **33**, 215–23.

Krampen, G., von Eye, A. and Brandtstädter, J. (1987) Konfigurationstypen generalisierter Kontrollüberzeugungen. *Z. Diff. Diagnost. Psychol.* **8**, 111–119.

Krause, B. and Metzler, P. (1984) *Angewandte Statistik*. Berlin: VEB Deutscher Verlag der Wissenschaften.

Krauth, J. (1973) Nichtparametrische Ansätze zur Auswertung von Verlaufskurven. *Biom. Z.* **15**, 557–66.

Krauth, J. (1980a) Ein Vergleich der Konfigurationsfrequenzanalyse mit der Methode der log-linearen Modelle. *Z. Sozialpsychol.* **11**, 233–47.

Krauth, J. (1980b) Nonparametric analysis of response curves. *J. Neurosci. Methods* **2**, 239–52.

Krauth, J. (1981a) Multivariate Behandlungsstabilität klinischer Skalen. *Psychol. Beiträge* **23**, 438–57.

Krauth, J. (1981b) Techniques of classification in psychology I: Factor analysis, facet analysis, multidimensional scaling, latent structure analysis. *Int. J. Classification* **8**(3), 126–32.

Krauth, J. (1982) Techniques of classification in psychology II: Cluster analysis, typal analysis, configural frequency analysis, discriminant analysis, regression analysis. *Int. J. Classification* **9**(1), 1–10.

Krauth, J. (1985a) Principles of configural frequency analysis. *Z. Psychol.* **193**, 363–76.

Krauth, J. (1985b) Typological personality research by Configural Frequency Analysis. *Pers. Indiv. Diff.* **6**, 161–68.

Krauth, J. and Kohnen, R. (1981) Die Konfigurationsfrequenzanalyse. XIVb. Behandlungsinduzierte Symptommuster-Abfolgen im Therapie-Wartegruppen-Vergleich. *Z. Klin. Psychol. Psychother.* **29**, 307–14.

Krauth, J. and Lienert, G. A. (1973a) *KFA Die Konfigurationsfrequenzanalyse und ihre Anwendung in Psychologie und Medizin.* Freiburg: Alber.

Krauth, J. and Lienert, G. A. (1973b) Nichtparametrischer Nachweis von Syndromen durch simultane Binomialtests. *Biom. Z.* **15**, 13–20.

Krauth, J. and Lienert, G. A. (1974) Zum Nachweis syndromgenerierender Symptominteraktionen in mehrdimensionalen Kontingenztafeln (Interaktionsstrukturanalyse). *Biom. Z.* **16**, 203–11.

Krauth, J. and Lienert, G. A. (1975) Konfigurationsfrequenzanalytische Auswertung von Verlaufskurven. In: W. H. Tack (Ed.), *Bericht über den 29. Kongress der DGfPs*, pp. 402–04. Göttingen: Hogrefe.

Krauth, J. and Lienert, G. A. (1978) Nonparametric two-sample comparison of learning curves based on orthogonal polynomials. *Psychol. Res.* **40**, 159–71.

Krauth, J. and Lienert, G. A. (1980) Die Konfigurationsfrequenzanalyse. XII. Symptommusterfolgen (Durchgangssyndrome). *Z. Klin. Psychol. Psychother.* **28**, 302–15.

Krauth, J. and Lienert, G. A. (1982a) Die Konfigurationsfrequenzanalyze. XVII. Dyslexie-Verdachtstypen bei Jungen und Mädchen. *Z. Klin. Psychol. Psychother.* **30**, 196–201.

Krauth, J. and Lienert, G. A. (1982b) Fundamentals and modifications of configural frequency analysis (CFA). *Interdisciplinaria* **3**(1), 1–14.

Krauth, J. and Lienert, G. A. (1984) Basic concepts and applications of configural frequency analysis (CFA). *Psychol. J.* **5**, 26–34 (in Russian).

Krippendorff, K. (1986) *Information Theory. Structural Models for Qualitative Data.* Beverly Hill: Sage.

Krüger, H.-P. (1979) Zur Anwendungsindikation von nonparametrischen Prädiktionsverfahren. *Z. Sozialpsychol.* **10**, 94–104.

Krüger, H.-P., Lehmacher, W. and Wall, K.-D. (1980) *The Fourfold Table up to N = 80.* Stuttgart: Gustav Fischer.

Küchenhoff, H. (1986) A note on a continuity correction for testing in three-dimensional configural frequency analysis. *Biom. J.* **28**(4), 465–68.

Kuda, M. (1985) Konfigurationsfrequenzanalyse von Items eines Suizidal-tendenzfragebogens. *Z. Klin. Psychol. Psychother.* **33**, 224–31.

Kullback, S. (1959) *Information Theory and Statistics.* New York: John Wiley.

Lancaster, H. D. (1969) *The Chi-squared Distribution.* New York: John Wiley.

Lange, H.-J. and Vogel, Th. (1965) Statistische Analyse von Symptom-korrelationen bei Syndromen. *Methods Inform Med.* **4**(2), 83–89.

Larntz, K. (1978) Small sample comparisons of exact levels for chi-squared goodness-of-fit statistics. *J. Am. Statist. Assoc.* **73**, 253–63.

Lautsch, E. (1983) Zur Anwendung der Konfigurationsfrequenzanalyse (KFA) in der empirisch-soziologischen Forschung. *Jahrbuch für Soziologie und Sozialpolitik*, pp. 198–212. Berlin: Akademie-Verlag.

Lautsch, E., Lienert, G. A. and von Eye, A. (1988) Strategische Überlegungen zur Anwendung der Konfigurationsfrequenzanalyse. *EDP Med. Biol.* **19**, 26–30.

Lautsch, E., Lienert, G. A. and von Eye, A. (In press) Küchenhoff-Stetigkeitskorrektur des Lehmacher KFA-Tests in der Suche nach Typen soziogener Neuropathologie. *Z. Klin. Psychol. Psychopathol. Psychother.*

Lautsch, E. and von Weber, S. (In press) SICFA—Simulation Configural Frequency Analysis. *Statist. Software Lett.*

Lehmacher, W. (1980a) Die Konfigurationsfrequenzanalyse qualitativer Daten als explorative Methode. In: N. Victor, W. Lehmacher and W. van Eimeren (Eds.), *Explorative Datenanalyse*, pp. 147–55. Berlin: Springer.

Lehmacher, W. (1980b) Nichtparametrischer Vergleich zweier Scharen von Verlaufskurven. In: J. Horbach and C. Duhme (Eds.), *Nachsorge und Krankheitsverlaufsanalyse.* Heidelberg: Springer.

Lehmacher, W. (1981) A more powerful simultaneous test procedure in configural frequency analysis. *Biom. J.* **23**(5), 429–36.

Lehmacher, W. (1984) Die Beziehung der Konfigurationsfrequenzanalyse zu anderen Methoden der Analyse qualitativer Daten. In: H. Enke and J. Haerting (Eds.), *Biometrie und Biostatistik in der Medizin und ver-*

wandten Gebieten, pp. 83–91. Halle: Martin Luther Universität, Wissenschaftliche Beiträge.

Lehmacher, W. and Lienert, G. A. (1980) Nichtparametrischer Vergleich von Testprofilen und Verlaufskurven vor und nach einer Behandlung. *Psychol. Beiträge* **22**, 432–48.

Lehmacher, W. and Lienert, G. A. (1982) Die Konfigurationsfrequenzanalyse. XVI. Neue Tests gegen Typen und Syndrome. *Z. Klin. Psychol. Psychother.* **30**, 5–11.

Lehmann, E. and Lienert, G. A. (In preparation) Differential improvements from haloperidol in two types of schizophrenics.

Lemke, R. and Rennert, H. (1970) *Neurologie und Psychiatrie*. Leipzig: Barth.

Leuner, H. C. (1962) *Die experimentelle Psychose*. Berlin: Springer.

Lienert, G. A. (1969) Die "Konfigurationsfrequenzanalyse" als Klassifikationsmethode in der Klinischen Psychologie. In: M. Irle (Ed.), *Bericht über den 26. Kongress der Deutschen Gesellschaft für Psychologie in Tübingen 1968*, pp. 244–53. Göttingen: Hogrefe.

Lienert, G. A. (1971a) Die Konfigurationsfrequenzanalyse. I. Ein neuer Weg zu Typen und Syndromen. *Z. Klin. Psychol. Psychother.* **19**, 99–115.

Lienert, G. A. (1971b) Die Konfigurationsfrequenzanalyse. II. Hierarchische und agglutinierende KFA in der klinischen Psychologie. *Z. Klin. Psychol. Psychother.* **19**, 207–20.

Lienert, G. A. (1971c) Die Konfigurationsfrequenzanalyse. III. Zwei- und Mehrstichproben KFA in Diagnostik und Differentialdiagnostik. *Z. Klin. Psychol. Psychother.* **19**, 291–300.

Lienert, G. A. (1972) Die Konfigurationsfrequenzanalyse. IV. Assoziationsstruktur klinischer Skalen und Symptome. *Z. Klin. Psychol. Psychother.* **20**, 231–48.

Lienert, G. A. (1978) *Verteilungsfreie Methoden in der Biostatistik*, Vol. II. Meisenheim am Glan: Hain.

Lienert, G. A. (1980) Nonparametric cluster analysis of learning curves based on orthogonal polynomials. In: Hungarian Academy of Sciences, *Proceedings of the 4th Meeting of Psychologists from the Danubian Countries*, pp. 595–609. Budapest: Akadémiai Kiadó.

Lienert, G. A. (1987) Vergleich unabhängiger Stichproben von qualitativen Variablen mittels geschlossener k-Stichproben-Konfigurationsfrequenzanalyse. In: E. Raab and G. Schulter (Eds.), *Perspektiven psychologischer Forschung. Festschrift zum 65. Geburtstag von Erich Mittenecker*. Wien: Deuticke.

Lienert, G. A. (Ed.) (1988) *Angewandte Konfigurationsfrequenzanalyse*. Frankfurt/M.: Athenäum.

Lienert, G. A. and Bergman, L. R. (1985) Longisectional interaction structure analysis (LISA) in psychopharmacology and developmental psychopathology. *Neuropsychobiology* **14**, 27–34.

Lienert, G. A. and Klauer, K. J. (1983) Kohortenanalyse von Erfolgsbeurteilungen mittels multivariater Prädiktions-KFA (Konfigurations-Frequenz-Analyse). *Psychol. Beiträge* **25**, 297–314.

Lienert, G. A. and Krauth, J. (1973a) Die Konfigurationsfrequenzanalyse. V. Kontingenz- und Interaktions-Strukturanalyse multinär skalierter Merkmale. *Z. Klin. Psychol. Psychother.* **21**, 26–39.

Lienert, G. A. and Krauth, J. (1973b) Die Konfigurationsfrequenzanalyse. VI. Profiländerungen und Symptomverschiebungen. *Z. Klin. Psychol. Psychother.* **21**, 100–09.

Lienert, G. A. and Krauth, J. (1973c) Die Konfigurationsfrequenzanalyse. VII. Konstellations-, Konstellationsänderungs- und Profilkonstellationstypen. *Z. Klin. Psychol. Psychother.* **21**, 197–209.

Lienert, G. A. and Krauth, J. (1973d) Die Konfigurationsfrequenzanalyse. VIII. Auswertung multivariater Versuchspläne. *Z. Klin. Psychol. Psychother.* **21**, 298–311.

Lienert, G. A. and Krauth, J. (1973e) Die Konfigurationsfrequenzanalyse als Prädiktionsmodell in der angewandten Psychologie. In: H. Eckensberger (Ed.), *Bericht über den 28. Kongress der Deutschen Gesellschaft für Psychologie in Saarbrücken 1972*, pp. 219–28. Göttingen: Hogrefe.

Lienert, G. A. and Krauth, J. (1974a) Die Konfigurationsfrequenzanalyse. XI. Auswertung multivariater klinischer Untersuchungspläne (Teil 1). *Z. Klin. Psychol. Psychother.* **22**, 3–17.

Lienert, G. A. and Krauth, J. (1974b) Die Konfigurationsfrequenzanalyse. IX. Auswertung multivariater klinischer Untersuchungspläne (Teil 2). *Z. Klin. Psychol. Psychother.* **22**, 108–21.

Lienert, G. A. and Krauth, J. (1975) Configural frequency analysis as a statistical tool for defining types. *Educ. Psychol. Meas.* **35**, 231–38.

Lienert, G. A. and Lehmann, E. (1984) Differential drug effects identified by 3-way configural frequency analysis. *Neuropsychobiology* **11**, 247–250.

Lienert, G. A. and Netter, P. (1986) Nonparametric evaluation of repeated measurement designs by point-symmetry testing. *Biom. J.* **28**(1), 3–10.

Lienert, G. A. and Netter, P. (1987) Nonparametric analysis of treatment response tables by bipredictive configural frequency analysis. *Methods Inform. Med.* **26**, 89–92.

Lienert, G. A. and Netter, P. (In press) Die Konfigurationsfrequenzanalyse. XXIb. Typenanalyse bivariater Verlaufskurven von Hyper- und Normotonikern. *Z. Klin. Psychol. Psychopathol. Psychother.*

Lienert, G. A., Netter, P. and von Eye, A. (1987) Die Konfigurationsfrequenzanalyse. XXV. Typen und Syndrome höherer Ordnung. *Z. Klin. Psychol. Psychopathol. Psychother.* **35**, 344–352.

Lienert, G. A. and Rey, E.-R. (1982) Die Konfigurationsfrequenzanalyse.XV. Typenexploration und -inferenz (Hybride und agglutinierende Prädiktions-KFA). *Z. Klin. Psychol. Psychother.* **30**, 209–15.

Lienert, G. A., Reynolds, J. and Wall, K.-D. (1979) Comparing associations in two independent fourfold tables. *Biom. J.* **21**, 473–491.

Lienert, G. A. and Rudolph, J. (1983) Die Konfigurationsfrequenzanalyse. XIX. Remissions-kontrollierte Inkrementen-KFA. *Z. Klin. Psychol. Psychopathol. Psychother.* **31**, 245–53.

Lienert, G. A. and Straube, E. (1980) Die Konfigurationsfrequenzanalyse. XI. Strategien des Symptom-Konfigurations-Vergleichs vor und nach einer Therapie. *Z. Klin. Psychol. Psychother.* **28**, 110–23.

Lienert, G. A. and von Eye, A. (1984a) Multivariate Änderungsbeurteilung mittels Inkrementen-Konfigurationsclusteranalyse. *Psychol. Beiträge* **26**, 363–71.

Lienert, G. A. and von Eye, A. (1984b) Testing for stability and change in multivariate t-point observations by longitudinal Configural Frequency Analysis. *Psychol. Beiträge* **26**, 298–308.

Lienert, G. A. and von Eye, A. (1985) Die Konfigurationsclusteranalyse (KCA) und ihre Anwendung in der klinischen Psychologie. In: D. Albert (Ed.), *Bericht über den 34. Kongress der Deutschen Gesellschaft für Psychologie in Wien 1984*, pp. 167–69. Göttingen: Hogrefe.

Lienert, G. A. and von Eye, A. (1986) Nonparametric two sample CFA of incomplete learning curves. In: F. Klix and H. Hagendorf (Eds.), *Human Memory and Cognitive Capabilities*, pp. 123–38. New York: Elsevier.

Lienert, G. A. and von Eye, A. (1987a) Nonparametric identification of multivariate improvement effects using configural analysis of complementary increments (CAC) from pre-post treatment designs. *Biom. J.* **29**, 429–37.

Lienert, G. A. and von Eye, A. (1987b) Nonparametric comparison of longitudinal response patterns from unpaired samples using configural frequency analysis. *Biom. J.* **29**, 675–88.

Lienert, G. A. and von Eye, A. (1988) Syndromaufklärung mittels generalisierter Interaktionsstrukturanalyse. *Z. Klin. Psychol. Psychopathol. Psychother.* **36**, 25–33.

Lienert, G. A. and von Kerekjarto, M. (1969) Möglichkeiten der Ex-post-Klassifizierung depressiver Symptome und Patienten mittels Faktoren- und Konfigurationsanalyse. In: H. Hippius and H. Selbach (Eds.), *Das depressive Syndrom*, pp. 219–56. Berlin: Urban & Schwarzenberg.

Lienert, G. A. and Wolfrum, C. (1979) Die Konfigurationsfrequenzanalyse. X. Therapiewirkungsbeurteilung mittels Prädiktions-KFA. *Z. Klin. Psychol. Psychother.* **27**, 309–16.

Lienert, G. A. and zur Oeveste, H. (In press) Configural frequency analysis as a statistical tool for development research. *Educ. Psychol. Meas.*

Lindner, K. (1979) Das maximale Signifikanzniveau bei Simultantests. *Proc. Op. Res.* **9**, 330–35.

Lindner, K. (1984) Eine exakte Auswertungsmethode zur Konfigurationsfrequenzanalyse. *Psychol. Beiträge* **26**, 393–415.

Lösel, F. (1978) Konfigurationen elterlicher Erziehung und Dissozialität. In: K. A. Schneewind and H. Lukesch (Eds.), *Familiäre Sozialisation*, pp. 233–45. Stuttgart: Klett.

Ludwig, O., Gottlieb, R. and Lienert, G. A. (1986) Tables of Bonferroni-limits for simultaneous F-tests. *Biom. J.* **28**, 25–30.

Marcus, R., Peritz, E. and Gabriel, K. R. (1976) On closed testing procedures with special reference to ordered analysis of variance. *Biometrika* **63**, 655–60.

Maxwell, A. E. (1961) *Analyzing Qualitative Data.* London: Methuen.

McCullagh, P. and Nelder, J. A. (1983) *Generalized Linear Models.* London: Chapman and Hall.

Meehl, P. E. (1950) Configural scoring. *J. Consult. Psychol.* **14**, 165–71.

Mendelsohn, G. A., Weis, D. S. and Feimer, N. R. (1982) Conceptual and empirical analysis of the typological implications of patterns of socialization and femininity. *J. Pers. Social Psychol.* **42**, 1157–70.

Metzler, P. and Nickel, B. (1986) *Zeitreihen- und Verlaufsanalysen.* Leipzig: Hirzel.

Miller, R. G. (1966) *Simultaneous Statistical Inference.* New York: McGraw-Hill.

Miller, R. G. (1977) Developments in multiple comparisons. *J. Am. Statist. Assoc.* **79**, 779–88.

Nelder, J. A. (1974) Log-linear models for contingency tables: A generalization of classical least squares. *J. Am. Statist. Assoc.* **81**, 826–31.

Nesselroade, J. R. (1983) Temporal selection and factor invariance in the study of development and change. In: P. B. Baltes and O. G. Brim, Jr. (Eds.), *Life-span Development and Behavior*, Vol. 5, pp. 59–87. New York: Academic Press.

Nesselroade, J. R. (In press) Sampling and generalizability: Adult development and aging research issues examined within the general methodological framework of selection. In: K. W. Schaie, R. T. Campbell, W. Meredith and S. C. Rawlings (Eds.), *Methodological Issues in Aging Research.* New York: Springer.

Nesselroade, J. R., Pruchno, R. and Jacobs, A. (1986) Reliability and stability in the measurement of psychological states: An illustration with anxiety measures. *Psychol. Beiträge* **28**, 252–64.

Neter, J., Wasserman, W. and Kutner, M. H. (1985) *Applied Linear Statistical Models*, 2nd edn. Homewood, IL: Irwin.

Netter, P. (1981) KFA von funktionellen Beschwerden bei Spontanangabe und standardisierter Befragung. In: W. Janke (Ed.), *Beiträge zur Methodik in der differentiellen, diagnostischen und klinischen Psychologie. Festschrift zum 60. Geburtstag von G. A. Lienert*, pp. 393–420. Königstein/TS: Hain.

Netter, P. (1982) Typen sympathomedullärer Aktivität und ihre psychischen Korrelate. In: H. Studt (Ed.), *Psychosomatik in Forschung und Praxis*, pp. 216–33. München: Urban & Schwarzenberg.

Netter, P. (1983) Activation and anxiety as represented by patterns of catecholamine levels in hyper- and normotensives. *Neuropsychobiology* **10**, 148–55.

Netter, P. and Lienert, G. A. (1984) Die Konfigurationsfrequenzanalyse. XXIa. Stress-induzierte Katecholamin-Reaktionen bei Hyper- und Normotonikern. *Z. Klin. Psychol. Psychopathol. Psychother.* **32**, 356–64.

Nie, N. H., Hull, C. H., Jenkins, J. G., Steinbrenner, K. and Bent, D. H. (1975) *Statistical Package for the Social Sciences*. New York: McGraw-Hill.

Osselmann, J. (1979) Konfigurationsfrequenzanalyse von subjektiven Bedingungen depressiver Reaktionen. *Z. Klin. Psychol. Psychother.* **27**, 116–34.

Osterkorn, K. (1975) Wann kann die Binomial- und Poissonverteilung hinreichend genau durch die Normalverteilung ersetzt werden. *Biom. Z.* **17**, 33–34.

Oswald, W.-D. and Roth, E. (1978) *Der Zahlen-Verbindungs-Test*. Göttingen: Hogrefe.

Overall, J. E. and Gorham, D. R. (1962) The brief psychiatric rating scale. *Psychol. Rep.* **10**, 799–812.

Perli, H.-G. (1985) *Testverfahren in der Konfigurationsfrequenzanalyse bei multinomialem Versuchsschema*. Erlangen: Palm und Enke.

Perli, H.-G., Hommel, G. and Lehmacher, W. (1985) Sequentially rejective test procedures for detecting outlying cells in one- and two-sample multinomial experiments. *Biom. J.* **27**, 885–93.

Perli, H.-G., Hommel, G. and Lehmacher, W. (1987) Test procedures in configural frequency analysis (CFA) controlling the local and multiple level. *Biom. J.* **29**, 255–67.

Rauchfleisch, U. (1972) Soziale und affektive Probleme in der Selbstbeurteilung Verwahrloster. *Praxis Kinderpsychol. Kinderpsychiatr.* **21**, 246–56.

Rauchfleisch, U. (1973) Frustrationsreaktionen verwahrloster Jugendlicher im Rosenzweig-Picture-Frustration-Test. *Z. Klin. Psychol. Psychother.* **21**, 18–25.

Rauchfleisch, U. (1974) Beziehungen zwischen Frustrationsreaktionen und Intelligenzfunktionen bei verwahrlosten Jugendlichen. *Psychol. Beiträge* **16**, 365–97.

Rindskopf, D. (1987) A compact BASIC program for log-linear models. In: R. M. Heiberger (Ed.), *Computer Science and Statistics. Proceedings of the 19th Symposium on the Interface*, pp. 381–85. Alexandria, VA: American Statistical Association.

Roeder, B. (1974) Die Konfigurationsfrequenzanalyse (KFA) nach Krauth und Lienert, ein handliches Verfahren zur Verarbeitung sozialwissenschaftlicher Daten, demonstriert an einem Beispiel. *Kölner Z. Soziol. Sozialpsychol.* **26**, 819–44.

Roeder, B. (1976) Parameterfreier Vergleich verschiedener Konfigurationsfrequenzanalysen. *Kölner Z. Soziol. Sozialpsychol.* **28**, 152–55.

Roeder, B. (1977) *KFA-Programm, Version 3.* Unpublished program manual.

Rushton, J. P., Jackson, D. N. and Paunonen, S. V. (1981) Personality: Nomothetic or idiographic? A response to Kendrick and Stringfield. *Psychol. Rev.* **88**, 582–89.

Sackett, G. P. (1977) Log sequential analysis of contingency and cyclicity in behavioral interaction research. Int: J. Osowski (Ed.), *Handbook of Infant Development*, pp. 623–49. New York: Wiley.

Shaffer, J. P. (1986) Modified sequentially rejective multiple test procedures. *J. Am. Statist. Assoc.* **81**, 826–31.

Siegel, S. (1956) *Nonparametric Statistics for the Behavioral Sciences.* New York: McGraw-Hill.

Silbereisen, R. K. (1976) Untersuchungen zur Klassifikation von Klienten der Sozialhilfe nach ihren Erfahrungen, Einstellungen und Forderungen. *Soziale Welt* **27**, 303–22.

Silbereisen, R. K. (1977) Konfigurationen der Einstellungen, Erfahrungen und Forderungen von Sozialhilfeempfängern. *Z. Klin. Psychol. Psychother.* **25**, 256–63.

Snedecor, G. W. and Cohran, W. G. (1967) *Statistical Methods*, 6th edn. Ames, IA: The Iowa State University Press.

Sonnemann, E. (1982) Allgemeine Lösungen multipler Testprobleme. *EDV Med. Biol.* **13**, 318–28.

Steiger, J. H., Shapiro, A. and Browne, M. W. (1985) On the multivariate asymptotic distribution of sequential chi-square statistics. *Psychometrika* **50**, 253–64.

SYSTAT (1986) *SYSTAT: The System for Statistics.* Evanston: SYSTAT.

Tomizawa, S. (1986) Four kinds of symmetry models and their decompositions in a square contingency table with ordered categories. *Biom. J.* **28**(4), 387–93.

von Eye, A. (1981) Die Assoziationsstrukturanalyse auf informationstheoretischer Basis. *Z. Klin. Psychol. Psychother.* **29**, 216–27.

von Eye, A. (1982) Beschreibung der Programme "KFA" und "THO" für Taschenrechner. Unpublished manual.

von Eye, A. (1984) Konfigurationsanalytische Typisierung multivariater Verlaufskurven. *Psychol. Beiträge* **26**, 37–51.

von Eye, A. (1985) Konfigurationsfrequenzanalyse bei gerichteten Variablenbeziehungen (GKFA). *EDV Med. Biol.* **16**, 37–40.

von Eye, A. (1986) Strategien der Typen- und Syndromaufklärung mit der Interaktionsstrukturanalyse. *Z. Klin. Psychol. Psychopathol. Psychother.* **34**, 54–68.

von Eye, A. (1987) BASIC programs for configural frequency analysis. Unpublished computer programs.

von Eye, A. (1988) The general linear model as a framework for models in configural frequency analysis. *Biom. J.* **30**, 59–67.

von Eye, A. and Bergman, L. R. (1987) A note on numerical approximations of the binomial test in configural frequency analysis. *EDP Med. Biol.* **17**, 108–11.

von Eye, A. and Brandtstädter, J. (1982) Systematization of results of Configural Frequency Analysis by minimizing Boolean functions. In: H. Caussinus, P. Ettinger and J. R. Mathieu (Eds.), *Compstat 1982, Part II: Short Communications, Summaries of Posters*, pp. 91–92. Wien: Physica.

von Eye, A., Gebert, A. and Lienert, G. A. (1981) Testskalenbeurteilung nach multivariater Punktsymmetrie. *Psychol. Beiträge* **23**, 208–25.

von Eye, A. and Hussy, W. (1980) Zur Verwendung der polynomialen Approximation in der Psychologie. *Psychol. Beiträge* **22**, 163–81.

von Eye, A. and Lienert, G. A. (1984) Die Konfigurationsfrequenzanalyse. XX. Typen und Syndrome zweiter Ordnung. *Z. Klin. Psychol. Psychopathol. Psychother.* **32**, 345–55.

von Eye, A. and Lienert, G. A. (1985) Die Konfigurationsfrequenzanalyse. XXIIa. Typen normativer Skalenmuster. *Z. Klin. Psychol. Psychopathol. Psychother.* **33**, 173–81.

von Eye, A. and Lienert, G. A. (1987) Nonparametric comparison of longitudinal response patterns from paired samples using configural frequency analysis. *Biom. J.* **29**, 615–24.

von Eye, A. and Lienert, G. A. (In press) Die Konfigurationsfrequenzanalyse. XXIV. Konfigurationsclusteranalyse als Alternative zur KFA. *Z. Klin. Psychol. Psychopathol. Psychother.*

von Eye, A. and Nesselroade, J. R. (In press) Types of change: Application of configural frequency analysis to repeated observations in development research. *Exp. Aging Res.*

von Eye, A. and Rovine, M. J. (1988) A comparison of significance tests for Configural Frequency Analysis. *EDP Med. Biol.* **19**, 6–13.

von Eye, A., Rovine, M. J. and Wood, P. K. (1990) A comparison of tests for residual analysis of cross-classifications. In: K. Berk and L. Malone (Eds.), Computing Science and Statistics, 21st Symposium on the Interface. Alexandria, VA: American Statistical Association.

Wall, K.-D. (1977) Statistical models to study WILDER'S law of initial values. *Biom. J.* **19**, 613–28.

Wall, K.-D. and Lienert, G. A. (1976) A test for point-symmetry in J-dimensional contingency-cubes. *Biom. Z.* **18**, 259–64.

Ward, J. H. (1963) Hierarchical grouping to optimize an objective function. *J. Am. Statist. Assoc.* **58**, 236–44.

Weber, A. C. and Scharfetter, C. (1984) The syndrome concept: History and statistical operationalizations. *Psychol. Med.* **14**, 315–25.

Weber, E. (1967) *Grundriss der Biologischen Statistik*, 6th edn. Jena: Gustav Fischer.

Wermuth, N. (1976) Anmerkungen zur Konfigurationsfrequenzanalyse. *Z. Klin. Psychol. Psychother.* **23**, 5–21.

Westermann, R. and Hager, W. (1986) Error probabilities in educational and psychological research. *J. Educ. Statist.* **11**, 117–46.

Wise, M. E. (1963) Multinomial probabilities and the χ^2 and the X^2 distributions. *Biometrika* **50**, 145–54.

Yates, F. (1934) Contingency tables involving small numbers and the X^2-test. *Suppl. J. R. Statist. Soc.* **1**, 217–35.

Zerbe, G. O. (1979) Randomization analysis of the completely randomized design extended to growth and response curves. *J. Am. Statist. Assoc.* **74**, 215–21.

Zerges, K. (1982) *Sozialdemokratische Presse und Literatur: Empirische Untersuchungen zur Literaturvermittlung in der sozialdemokratischen Presse.* Stuttgart: Metzler.

zur Oeveste, H. and Lienert, G. A. (1984) Methoden der Entwicklungs-Konfigurationsfrequenzanalyse. *Psychol. Beiträge* **26**, 372–81.

Subject Index

alpha control, 35–7, 208
  Bonferroni, 37–9, 40–2, 43, 70, 77, 79, 93, 98–100, 101, 106, 111, 122, 126, 130, 139, 147, 155, 157, 161–2, 171, 180, 184
  comparison of methods, 41–3
  global level, 36–7
  Holm, 38–40, 40–2, 43, 65, 92, 126, 199, 213, 244–8
  local level, 36–8, 39
  multiple level, 37, 40
  modified Holm procedure, 39–40, 43–5

Bernoulli experiment, 17
binomial rest, 16–18, 19, 31–2, 64, 68, 70, 76, 79, 111, 148, 160, 167, 171–2, 180
  approximation via F-test, 16, 26–8, 28, 31–2, 64, 70, 155
  approximation via chi-square test, 16, 20, 23, 25–6, 64, 70, 121
  approximation via z-test, 16, 20, 64, 68, 100–1, 106–7, 120–1, 130, 157
  numerical approximation, 16, 19–21, 21, 31–2
  Stirling's formula, 19–21, 21–2, 31–2
BMDP, 75, 79, 230–5, see CFA programs
bootstrap CFA, 208–13
Box-Jenkins models, 173

Cardani's formula, 75, Appendix B
causality, 86, 97
CFA models, 46–8, 59–61, 67
  choice of model, 47
  global models, 47–51, 59, 82
  regional models, 47, 51–7, 59, 82–4
CFA of differences, 146
  and first order CFA, 165
  difference scores, 146–7, 149, 151–2, 153, 159–60, 164–6, 166–8

difference scores and polynomials, 164–5
  first differences, 159–61, 162–3, 168
  second differences, 168
CFA of directed relationships (DCFA), 54–6, 57, 82, 136–8, 139–40, 220
CFA programs
  estimation of tail probability for, F 240–1
  estimation of tail probability for z, 239–40
  main frame computers, 227–38
  mini computers, 223–7
  pocket calculators, 222–3
CFA, steps of analysis, 47
chi-square decomposition, 4, 35, 52, 55, 83
cluster analysis, 5, 63
clusters, zero order (anti)types, 63, 67
conditional CFA, 82, see prediction CFA
configural (anti)clusters, 48–9
configural cluster analysis, see zero order CFA
configurations, 4, 46, 49
confirmatory CFA, 7, 16, 37, 40, 95, 207–9, 213–5
  hybrid approach, 208
conservative testing, 29, 40
cross-classification, 3, 4

descriptive CFA, 6
diagonal half sign test, 190–1

estimation, 59
  expected frequencies, 46–7
  maximum likelihood (ML), 59, 61–2, 64, 69, 75, 79
  ordinary least squares (OLS), 59–60, 64, 69, 75–6, 79
  weighted OLS, 60

265

Euclidean distance, 201, 203
exploratory CFA, 7, 16, 37, 95, 111, 207–213

factor analysis, 74
first order CFA, 49–50, 68–70, 71–3, 74, 80–1, 146, 151, 155, 160–1, 162–3, 165–7, 170–2, 173, 218, 222
Fisher's exact test 118–20, 121, 133–5, 159, 194
fixed margins model, 28
fourfold tests of homogeneity, 118, 126–8, 191, 193, 196

general linear model (GLM), 40, 45, 59, 69, 75–6, 79, 85, 117, 129, 138, 147, 155, 160
    analysis of variance (ANOVA), 69, 76, 79, 103, 151–2
    regression, 103, 137, 175, 183
goals of CFA, 46, 218–20, 221
goals of ISA, 86
goals of log-linear modeling, 46, 216–8, 219–21
grouping criteria, 5

hierarchical CFA, 6
higher order CFA, 51, 74, 81
hypergeometric test, 28–30, 31–3, 41, 65, 70, 76, 93–4, 98–9, 149, 199, 222
    continuity correction 30–1, 33, 41, 65, 70, 76, 93–4, 98–9, 149, 199, 213, 222

inferential CFA, 6
information theory, 4, 13, 52, 82–3
interactions, 82–4
interaction structure analysis (ISA) 51–3, 82–4, 128–38, 218
    and ANOVA/regression, 103
    and k-sample CFA, 128–36
    df in ISA, 87–9
    generalized ISA, 54, 56–7, 136
    hierarchical ISA, 95–6
    interactions, 52
    prediction CFA as ISA variant see prediction CFA
    strategies, 92–4
    variants 53, 56–7

k-sample CFA, 116–18, 124–8, 128–36, 143, 197
    2-sample CFA, 116–27, 125, 146, 162–3, 184, 188
    2-stage testing, 124–6
Kimball's formula, 108–9

Leuner's syndrome, 34, 214–15
Likelihood ratio chi-square, 217, 220
log-linear model V, VI, 4, 13, 45–7, 48, 55, 62, 68–9, 72, 74–5, 78–9, 81, 85f, 102, 105, 108, 117, 129, 138, 147, 154, 160, 171
    relationship to CFA, 216–21
    residual analysis, 5, 217–18
    saturated model, 216
    standardized residuals, 14
longitudinal CFA, 143

Mann-Whitney U-test, 35
McNemar's test, 191
Meehl's paradox, 14, 77–9
multiple tests, dependence, 35–6, 46

Newman-Keuls procedure, 39, 125–6
nonconservative testing, 40
null hypothesis (assumptions), 16–18, 28, 35, 39–40, 46, 51, 55, 111–12, 116–17, 119, 121–2, 124, 129, 137–8, 157, 169, 214, 218
    local, 129, 218
number of cells, 152, 154, 169–70

omega squared, 112
omnibus tests, 49, 67, 75

patterns of characteristics, 5, 46
    complementary, 114
    mono- and trisymptomatic, 34
phi coefficient, 12–13, 112–14, 193
phi squared, 113–14
polynomials, 173–4, 176–8, 179–81, 182–84, 197
    coefficients, 176–8, 183
    equidistant time points, 173–82
    nonequidistant time points, 182–4
prediction analysis, 5, 194
prediction CFA (PCFA) 53–4, 56–7, 82, 99–101, 102–4, 114–15, 194, 220
    and ANOVA and regression, 103–4

biprediction CFA, 104, 108, 114–15, 184, 186
classification of models, 102
conditional PCFA, 104–6, 107–8
prediction coefficients, 104, 112–14, 115–16
point fourfold phi 112–13
phi association, 115–16
phi discriminant, 113–14

relationships, 4, 8, 13

sample size, 64, 69–70, 76, 120, 170, 197
SAS, 75, *see* CFA programs
scaling, 74
second order CFA, 50–2, 74–6, 79–80, 171–3
shifts, 145–6, 153–5, 156–8
simultaneous testing, 35–7, 38, 46
SPSSX, 75, 230, 236–8, *see* CFA programs
syndrome, 14, 49
SYSTAT, 75, 120, 223, 225–7, *see* CFA programs

test comparison, 31–3
third order CFA, 51, 78–80, 81
time series differing in length, 186–8
classification criteria, 187–8

treatment effects, 189–91
control group designs, 195–7
trend, 145, 154, 162–3, 164–6, 168–70
and level information, 168–70
patterns, 154
patterns of correlation, 197–9
patterns of distance, 201–3
types/antitypes, 7–9, 16, 45, 48–9, 55, 63, 74–5, 78–9, 81, 84, 86, 105, 118, 136–8, 146, 157, 170, 218
aggregation of types, 140–1
discrimination types, 121–2

variability accounted for 112–13, 115–16

Wilcoxon test, 35

X-square test, 24, 26, 29, 31–3, 40, 44, 69, 72, 76, 79, 87–9, 92–3, 111, 120–1, 122, 124–6, 139, 162, 166–7, 173, 184–6, 188, 194, 196, 209, 217, 222–3

zero order CFA, 48–50, 63–5, 67, 69, 72–4, 80–1, 146, 151, 160–1, 162–3, 166–7
z-test, 23–5, 31–2, 64–5, 70, 93, 120–1
Chi-square approximation, 23–5, 34, 64–5, 70, 121

Author Index

(Only references from the text are included: references from the list of references are omitted)

Abramowitz, M., 175, 222–3, 239
Abt, K., 207
Agresti, A., 46, 216, 218
Anderson, T. W., 145
Arminger, G., 59

Bartoszyk, G. D., 159, 161, 165
Bauer, P., 41
Bent, D. H., 230
Benton, A. L., 97
Berchtold, H., 121
Bergman, L. R., 16–7, 20–1, 22, 24, 54, 227
Bierschenk, B., 153
Bishop, Y. M. M., 4, 46, 62, 216
Bliss, C. I., 174
Bock, H. H., 213
Box, G. E. P., 173
Brandtstädter, J., 74, 140
Browne, M. W., 35

Chapius, F., 97
Chipuer, H., 100, 223
Cochran, W. G., 178
Copenhaver, D. M., 41

Deming, W. E., 47
Dixon, W. J., 230
Dobbins, L., VI

El-Khouri, B., 227
Enke, H., 208
Everitt, B. S., 26

Feller, W., 20, 22
Ferguson, G. A., 154
Fienberg, S. E., 4, 24, 46, 51, 62, 74, 105, 216

Fisher, R. A., 118–20, 121, 133–5, 159, 176, 194
Fleischmann, U. M., 92, 97
Funke, J., 54, 104, 112–13, 115, 170
Funke, W., 54, 104, 112–13, 115

Görtelmeyer, R., 74
Gabriel, K. R., 39
Gilula, Z., 24
Gokhale, D. V., 52
Goodman, L. A., 37, 46, 216
Gorham, D. R., 190
Gottlieb, R., 31

Hütter, U., 54, 100, 105
Haberman, S. J., 5, 14, 17, 29, 40, 46–7, 216–17
Hackl, P., 41
Hager, W., 36
Hald, A., 26
Harter, H. L., 37
Hartigan, J. A., 5
Havránek, T., 92, 100, 108
Hawkins, M. M., 108
Hays, W. L., 27, 112
Heilmann, W.-R., 16, 26–8, 31, 33, 54, 100, 121
Heilweil, M. F., 140
Hildebrand, D. K., 5, 194
Hoernes, G. E., 140
Holland, B. S., 41
Holland, P. W., 4, 46, 62, 216
   Holm, S. 38–40, 41, 43–4, 92, 126, 199, 213, 244
Hommel, G., 23, 30, 36–7, 39–41, 43–5, 149, 166
Hommers, W., 8

268

Hu, T.-C., 20
Hull, C. H., 230
Hussy, W., 170, 173–4, 182–3

Jacobs, A., 180
Jannarone, R. J., 9
Jenkins, G. M., 173
Jenkins, J. G., 230
Jones, C., VI

Küchenhoff, H., 30, 33, 41, 65, 76, 93, 98–9
Keuchel, I., 153
Keuls, M., 39, 125
Kimball, A. W., 108
Kirk, R. E., 27, 176, 222–3, 239
Klauer, K. J., 54, 70
Koehler, K. J., 26
Kohnen, R., 100, 128
Kotze, P. J. V., 108
Krüger, H.-P., 120
Krampen, G., 74
Krause, B., 120–1
Krauth, J., V, 58–9, 14, 16–17, 23–4, 31, 33–5, 37–8, 46–7, 49, 52–4, 74, 82–3, 86–7, 100, 104–5, 116, 121, 124, 126, 139, 146–7, 149, 154–5, 159, 173–4, 182, 184, 189
Krieger, A. M., 24
Krippendorff, K., 4, 82
Kullback, S., 4, 52
Kutner, M. H., 60–1

Lösel, F., 74, 122
Laing, J. D., 5, 194
Lancaster, H. D., 4, 52, 55, 82
Larntz, K., 26, 33, 64, 76
Lautsch, E., 30, 208–9
Lehmacher, W., 17, 23, 28–30, 31, 33, 36–7, 39–41, 43–5, 46, 65, 76, 93, 98–9, 120, 149, 166, 183, 199, 208, 213, 222
Lemke, R., 65
Lerner, R., VI
Leuner, H. C., 34, 214–15
Lienert, G. A., V, VI, 4–5, 8–9, 14, 16–17, 23–4, 29–30, 31, 33–5, 37–8, 47–9, 50, 52–4, 63, 65, 68, 70, 74–6, 78, 82–3, 86–7, 92–3, 97, 100, 104–5, 108–9, 112–13, 115–16, 121–2, 124, 126, 128–9, 130, 139, 146, 149, 153–5, 159, 161, 165, 168,

170, 173–4, 182, 184, 187, 189–90, 193–4, 197, 208–9
Lindner, K., 28, 30–1, 41, 208
Ludwig, 0:., 31

Müller, U. 54, 100, 105
Maly, V., 54, 100
Mann, H. B., 35
Marcus, R., 39
Maxwell, A. E., 126
McCluskey, 140, 142
McCullagh, P., 60
McNemar, Q., 191
Meehl, P. E., 9
Metzler, P., 120–1, 145
Miller, R. G., 37
Milmoe, S., VI

Nelder, J. A., 23, 60
Nesselroade, J. R., 151, 168–9, 170, 173, 179–80, 182, 214
Neter, J., 60–1
Netter, P., 54, 75, 104, 108–9, 122, 128–9, 130
Newman, D., 39, 125
Nickel, B., 145
Nie, N. H., 230

Osterkorn, K., 23
Oswald, K.-D., 97
Overall, J. E., 190

Pearson, K., 12, 24, 26, 87, 92, 112, 139, 162–3, 173, 203, 209, 217, 222–3
Peritz, E., 39
Perli, H.-G., 23, 30, 36–7, 39–41, 43–5, 149, 166
Pruchno, R., 180

Quine, M. V., 140, 142

Rennert, H., 65
Rey, E.-R., 54, 100, 208
Reynolds, J., 75
Rindskopf, D., 227
Roberts, J. S., 9
Roeder, B., 227
Rosenthal, H., 5, 194
Roth, E., 97
Rovine, M. J., VI, 24, 76, 152
Rudolf, J., 128, 197

Sackett, G. P., 194
Schütt, W., 16, 26–8, 31, 33
Shaffer, J. P., 41
Shapiro, A., 35
Siegel, S., 41
Snedecor, G. W., 178
Sonnemann, E., 38
Stegun, I. A., 175, 222–3, 239
Steiger, J. H., 35
Steinbrenner, K., 230
Stephan, F. E., 47
Straube, E., 189–90, 193–4

von Eye, A., 4, 16–17, 20–1, 22, 24, 30,
    47–8, 50, 54, 59, 63, 65, 74–6, 78,
    82, 92–3, 95, 100, 136, 139–40,
    151, 153, 168–9, 170, 173–4, 179–
    80, 182–4, 187, 197, 208–9, 222–3
von Eye, D., VI
von Eye, J., VI
von Eye, M., VI

von Eye, V., VI
von Kerekjarto, M., 65
von Weber, S., 209

Wall, K.-D., 75, 120, 143
Ward, J. H., 63
Wasserman, W., 60–1
Weber, E., 20, 27
Wermuth, N., 105
Westermann, R., 36
Whitney, D. R., 35
Wilcoxon, F., 35
Wise, M. E., 26
Wolfrum, C., 54, 100, 105
Wood, P. K., VI, 24

Yates, F., 30, 176

Zerbe, G. O., 184
Zerges, K., 74